Fronto: Selected Letters

CLASSICAL STUDIES SERIES

Also available from Bloomsbury:

The Aeneid of Virgil, R. D. Williams
Sophocles: Antigone and Oedipus the King, John Wilkins and Matthew Macleod
Sallust: Conspiracy of Catiline, Patrick McGushin
Euripides: Medea and Electra, John Ferguson
Herodotus: Persian Wars, Stephen Usher
Aristophanes: Clouds, Acharnians, Lysistrata, K. J. Dover and Simon Tremewan

Fronto: Selected Letters

Caillan Davenport and Jennifer Manley

B L O O M S B U R Y

LONDON • NEW DELHI • NEW YORK • SYDNEY

Bloomsbury Academic
An imprint of Bloomsbury Publishing Plc

50 Bedford Square
London
WC1B 3DP
UK

1385 Broadway
New York
NY 10018
USA

www.bloomsbury.com

Bloomsbury is a registered trade mark of Bloomsbury Publishing Plc

First published 2014

British Library Cataloguing-in-Publication Data
A catalogue record for this book is available from the British Library.

ISBN: PB: 978-1-78093-442-6
ePDF: 978-1-47250-406-7
ePub: 978-147250-405-0

Library of Congress Cataloging-in-Publication Data
A catalog record for this book is available from the Library of Congress.

Typeset by RefineCatch, Bungay, Suffolk

For our families

Contents

Preface

This book consists of a translation and commentary on fifty-four letters of Marcus Cornelius Fronto and his social circle dating from the second century AD. Fronto was one of the most prominent Romans in the age of the Antonines (*c.* 138–92): he was a senator and consul, a renowned advocate in Rome's law-courts, and most famously, tutor in Latin rhetoric to the future emperors Marcus Aurelius (reigned 161–180) and Lucius Verus (reigned 161–169). Fronto's correspondence ranges across a period of more than twenty-five years (*c.* 139–166), during which his illustrious pupils grew up to claim the throne and wage war with the Parthian empire, and Fronto himself became embroiled in famous legal cases. Yet there is much more to these letters than the world of high politics, with many of them providing intimate insights into their authors' lives. We are privy to Marcus' infatuation with his talented tutor and Fronto's own deepening feelings for his pupil; we see Marcus grow up, and feel Fronto's pain as the prince needs him less and less; we read of Fronto's recurrent health problems, his embarrassing friends, and his love for partridges; we beam with pride as Marcus and Fronto raise children and grandchildren; and we sense their pain as they grieve for ones they have lost.

We have aimed to collect and translate a selection of Fronto's letters that tell the story of his life in a single volume. The letters have also been chosen for their potential to offer insights into the politics and society of the Roman world. The work is designed to be easily intelligible to undergraduate students of ancient history in the English-speaking world, but we hope graduate students and scholars, especially those unfamiliar with the Antonine period, will also profit from our work. Haines' two-volume Loeb translation is still the standard English version of Fronto's letters. Although it has many virtues, it is based on an out-dated edition of the Latin text and some of the language is quite archaic. We have used van den Hout's 1988 edition of the Latin, and aimed to make the translations as comprehensible and vibrant as possible. Our commentary is primarily historical, rather than linguistic or literary, though there are remarks on points of style. We cannot better van den Hout's monumental commentary of 1999, but we have tried to complement it. We wish to make clear our debt to both van den Hout and Haines in preparing this edition, as well as scholars such as Mai, Naber, and Hauler, whose labours restored Fronto's letters to the world after centuries buried under the Acts of the Council of Chalcedon. As far as more recent scholars are concerned, we must acknowledge Champlin's authoritative book on Fronto, Birley's excellent biography of Marcus Aurelius, and Richlin's stimulating scholarship on the Marcus–Fronto relationship. Their works have been our near constant companions.

There are many people to thank. We are grateful to our successive editors at Bloomsbury, Deborah Blake and Charlotte Loveridge, for their help and support, to John Whitehorne for reading the manuscript, and to Chris Mallan and Yvette Hunt for their advice on specific points. We would like to thank the anonymous referees for the press for their feedback, especially the reader who devoted significant time and energy to offering detailed comments on the text, which led to many improvements. Janette McWilliam kindly granted us permission to use coins from the R. D. Milns Antiquities Museum at The University of Queensland for the cover, and we thank Jessica Dowdell for her assistance with the images. We have benefited enormously from the erudition and patience of our own Latin and Greek teachers, who taught us to render the languages into English rather than 'translationese'. Even though we have never written them the sort of letters that Marcus sent to Fronto, we are grateful nonetheless. Our own students have always inspired us with their intelligence and perseverance (especially when faced with yet another use of the subjunctive). The curious may wish to know who was responsible for which letters: although there was an initial division of labour, we have changed, corrected, and commented on each other's work to the extent that the finished product is truly a joint effort.

Caillan Davenport and Jennifer Manley
Brisbane, February 2013

Abbreviations

AE	*L'Année Epigraphique* (Paris, 1888–)
BMCRE	H. Mattingly et al., *Coins of the Roman Empire in the British Museum* (London, 1923–)
CIL	*Corpus Inscriptionum Latinarum* (Berlin, 1863–)
IG	*Inscriptiones Graecae* (Berlin, 1873–)
ILS	H. Dessau (ed.), *Inscriptiones Latinae Selectae* (Berlin, 1892–1916)
ILTun.	*Inscriptions Latines de la Tunisie* (Paris, 1944)
Inscr. It.	*Inscriptiones Italiae* (Rome, 1931–)
*LSJ*⁹	H. G. Liddel, R. Scott, H. Stuart-Jones (eds), *A Greek-English Lexicon* (9th edition)
OED	*Oxford English Dictionary* (2nd edition) (Oxford, 1989)
OLD	*Oxford Latin Dictionary* (2nd edition) (Oxford, 2012)
Pan. Lat.	R. A. B. Mynors (ed.) *Panegyrici Latini* (Oxford, 1964)
*PIR*²	*Prosopographia Imperii Romani Saec. I, II, III* (2nd edition) (Berlin 1933–)
TLL	*Thesaurus Linguae Latinae* (Leipzig, 1900–)

Cicero's Letters

Ad Att.	*Letters to Atticus*

Ad Fam.	*Letters to his friends*
Ad Q. Fr.	*Letters to his brother Quintus*

Historia Augusta (HA)

Hadrian	*Life of Hadrian*
Pius	*Life of Antoninus Pius*
Marcus	*Life of Marcus Aurelius*
Verus	*Life of Lucius Verus*
Commodus	*Life of Commodus*

Conventions

The numbering system of Fronto's letters is notoriously convoluted. Cross-references to letters in this collection are highlighted in bold, in the following form: **Letter 24**. Under the entry for each letter, the reader will find a full reference to the Latin text in van den Hout's second edition of the 1988 volume (VdH^2) and to Haines' two-volume English translation of 1919–20 (Haines I or II).

The references are given in the following format: *Ad M. Caes.* 4.6, VdH^2 pp. 62–3 = Haines I, pp. 180–3. It is often the case that the letters are numbered differently in both van den Hout and Haines, in which case, both references are given: *Ad M. Caes.* 5.55, VdH^2 pp. 80–1 = *Ad M. Caes.* 5.40, Haines I, pp. 240–3. This system is also used throughout the book to refer to letters we have not translated here. We acknowledge that this is a cumbersome system, but it is the only way to direct the reader to both the Latin text and a translation. Readers should note that if they wish to consult van den Hout's 1999 commentary his comments are keyed directly to the page and line numbers of his 1988 Teubner.

All dates are AD unless otherwise indicated. The emperor Marcus Aurelius is generally referred to as 'Marcus' throughout.

Map of Central Italy

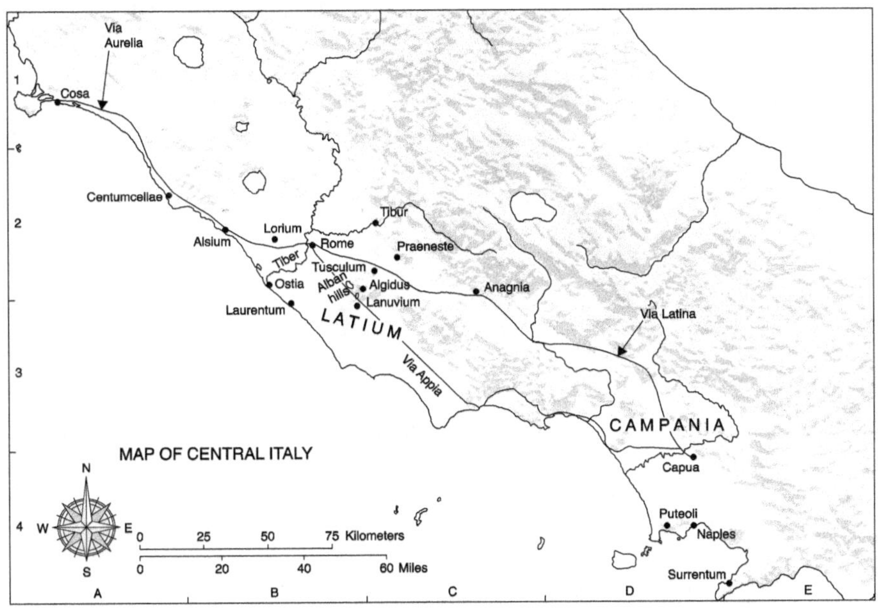

Introduction

Introducing Fronto

M. Cornelius Fronto was born at the end of the first century in Cirta (modern-day Constantine) in North Africa. Little is known about his family, but they were probably of equestrian status and members of the local municipal aristocracy of Cirta. Fronto would have left to study in Rome when he was in his late teens. His tutors included the philosopher Athenodotus and the orator Dionysius (**Letters 19, 24**). Fronto and his brother Q. Cornelius Quadratus both went on to become Roman senators, part of a wave of new men from Africa who entered the senatorial order in the second century (Champlin 1980: 5–19).

Fronto's government career, partially recorded on an inscription from Africa (*CIL* VIII 5350 = *ILS* 2928), encompassed a range of administrative and judicial positions. He was initially a member of the board of three for capital crimes (*triumvir capitalis*) before entering the senate and becoming a quaestor. As quaestor, Fronto was sent to Sicily to assist the senatorial proconsul, the only time he served outside Italy on an official posting. After returning to Rome, he became a plebeian aedile, a post mainly concerned with the oversight of the markets and public amenities in the city. During these early years, Fronto married Cratia, and he began to earn a reputation as an advocate representing clients in the courts. By the time he was elected praetor in the late 120s, Fronto was renowned as the foremost advocate in Rome (Dio 69.18.3).

The relationship between Fronto and Hadrian (117–138) appears to have been a difficult one, although he continued to praise the emperor in the senate as required for his career (**Letter 12**). The reign of Antoninus Pius (138–161) marked a significant turning point in Fronto's life, as Pius appointed him tutor to his adopted sons, Marcus Aurelius and Lucius Verus. The earliest correspondence between Marcus and Fronto can be dated to 139 (**Letter 1**), indicating that Fronto's employment began shortly after Pius' accession (Champlin 1974: 143–4; cf. Richlin 2011: 165). The young princes had numerous tutors, many of them prominent senators and equestrians, who schooled them in Greek and Latin language and literature, law, philosophy, music, and geometry. Marcus had four teachers in the arts of oratory and rhetoric: three in the Greek language, and one, Fronto, for Latin (*HA Marcus* 2.1–4; Dio 72.35.1–2). The post came with no salary, but Fronto earned his due reward in 142, when he was appointed to the suffect consulship for the months of July and August (Eck 1998). On 13 August of the same year, Fronto delivered a speech of thanks to Pius in the senate, praising the emperor's virtues and accomplishments (**Letters 12–14**).

Throughout Pius' reign, Fronto remained active in the courts and in the senate, representing clients based as far afield as Asia Minor (**Letters 18, 44**). He also delivered a speech of gratitude to the emperor on behalf of the African city of Carthage, on which Pius had lavished attention after an earthquake (Champlin 1980: 86–8). As a leading senator and advocate, Fronto had numerous pupils, clients and associates for whom he wrote letters of recommendation, and obtained posts and favours (**Letters 28–29**). Fronto owned numerous residences, including a magnificent house with pleasure gardens on the Esquiline hill in Rome (it had previously belonged to Augustus' intimate associate Maecenas). He also had at least two country villas: one located outside Rome near the Via Aurelia, which ran northwards towards Cosa in Etruria, and another at Surrentum (modern-day Sorrento) on the Bay of Naples (Champlin 1980: 21–4).

Fronto and Cratia had six children. Only their daughter, Cornelia Cratia, survived to adulthood. She married one of Fronto's pupils, the senator Aufidius Victorinus, who was also a close friend of Marcus (*HA Marcus* 3.8). Fronto was very fond of Victorinus, praising his character and his talent for eloquence (**Letter 33**). Victorinus was suffect consul in 155 and went on to have a successful senatorial career as a provincial governor and general. Fronto was himself appointed governor of the province of Asia in the late 150s, but was forced to decline on grounds of ill health (**Letter 34**). The excuse was a believable one, since he suffered from chronic illnesses, possibly gout and rheumatoid arthritis, and he made frequent references to his health complaints in his correspondence (**Letters 20, 34, 50**).

Marcus and Verus became joint emperors in 161 following Pius' death. Fronto continued to have a good relationship with his former pupils, regularly visiting the imperial palace and exchanging details of family life in his letters (**Letters 36–39**). In contrast with the relatively peaceful reign of Pius, the 160s were marked by near-constant warfare on the northern and eastern frontiers of the Roman empire. When war with the Parthian empire broke out in 161, Verus was sent to Syria to take charge of the campaign. Verus gave Fronto the task of writing an official history of the Parthian War, with special emphasis on his own valiant conduct (**Letter 47**). However, it was never finished: Fronto only seems to have written a brief treatment, which he sent to Marcus as a sample of the final work (**Letter 49**).

Fronto was by now a very old man and probably died shortly after 166, when his correspondence ends. The last years of Fronto's life cannot have been happy ones, since his wife Cratia and three-year-old grandson died a few months apart in 165 (**Letters 50–54**). Though there is no definite evidence, it is possible that Fronto died from the Antonine plague, which Verus' troops had brought back with them from the eastern front (Champlin 1980: 139–42).

Roman Letters

A letter is, at its simplest, a written communiqué from one person to another (*OED*, s.v. 'letter'). Letters are addressed to a particular individual, or group, from someone who is geographically distant and unable to communicate face-to-face, and they usually feature formulaic greetings (Trapp 2003: 1). They are more complex than they may initially appear: the style, content, and subtext of letters can be influenced by the social context in which the letter was written, the environment and background of its author, and his or her aim in sending the letter. The epistolary form itself invites a level of intimacy between author and reader, allowing us to imagine that we are interacting directly with people from the ancient world. Early modern historians were particularly fascinated with the insight letters provided into Roman historical figures, a trend that has continued today, albeit with a higher level of sophistication in the approach (compare, for example, Church 1884 and Hoffer 1999).

Many different kinds of letters survive from the Roman world. Papyri discovered in the sands of Egypt have revealed bureaucratic letters ordering supplies and provisions, complaints to officials, letters written by soldiers, petitions to emperors, as well as much more personal correspondence (Parsons 1980; Trapp 2003: 7–8). These records are complemented by the Vindolanda tablets from northern England, which were written on thin wooden leaf tablets. These shed vital light on the lives of soldiers and the military community (Bowman 1994a, 1994b). But letter writing was not just for everyday correspondence: it could also be an elevated literary genre. Horace and Ovid both wrote collections of letter poems, and the philosopher Seneca was the author of a series of didactic epistles on moral themes (Trapp 2003: 23–6). There was a wealth of theoretical discussion from the classical and Hellenistic periods onwards concerning how letters should be written (Demetrius, *On Style* 223–235 = Trapp 2003: no. 73).

Fronto especially admired the correspondence of M. Tullius Cicero, the famous senator and orator of the late Republic. Cicero's letters were not originally intended to be published, although he did begin to think about collecting and editing them in the late 40s BC (*Ad Att.* 16.5). His correspondence was edited and circulated after his death, either by his secretary Tiro or his friend Atticus (White 2010: 33–40). In contrast, the *Letters* of Pliny the Younger, a senator of the Flavio-Trajanic period, were self-consciously composed with an eye to publication, perhaps in order to draw greater attention to Pliny as an orator (Mayer 2003: 227–34). Even the tenth book of letters to the emperor Trajan shows evidence of editorial intervention and arrangement (Gibson and Morello 2012: 251–3). Through their letters we can observe Cicero and Pliny developing their relationships with patrons, clients and friends, asking for favours, affecting introductions, making political deals, and grieving over lost relatives.

Letters were originally written on papyrus or thin wooden tablets by the authors themselves, though they could also be dictated to an educated slave, especially if the writer was unwell (McDonnell 1996: 474–5). They were then folded and sealed (in the case of papyrus) or tied together, if they were tablets. The letters were usually dispatched in the hands of a friend, slave or freedman, but could also be entrusted to a traveller who just happened to be heading in the right direction (White 2010: 11–12). Official letters were sent through the imperial postal service, known as the *cursus publicus*, if appropriate permission had been obtained (Wilcox 2012: 17–18). Roman aristocrats made copies of their letters, which enabled them to be assembled into collections, either by the writers themselves or other editors. Although it may seem strange to us today, the letters were not usually ordered chronologically, but by topics such as theme or addressee. For example, book thirteen of Cicero's *Ad Familiares* is a collection of letters of recommendation (White 2010: 46). These arrangements were designed to highlight different aspects of the author's character or public life (see Beard 2002 on Cicero). Therefore, we need to be aware that the arrangements of letters in many modern translations and anthologies (including this one) are not the same as the original collection (Gibson 2012).

The letter collections have reached us today because interested parties, such as church authorities, diligently copied the manuscripts in the medieval period (Trapp 2003: 2). This explains why letters with moral or religious content survived in such quantities, notably Seneca's *Moral Letters*, and the collections of Augustine, Basil, Gregory of Nazianzus, and Jerome. Sometimes different manuscripts have gaps (known as 'lacunae') or variant readings, which modern editors have to collate in an attempt to determine the original version of the Latin or Greek text. It is important to emphasise, therefore, that there is a long 'production line' between the original letter being written and its arrival centuries later, edited, re-ordered and translated into a collection such as this one (Gibson 2012: 70–1).

Fronto's Correspondence

Fronto's letters were unknown before 1815, when Cardinal Angelo Mai, prefect of the Ambrosian Library in Milan, discovered the first fragments of the codex on which they were written. A few years later, Mai uncovered the rest of the codex in the Vatican Library; the two halves had apparently been separated in the seventeenth century (Richlin 2006a: 2–3; Reynolds 1983: 173). Examination of the manuscripts showed that the text was originally copied out in the fifth century, with the original codex being made up of approximately 680 pages. However, only 282 pages survived in the Milan manuscript and 106 in the Vatican, which serves as a stark reminder of how much of the correspondence has been lost (Fleury 2012: 63). We currently have around two hundred letters of Fronto and his correspondents, including fragments; the great majority of these were written in Latin, though there are also some in Greek (**Letters 17, 19**). Parts of one of Fronto's speeches, *For the Carthaginians*, were discovered by Mai in a separate manuscript in the Vatican Library, and fragments of the correspondence between Fronto and Lucius Verus subsequently appeared in Paris (Reynolds 1983: 173–4; Champlin 1980: 86–8).

Mai uncovered Fronto's letters on a palimpsest, which has important implications for the survival and reconstruction of the text. A palimpsest is a manuscript from which one text has been removed (washed or scraped off) and another written over the top. The underlying text is usually very difficult to restore, depending on the vigour with which it was erased, and the restoration of the original manuscript usually results in numerous lacunae and uncertain words and passages. In the case of Fronto's letters, the manuscript was reused in the seventh century to preserve the Acts of the Council of Chalcedon. Mai used chemical reagent to read Fronto's work, but in the process destroyed much of the text. Scholars have had to rely heavily on his original reconstruction and the subsequent efforts of nineteenth and early twentieth-century scholars, notably Naber, Niebuhr, and Hauler (Haines 1919: xi–xii; Champlin 1980: 2). Haines' translation of 1919–20, which is the standard text in the English-speaking world, is based primarily on the edition of Naber, but incorporates emendations of later editors. Van den Hout's Teubner edition of 1954 was a landmark publication, providing scholars with an up-to-date critical edition that underpinned all research on Fronto in the second half of the twentieth century. Van den Hout later released a second, revised edition of 1988, and an exhaustive scholarly commentary followed in 1999. These will be the standard research tools for all scholars for the foreseeable future, despite some drawbacks (for reviews, see Holford-Strevens 1991 and 2000).

Prior to Mai's discovery, Fronto was known only by his ancient reputation as an outstanding orator and Marcus' tutor (*Meditations* 1.11). When Mai published the letters for the first time, they did not live up to popular expectations of Fronto's rhetorical prowess (Champlin 1980: 2–3). They were considered to be very poorly written and largely concerned with trivialities, such as the author's near-continuous health complaints, or featured unexpectedly amorous letters between Fronto and Marcus (Richlin 2006b).

Their unfavourable reception coloured scholars' views of them for well over one hundred years, perhaps because their contents threatened to shatter the golden image of Marcus Aurelius (Richlin 2012: 497–8). They have, however, proved invaluable for research into the social, cultural, and political environment of the Antonine age, as well as the lives of its leading personalities (Champlin 1980; Birley 1993; Richlin 2006a).

The collection of Fronto's correspondence includes letters to and from the emperors Antoninus Pius, Marcus Aurelius and Lucius Verus, as well as Marcus' mother, Domitia Lucilla, Fronto's son-in-law Aufidius Victorinus, and numerous other notables of the Antonine age. The letters were probably not intended for publication, although there was some informal circulation. For example, Marcus read one of Fronto's letters aloud to Pius (**Letters 38–39**), and Fronto forwarded a copy of a letter he originally sent to Marcus to Victorinus (**Letters 42, 44**). Fronto did circulate his speeches during his lifetime, and was concerned to revise them until they were at the appropriate standard (Champlin 1980: 51–2; **Letter 44**). However, many of the letters seem genuine and unguarded, revealing the insecurities and anxieties of Fronto and his correspondents. Others, especially those to Pius, are clearly written in a more self-aware and official tone (**Letters 30, 34–35**). At least some of Fronto's correspondence had been collected and published by the fourth century, although it was not very popular (Fleury 2012: 64). The identity of the editor (or editors) has been the subject of some speculation, with candidates including Victorinus or another male descendant, concerned to revive the family's fortunes (Haines 1919: xxi–xxii; Champlin 1974: 157; Fleury 2012: 64), although Richlin (2011: 166–7) has recently suggested Fronto's daughter Cratia as a possibility.

The editor(s) of the correspondence, whoever they were, did not organise it in strictly chronological order, in keeping with the usual practice of ancient letter collections. Van den Hout's second edition has the following divisions:

Ad M. Caes. et invicem: 'To Marcus as Caesar, and his replies' (five books)
Ad M. Antoninum Imp. et invicem: 'To Marcus as Augustus, and his replies' (four books)
Ad Verum Imp.: 'To Verus as Augustus' (two books)
Ad Antoninum Pium: 'To Antoninus Pius' (one book)
Ad amicos: 'To his friends' (two books)

There were several smaller collections or individual letters given their own title:

Ad M. Antoninum de eloquentia: 'To Marcus as Augustus: On eloquence'
Ad M. Antoninum de orationibus: 'To Marcus as Augustus: On speeches'
Principia historiae: 'The beginnings of a history'
Laudes fumi et pulveris: 'Praise of smoke and dust'
Laudes neglegentiae: 'Praise of carelessness'
De bello Parthico: 'On the Parthian War'
De feriis Alsiensibus: 'On holidays at Alsium'
De nepote amisso: 'On the loss of his grandson'
Arion: 'The story of Arion'
Additamentum: Letters without a title

Earlier editions had a separate section for the Greek letters (*Epistulae Graecae*), but van den Hout distributes them among the categories above.

There are some obvious elements of chronological organisation: the five books to Marcus as Caesar must be dated *c.* 138–161, and those written to him as Augustus between 161 and *c.* 166. Within these limits, most of the letters in *Ad M. Caes.* books 1–2 are dated to the early 140s, including a group in *Ad M. Caes.* 2 focusing on Fronto's consulship, held in 142 (Champlin 1974: 139–40; **Letters 12–13, 15–17**). This was perhaps designed to foreground Fronto's role as Marcus' tutor, and his appointment to the consulship (van den Hout 1999: 3). Clear thematic arrangements are also apparent, such as the correspondence concerned with Herodes Atticus in *Ad. M. Caes.* book 3 (**Letters 7–11**). Many of the very brief letters dealing with health and illness were collected together in *Ad M. Caes.* book 5 (**Letters 20–21, 25–27**). Thematic organisation is also apparent in the two books *Ad amicos*, where there are discrete groups featuring letters of recommendation and consolation (Champlin 1974: 153). The fact that the letters concerning the death of Fronto's three-year-old grandson in 165 were placed in their own section indicates that the editor recognised this was an important moment in his life (**Letters 52–54**).

Fronto and Marcus Aurelius

Fronto's relationship with the Antonine emperors dominates the collection. Of the extant letters, 88 are written by Marcus Aurelius, and 72 of these are dated to the period in which he was Caesar (Fleury 2012: 65). This correspondence is varied in its emotional content. Fronto's letters to Marcus include discussion of Latin literary forms and style as part of his instructional programme (**Letter 1**): these educational letters usually have a rather elevated tone, though his writing is not without affection. In contrast, Marcus' replies are casual, and are often more effusive than one would expect of letters between pupil and teacher (Richlin 2006a: 5–6; Fleury 2012: 65–6; **Letter 6**). Richlin's scholarship has raised the issue of whether the two men were in love or had a physical relationship (see Richlin 2006a, 2006b, 2011). It is clear that at the very least Marcus and Fronto enjoyed a close bond, which grew over time. In some of the more emotionally charged letters, Marcus calls Fronto his 'inspiration' and writes that he is 'ablaze with affection' for his teacher (**Letter 2**), and finishes his letters by calling him 'as sweet as honey, my love, my joy' (**Letter 6**). In return, Fronto uses affectionate expressions, saying 'I truly love your little letters twice as much' (**Letter 8**), and he writes of his desire to leave Rome so he can embrace his pupil (**Letter 16**). Although this language might seem strange and overly effusive to the modern English-speaker, it is reflective of the emotive discourse that typified Roman letter writing (Williams 2012: 243). The expressions of affection could have different connotations depending on the circumstances. For example, when Antoninus Pius calls Fronto 'dearest' (**Letter 14**), this is not a declaration of love, but a sign of the orator's standing in the emperor's favour. Likewise, when Fronto states that he loves Pius 'as I do the sun, the day, my life and very breath' (**Letter 12**), he is playing the part of the devoted and flattering courtier. But the language used by both Marcus and Fronto clearly indicates a closer relationship than that shared by Fronto and Pius. In her provocative book *Marcus Aurelius in Love*, Richlin (2006b: 112) describes the language as 'pervasively amatory', though she leaves it up to her readers to decide whether the two men were actually in love.

We stop short of thinking that Marcus and Fronto had an actual love affair: Marcus' own remarks about his sexual experiences in the *Meditations* (1.17.2, 7) would seem to tell against this. Two Latin words that feature prominently in the correspondence – *amor* ('love') and *desiderium* ('longing, desire') – can be used to refer to both sexual and non-sexual love, and are equally applicable to friends and family members as they are to lovers. As Williams (2012: 252–3) has recently observed, *amor* is the expression of the bond of *amicitia* ('friendship') between Marcus and Fronto. Another important word used by Marcus to describe Fronto, *mellitus* ('honey sweet'), occurs in the love poetry of Catullus (*Poems* 3, 48, 99), but is also used by Cicero to describe his son (*Ad Att.* 1.18). The fact that this language can be interpreted in more than one way seems to be intentional: on one level, it is a self-conscious literary choice, displaying the depth of Marcus and Fronto's learning and their familiarity with a wide range of Latin literature, but this does not preclude it being representative of real human emotion. Marcus was clearly enamoured with his teacher, admiring his intellect, erudition, and eloquence. He wrote about Fronto's way with words with wide-eyed admiration, as we might expect of an ingénue being educated at the feet of a distinguished literary master (**Letters 13, 18**). In return, Marcus wanted to use language and word play that would impress Fronto and demonstrate the results of his own wide reading (see **Letters 5–6**).

The manner in which these feelings of infatuation are expressed is indebted to the pederastic language of classical Greek education, in which the teacher is the *erastês* ('lover') and the student is the *erômenos* ('beloved') (Dover 1989: 16). Fronto himself explicitly used such language in the *Treatise on Love* he sent to Marcus – brilliantly translated by Richlin (2006a: 36–9) – and in a letter to Herodes Atticus, Marcus' teacher in Greek rhetoric, in which he declared himself to be Herodes' rival for the prince's affections (*anterastês*) (**Letter 19**). We need to consider the cultural and intellectual context in which these letters were written: the imperial court had only recently witnessed the emperor Hadrian conducting a homosexual affair with his lover Antinoüs (Laes 2009: 1; Richlin 2011: 166). The flowering of Greek culture known as the 'Second Sophistic' saw writers such as Plutarch, Dio Chrysostom, Philostratus, and Achilles Tatius imitate and allude to the works of Plato, especially those dialogues that dealt with sexual relationships between men (Trapp 1990; Richlin 2006a: 14–17; Yunis 2011: 26–7). In choosing to use such language, Marcus and Fronto do so knowingly, and employ it to show off their own literary and rhetorical prowess (see **Letter 13**). This does not mean that their affection is merely empty verbiage, devoid of real feeling – there are clearly real emotions at play here – but it is unlikely to be indicative of a sexual relationship between the two men.

Even as Marcus married and had children of his own, Fronto kept up the correspondence, though he ceased to provide formal tuition in Latin rhetoric from the mid-140s. Marcus began to explore his growing interest in philosophy (**Letter 21**), and there are signs that Fronto felt some anxiety that his former pupil did not rely on him as he had before (**Letter 24**). Although Marcus' language is less amorous and cloying in this period compared with the early letters, this can be attributed to the fact that he had matured, married, and had a family. The two men still shared an intimate relationship, as can be seen in the detailed letters about each other's health complaints, though more often than not, these are Fronto's afflictions, rather than Marcus' (Whitehorne 1977b). Their enduring friendship is further demonstrated by Fronto's teasing letter to Marcus concerning his 'holiday' at Alsium (**Letter 41**), and Marcus' compassion at the death of Fronto's grandson in 165 (**Letter 52**). Even then, more than twenty-five years after the start of their relationship, Fronto remained 'my sweetest teacher'.

This Translation and Commentary

This translation and commentary is based on van den Hout's 1988 edition of the Latin text. The eight chapters are in approximate chronological order, although some cover the same time period from different perspectives (for example Chapters 4–5, and Chapters 6–8). This arrangement is designed to enable the reader to take a journey through Fronto's life, from the late 130s to the mid-160s. We have endeavoured to make our translations easy to read for English speakers, while staying as close to the original Latin text as possible. Where Fronto or his correspondents used a pun or alliteration, we have tried to reflect this. When translating Latin into English, it is all too easy to make everyone sound like they are characters in a Jane Austen novel. So, in places where the Latin idiom is difficult to render into English, we have chosen to err on the side of readability. We have indicated places in which the Latin text is unreadable, or where the translation is based on restorations. We have not translated passages that are too fragmentary: scholars will of course be able to refer to van den Hout's edition to see what can be made of these.

It is necessary to say a few words about some Latin terminology. The word *dominus* appears frequently throughout the letters: we have translated this as 'lord' when Fronto is addressing Marcus, Pius, or Verus. However, *dominus* can also be used by social equals to refer to each other, and in this case it has been translated as 'dear'. In such a context the word indicates 'courtesy but little or no deference' (Dickey 2002: 90–1). The traditional opening form of address is in the form *Caesar Frontoni magistro suo salutem*, translated here as 'Caesar sends greetings to his teacher Fronto', although the original meaning is 'bids good health' (Trapp 2003: 35). Sometimes *have* is used as a greeting, which we have translated as 'hello'. The letters often end with *vale*, 'be well', which we have sometimes retained as a wish for good health, or translated as 'goodbye' or 'farewell', depending on the context. *Saluta*, an exhortation to greet another which comes at the end of a letter, we have rendered as 'give my best wishes'. Expressions thought worthy of special mention are discussed in the notes.

Dramatis Personae: Historical Figures in the Letters

This chapter features brief biographical sketches of Fronto's family, key members of the imperial house, and other prominent individuals. In each entry, we have listed the letters in this collection which the individual wrote or received, as well as any letters in which they are mentioned by third parties.

Fronto's family

Q. Cornelius Quadratus: Fronto's brother. He was a senator, governor of Numidia *c.* 142 and suffect consul in 147. He lived with Fronto in Rome; no wife or descendants are known. **Letters:** 45, 53. **References:** *PIR*[2] C 1426; Champlin 1980: 6; van den Hout 1999: 541.

Cratia the Elder: Fronto's wife. Champlin suggests Cratia came from Asia Minor or the former Greek colonies of southern Italy, while Richlin proposes North Africa. Fronto's correspondence reveals that she was a friend of Domitia Lucilla, Marcus' mother. She died in 165. **Letters:** 6, 13, 16, 26, 36, 50, 51, 54.

References: *PIR*² G 218; Champlin 1980: 25–6; van den Hout 1999: 277–8, 535; Richlin 2011: 177–98.

Cornelia Cratia (the Younger): Fronto's daughter, born *c.* 141. She married the senator Aufidius Victorinus *c.* 157, and they had three children, one of whom died in infancy while the couple were stationed in Germany. **Letters:** 6, 24, 33, 38, 40, 53. **References:** *PIR*² G 219; *AE* 1945, 38; Champlin 1980: 27–8; van den Hout 1999: 167, 605.

C. Aufidius Victorinus: Senator from Umbria. He studied under Fronto and was a friend of Marcus Aurelius. He held a suffect consulship in 155 and married Fronto's daughter Cratia *c.* 157. Victorinus was governor of Germania Superior *c.* 161/2–165/66 and later proconsul of Africa. He was ordinary consul in 183 and urban prefect under Commodus, but committed suicide rather than endure harassment by the emperor's stooges (Dio 72.11.1–4). **Letters:** 22, 26, 33, 40, 44, 45, 53. **References:** *PIR*² A 1393; *CIL* VI 41140; Alföldy 1977: 228–9; Champlin 1980: 27–8; van den Hout 1999: 411–12.

The children of Cratia and Victorinus: The question of Fronto's grandchildren is a complicated one. We know of three sons of Cratia and Victorinus:

(1) M. Aufidius (Victorinus) Fronto: *PIR*² A 1385
(2) C. Aufidius Victorinus: *PIR*² A 1394
(3) 'Decimanus' *PIR*² D 23

Fronto (1) is assumed to be the eldest of the boys, since he was consul in 199, a year before Victorinus (2). Fronto (1) was born *c.* 160, and remained in Rome with our Fronto while his parents were in Germany (**Letters 40, 53**). We also have good information about 'Decimanus' (3) from **Letters 50–54**. He was born while his parents were in Germany and died there in 165, aged three. Victorinus (2) was born *c.* 161, and was consul in 200. In **Letter 38,** dated to late 161, Marcus refers to Fronto's grandchildren in the plural. 'Decimanus' (3) could not have been born by then, so he must mean Fronto (1) and Victorinus (2). The natural conclusion is that Victorinus (2) travelled to Germany with his parents. In **Letter 40,** dated *c.* 162, Fronto himself writes of grandchildren in the plural, and the context may suggest that Cratia is about to give birth to

'Decimanus' (3). This reconstruction follows the arguments of van den Hout (1999: 417), but we cannot accept his hypothesis that **Letters 53–54** actually refer to two separate grandchildren, who both died in Germany. An alternative interpretation, proposed by Champlin (1974: 155–6; 1980: 28) is that Victorinus (2) was actually born after his parents returned from Germany. He argues that **Letter 38** refers to Fronto (1) and 'Decimanus' (3), which would place the latter's date of death somewhat earlier than 165, which is unlikely. Champlin believes that **Letter 40** should be dated *c.* 166, since he thinks that Fronto is caring for both Fronto (1) and Victorinus (2). However, Fronto only uses singular pronouns in the letter, which proves that only one child is staying with him, which must be Fronto (1) (see our commentary on **Letters 40** and **53**).

The imperial household

Antoninus Pius: Roman emperor from 138–161. He was a senator from a prominent family, though he held only a few government posts, including the proconsulship of Asia, in the course of his senatorial career. When Hadrian's original heir Aelius Caesar died suddenly in 138, the emperor adopted Antoninus instead. He then instructed Antoninus to adopt Marcus Aurelius and Lucius Verus (who was the son of Aelius Caesar). Hadrian was very unpopular with the senate at the time of his death in 138 and Antoninus gained the name Pius ('dutiful') for his determination in securing Hadrian's deification despite the senate's opposition. His wife was Annia Galeria Faustina the Elder, with whom he had one daughter, Faustina the Younger (see below). He never left Italy during the course of his reign, which was generally peaceful, though not without its conflicts (notably in Britain, Dacia, and Mauretania). **Letters:** 4, 6, 12–14, 18, 30, 32, 34–35, 37, 41, 45–46, 49, 53. **References:** *PIR*^{2} A 1513; Barnes 1967; Birley 1993.

Marcus Aurelius: Roman emperor from 161–180. He was born M. Annius Verus in 121 to M. Annius Verus the Elder and Domitia Lucilla. After his father died in the early 120s, Marcus, his mother and sister, moved into his grandfather's house. During Pius' reign, he held the rank of Caesar, which made him the heir apparent, and he married the emperor's daughter, Faustina the Younger, in 145. After the death of Pius in 161, he became M. Aurelius

Antoninus Augustus and ruled jointly with his adoptive brother, Lucius Verus, until the latter's death in 169. Marcus' reign saw war with the Parthian empire in 161–166, and conflicts with the Marcomanni and Quadi on the Danube subsequently occupied his attention from 168–174. The following year was marked by the revolt of the senatorial general Avidius Cassius and the death of Faustina. In 177, Marcus raised his only surviving son, Aurelius Commodus, to the rank of Augustus, effectively making him co-emperor. A further campaign on the Danube followed in 178–180. Marcus died in Sirmium in March 180, and was succeeded by Commodus. Marcus is famous for his philosophical work *To Himself*, which is better known today as *The Meditations*. **Letters:** 1–13, 15–16, 18–27, 29, 32, 36–39, 41–44, 46, 49, 52–54. **References:** *PIR*^{2} A 697; Birley 1993; McLynn 2009; Van Ackeren 2012.

Lucius Verus: Roman emperor from 161–169. Born in 130 as L. Ceionius Commodus, his name changed to Lucius Aurelius Verus Augustus when he became emperor in 161. He had a reputation as something of a playboy, though he married Marcus' daughter Lucilla in 163. From 162–166, he was based in the east as commander of the Parthian campaign, and celebrated a triumph on his return to Rome. In 168, he travelled with Marcus to northern Italy with a view to conducting a campaign against the barbarian tribes on the Danube. However, he died early in 169. **Letters:** 36–37, 43, 45–51. **References:** PIR^2 C 606; Barnes 1967; Birley 1993.

Domitia Lucilla: Marcus' mother. The wife of M. Annius Verus, with whom she had two children, Marcus and Annia Cornificia Faustina. Domitia was an integral part of the imperial court for many years: her sister-in-law Faustina the Elder was the wife of Antoninus Pius, and her son Marcus was Pius' heir apparent. She could read and write Greek, and was fabulously wealthy, owning numerous brick factories in Italy. Domitia did not live to see her son become emperor, dying *c.* 156. **Letters:** 2–4, 6, 16–17, 21, 25, 29. **References:** *PIR*^{2} D 183; Champlin 1980: 108–9; Birley 1993: 29–35, 45, 71–4, 107; Richlin 2011: 191–5.

Annia Galeria Faustina the Younger: Daughter of Pius and Faustina the Elder, and wife of Marcus. Born *c.* 130, she was originally betrothed to Verus under Hadrian's dynastic plan, but Pius changed the arrangements and she married Marcus in 145. She and Marcus had fourteen children, most of whom died in infancy; the only son to survive to adulthood was the future emperor Commodus. Her daughter Lucilla married Lucius Verus, and four other daughters were married to Roman senators. Faustina accompanied Marcus on his campaigns against the Marcomanni, and he had her deified on her death in 175. The nasty rumours that she was an adulteress are not to be believed (*HA Marcus* 19.1–11), although it is suspicious that she encouraged Avidius Cassius to seize the throne when Marcus was gravely ill (Dio 72.22[2], 29–30). **Letters:** 14, 22, 25–27, 29, 38, 42–44. **References:** *PIR*[2] A 716; Birley 1993; Burns 2007: 155–78.

Matidia (the Younger): Great-aunt of Marcus Aurelius (by adoption). Matidia was the sister of Hadrian's wife Sabina, and was styled the 'maternal aunt' of Antoninus Pius, although they were not blood relatives. She owned property in North Africa, Asia Minor, Campania, and in Rome and its vicinity, including several brickworks. Matidia never married, and died in the early 160s, at about the age of eighty. Her will generated significant controversy. **Letters:** 42–44. **References:** *PIR*[2] M 368; Champlin 1980: 71–2; Boatwright 1992.

Other individuals

C. Avidius Cassius: Roman senator, who served as legate of the Legion III Gallica in the Parthian war. He was responsible for sacking the Parthian cities of Seleucia and Ctesiphon (Xiphilinus = 'Dio' 71.2.2–4). Cassius was appointed suffect consul in 166, then governor of Syria, followed by a special command over the eastern provinces *c.* 172–175 (Dio 72.4.1). In 175, he made a bid for the imperial throne, allegedly because Faustina told him that the emperor was ill and not likely to survive (Dio 72.22.3). When news arrived that this was not the case, the uprising could not be stopped. The revolt was short-lived, since Cassius was murdered by one of his soldiers only a few months later. **Letters:** 47–48. **References:** *PIR*[2] A 1402; Whitehorne 1977a; Syme 1987; Birley 1993: 184–9.

C. Censorius Niger: Equestrian official, who was governor of Noricum and Mauretania Tingitana in the 130s. He died sometime between 146 and 158, and made Fronto the heir to five twelfths of his fortune. Unfortunately, he caused Fronto considerable embarrassment by attacking the praetorian prefect, M. Gavius Maximus, in his will. **Letters:** 30–32. **References:** *PIR*^{2} C 658; Champlin 1980: 100–2; van den Hout 1999: 386.

M. Gavius Maximus: Prominent member of the equestrian order. Maximus was governor of Mauretania Tingitana and prefect of the fleet before being appointed praetorian prefect, the highest-ranking equestrian official in the empire. Maximus served as Pius' prefect for twenty years until *c.* 158, an extraordinarily long and stable tenure given the more turbulent careers of some other occupants of this office (*HA Pius* 8.7). **Letters:** 30–32. **References:** *PIR*^{2} G 104; Champlin 1980: 100–2; Birley 1993: 112–3; 1997a: 296; van den Hout 1999: 386, 389.

Ti. Claudius Herodes Atticus: Wealthy Athenian orator and senator, the most prominent Greek political figure in the Antonine age. Herodes was born *c.* 100 at Marathon in Greece, but as a young man he stayed in the house of P. Calvisius Tullus Ruso, Marcus' maternal grandfather. Following in the footsteps of his father, who had been appointed consul by Hadrian, Herodes embarked on a senatorial career. In the early 140s, he married an Italian woman of a patrician family, Annia Regilla. At about this time, Herodes was put on trial in Rome because of his failure to honour his father's will; Fronto was the prosecuting counsel. Herodes was presumably acquitted (though the matter is quite obscure), and appointed ordinary consul in 143. He became one of Marcus' tutors in Greek rhetoric, and he and Fronto were eventually reconciled. Herodes' life continued to be turbulent: his pregnant wife was beaten to death by a freedman *c.* 160, allegedly on Herodes' orders. He was brought to trial in Rome by Regilla's brother, but was acquitted by Pius. In the 170s, Herodes was charged with tyranny by the people of Athens, and brought to trial before Marcus at Sirmium. His former pupil exonerated him (Philostratus, *Lives of the Sophists*, 554–9). Herodes died in 177, and was buried at the Panathenaic Stadium in Athens. **Letters:** 7–11, 18–19, 50. **References:** *PIR*^{2} C 802; Champlin 1980: 64–4, 104–5; Tobin 1997; van den Hout 1999: 94–7; Pomeroy 2007.

Family Trees

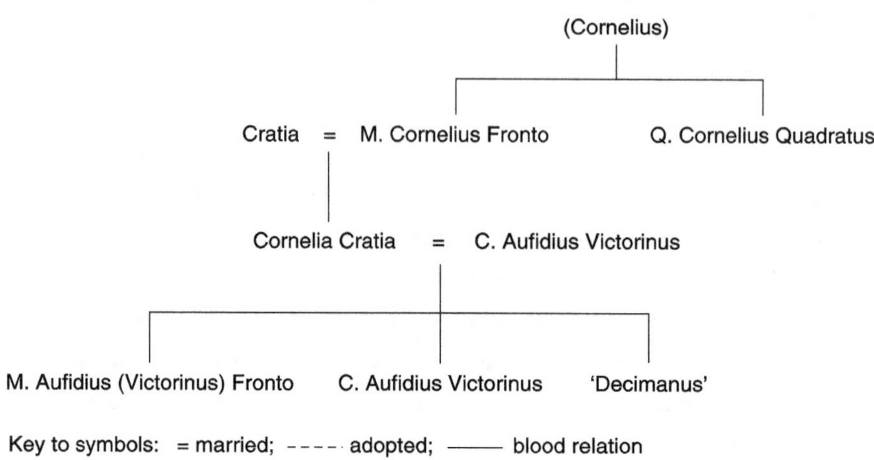

Figure 1: Fronto's Family

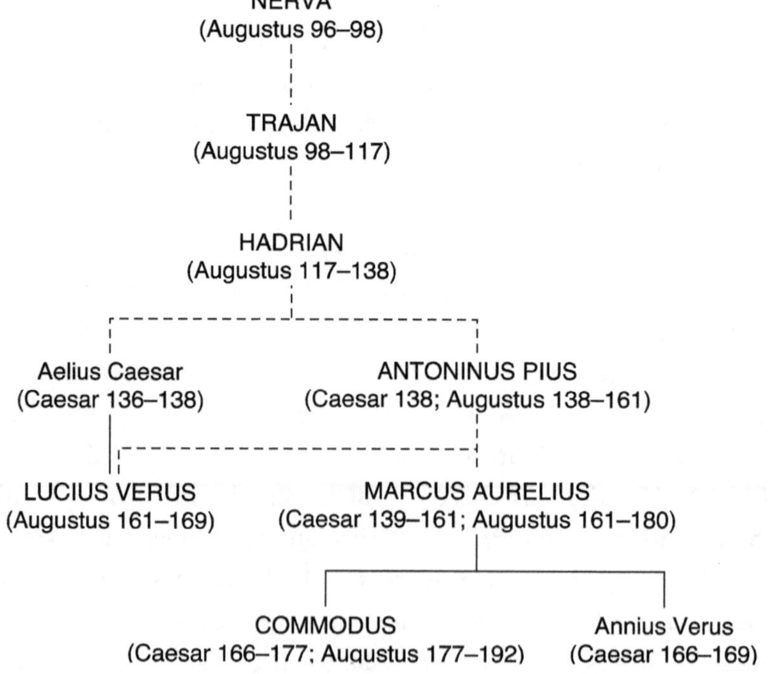

Figure 2: The Imperial Succession in the Second Century

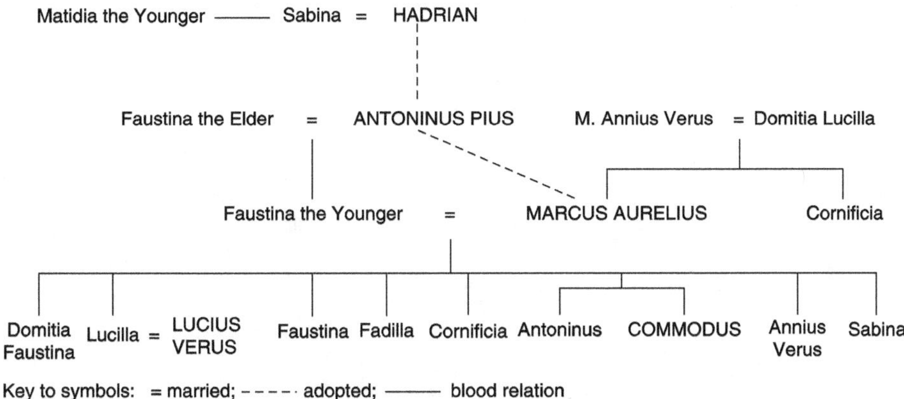

Figure 3: The Antonine Imperial Family

NB: Lucius Verus was adopted by Antoninus Pius, but it is not possible to represent that relationship on this stemma. For reasons of space, this stemma only includes one child of Pius and Faustina the Elder, and only nine of the fourteen children of Marcus and Faustina the Younger. For the complete family, see the diagrams in Birley (1993: 234–9).

1

Educating Caesar

Introduction

Soon after Antoninus Pius' accession to the throne in 138, Fronto was employed by the emperor to serve as Marcus Aurelius' tutor in Latin rhetoric. None of Fronto's surviving correspondence can be convincingly dated before this year (Champlin 1974: 158–9). **Letter 1** is one of the earliest letters from Fronto to his pupil, probably written in 139, and its tone is staid and formal compared with their later correspondence (Champlin 1974: 143–4; van den Hout 1999: 150). In the course of chastising the young Marcus for thoughtlessness and imprecision in his choice of words, Fronto reveals his own list of Latin literary greats whose use of language is to be admired. He wanted to instil in Marcus a love of the great works of Latin literature, especially of the Republican period, and to encourage him to take inspiration from them in his speeches and letters. The purpose of such an education was to socialise the prince in the ways of a Roman statesman (on this process, see Connolly 2011; see also Morgan 1998).

Fronto's principal method of instructing Marcus was to set him literary exercises, which required the prince to compose a piece of writing on a set theme or subject (usually of a historical nature). This was a standard technique for the teaching of rhetoric and composition in the Roman world (Bonner 1977: 250–76). Although these exercises could sometimes deal with philosophical or abstract questions, Fronto took after Cicero in his preference for exercises drawn from the world of Roman politics and law (Corbeill 2010: 72–4). We can observe this process in action in **Letter 2**, in which Marcus discusses an assignment to be inspired by the work of Coelius Antipater, and in **Letter 4**, where he is working on a piece concerning the trial of a Republican politician, Sulpicius Galba. Fronto was not a professional rhetorician, and his instruction never seems to have been of a very practical nature (Kennedy 1972:

597–600). In **Letter 3**, for example, he appears more concerned with rhetorical theory than in advising Marcus about preparing for, memorising, and then delivering a speech.

The letters also enable us to trace the developing relationship between teacher and pupil. In this, the difference in Fronto's tone between **Letters 1** and **3** is immediately apparent. In **Letter 3** we find him somewhat anxious that he is moving too quickly for his pupil, who is still a novice in the art of rhetoric. The letter ends with a friendly coda, including best wishes for Marcus' mother, Domitia Lucilla: this becomes a staple of the letters of the early 140s. **Letters 3–6** should all be dated to this period, in which the prince visits Lorium and Centumcellae, where he opens a new game park (**Letter 4**), and the *Villa Magna* at Anagnia, where he participates in the harvesting of grapes (**Letters 5–6**). The letters allowed Fronto and Marcus to keep each other informed of their various activities, while the prince was able to display the fruits of his education. **Letters 5** and **6** show Marcus engaging in literary word play and rhetorical flourishes, drawn from his reading in the classics of archaic Latin literature, which Fronto particularly favoured. Several of these letters (especially **2** and **6**) reveal the extent of Marcus' growing admiration and love for his tutor.

Letter 1. Fronto to Marcus (139)

Ad M. Caes. 4.3, VdH[2] pp. 56–9 = Haines I, pp. 2–13.

Fronto to my lord,

1. In all branches of learning, I consider that it is better for the pupil to be completely inexperienced and ignorant rather than to have some prior experience or education.* For someone who knows that he is a novice in the field sets less lofty goals, and consequently does not have as far to fall when he fails – for lack of confidence keeps audacity effectively in check. On the other hand, when a man tries to pass off his superficial acquaintance with a subject as evidence of real erudition, he is usually tripped up by his sham self-confidence. Generally, this is thought to be true for the study of philosophy too, for it is better to have avoided it completely rather than to have had only a little

taste, on the proverbial 'tips of the lips'. The very worst men of all turn out to be those who linger at philosophy's doorstep, but turn around before they have even crossed the threshold. However, in other areas of study, it is occasionally possible for someone to lie low and be regarded as knowledgeable for a time, when in fact he actually knows nothing at all. He is immediately exposed through his choice of words and the way he expresses himself. It is not possible for someone to employ language as a tool of deception for too long, since he will eventually reveal that he has no real knowledge of the words he uses, has judged them poorly, assessed them rashly, treated them ignorantly, and has failed to recognise their true weight or importance.

2. It was for this reason that few of our literary forefathers* diligently committed themselves to the hard work, dedication, and trial of searching for the right words. Looking at all those orators who have graced the earth, we can count among this select group only M. Porcius,* and C. Sallustius,* who often imitated his style. Out of the poets, this is true of Plautus,* of course, and even more so of Q. Ennius* and L. Coelius,* who matched him in erudition, as well as Naevius,* Lucretius,* Accius,* Caecilius* and Laberius.* Beyond these writers, we should give due credit to those who excel in their own genre, such as Novius,* Pomponius* and others of their ilk in the use of rustic, humorous, and farcical vocabulary. We can include Atta,* for his language appropriate for female performers, Sisenna,* for bawdy situations, and Lucilius,* for art and business.

3. You have probably been wondering where I would place M. Tullius,* who is famous as the font and source of Roman eloquence. I think that he always used the most beautiful language and surpassed all other orators in his structuring of the arguments that he wished to expound. However, it seems to me that he was not the most diligent man when it came to seeking out appropriate words.* This may have been the result of the greatness of his intellect or aversion to hard work. Or it could be that he believed that those rare words, which most men would be unlikely to find by searching for them, would simply appear before him without any effort to look for them. Thus I have established from a most careful reading of all his works over a sustained period that he used all types of words richly and profusely. There are literal and figurative words, simple and compound words, and words that are noble and really quite charming, which are on display throughout his works. However,

you will discover very few words that are unexpected or surprising in any of his speeches. I am referring to the sort of words that could not be tracked down without due application, care, alertness, and a great knowledge of ancient poetry.

I call a word unexpected and surprising when the reader or listener could not foresee or anticipate it. If one were to remove it from the sentence and challenge the reader to find a replacement, he would not be able to come up with a new word (or at least nothing that would suit the context as perfectly). And that is why I lavish praise on you when you employ skill and diligence in this matter, digging up a word from the depths of your learning and adapting it for the point you wish to make. But, as I said above, there is a great danger inherent in doing this, since you could use a word in an inappropriate fashion or without clarity or charm, like a man who is not yet fully proficient in his subject. For it is vastly preferable to use common and ordinary language rather than terms that are curious and unfamiliar, if they basically mean the same thing.

4. It might be useful for me to show how significant the problem of deciding which words to use actually is, and what precise and careful attention you must show in the process, so that this does not discourage the minds of young students or cripple their hopes of success. Often, the transposition, omission, or alteration of one single letter changes the power and polish of a word entirely, and makes the speaker's knowledge and refinement clear to all. In this regard, I have observed that when you have been reading your exercises aloud to me,* and I have changed one of the syllables in a word, you have decided to ignore me and not given it much thought. But I do not want you to be ignorant of the great difference that a single syllable can make. For example, one uses *colluere* to speak of 'rinsing' the mouth, but *pelluere* to refer to 'scrubbing' the floor in the baths. When we want to say that the cheeks are 'washed' with tears, we use *lavere*, not *pelluere* or *colluere*. But clothes are 'washed' with the verb *lavare*, not *lavere*, and sweat and dust are 'washed away' with *abluere*, not *lavare*. It is more appropriate to speak of a stain being 'washed clean' with *eluere*, rather than to use *abluere*. But if the stain has embedded itself and cannot be removed without some damage, I would use the Plautine word *elavere*, 'to scrub off'. Then there is also *diluere*, for 'watering down' mead, *proluere* for 'gargling' the throat, and *subluere* for 'washing under' horses' hooves.

5. There are numerous cases in which the change of a single syllable or letter can transform the meaning or sense of a word. So to give one example, I would be speaking correctly if I used *litam* to refer to a face 'decked out' with make-up, but then used *oblitum* to describe a body 'smeared' with filth, *delitum* for a cup 'coated' in honey, *praelitum* for the sword 'tipped' with poison, and *inlitum* for a stake 'daubed' with bird-lime – yes, all those, by Hercules!

6. Now, perhaps there is someone who will ask:* 'Who is going to stop me from using *lavere* instead of *lavare* when I want to speak of "washing" clothes, or if I say that I am "washing" away sweat with *lavare* rather than *abluere*?' Of course, there is no one who has the power to prevent or moderate your actions in this regard, since you are the offspring of free parents,* possess far more than the minimum census qualification for the equestrian order, and are even asked to give your opinion in the senate. But as for people like me, who have devoted our lives to servicing the ears of learned men,* it is necessary to follow these specific and precise rules with great care. Some men struggle to form words, going at them with hammers and tongs as if they were carving flints, while others labour over them like little gemstones using a small chisel and tiny hammer. In your case, since you need to gain greater facility in searching for words yourself, it will be more appropriate for you to take note of the mistake when you are corrected, rather than demur or be discouraged when you are caught out. For if you stop looking, you will never find anything, but if you persevere with your quest, you will be successful.

7. To take this point further, you seemed to have paid no attention to me when I changed the order of your words so that 'three-headed' came before the name Geryon.* Pay attention to this point: words can be necessary or superfluous depending on their order in a sentence. For example, I would be speaking correctly if I referred to a 'ship with three banks of oars' (*navis triremis*), but it would be unnecessary to add the word 'ship' to 'trireme' (*triremis navis*).* For there is no danger that someone would think that the word *triremis* referred to a litter, wagon, or cithara with three banks of oars. And then, when you were discussing why the Parthians have wide sleeves, you wrote, I think, that 'heat was suspended by the slits in their clothes'. But really, now, how was the heat 'suspended'?* Of course, I am not rebuking you for going out on a limb and using such a metaphor in a rather bold fashion, for I do concur with the sentiments of Ennius that an orator ought to be bold. So, let an orator be

bold then, as Ennius wanted, but do not let him stray from making his desired meaning clear. Therefore, I lavished approval and praise on your wish to embark on a search for a specific word, but I admonished your carelessness for selecting a word that sounded wrong. For it is not possible for heat to be 'suspended' through the openings of sleeves that are actually wide and flowing. However, it is possible for heat to be 'sent out' through the slits in clothes, and it can also be 'sent through', or 'sent down',* 'circulated', 'dissipated', or 'ventilated'. In fact almost anything works better than 'suspended', a word which means something is 'held from on high', not 'drawn off through vents'.

8. After this, I gave you advice on what you should do to prepare yourself for writing a work of history,* since that is what you wished. Since the exposition of such a matter would take quite a long time, I will bring matters to a halt here so I don't go beyond what is appropriate for a letter.* If you want me to write to you concerning this topic, be sure to keep reminding me.

Commentary

prior experience or education: From a young age, Marcus had received the appropriate education in reading, elocution, and Greek and Latin grammar (Fantham 1996: 239–41). Fronto is referring to the study of Latin rhetoric as appropriate for an orator, as he was the prince's sole tutor in this area.

our literary forefathers: Fronto was an admirer of the style of Latin written in the Republican period, as shown by the following list of authors. His enthusiasm in this area was shared by a number of other Romans of the second century, including Aulus Gellius and the emperor Hadrian. This was a movement that to some extent paralleled developments in the Greek world (Champlin 1980: 45–59; Holford-Strevens 2005: 3–6; 354–63). However, as Holford-Strevens (2005: 6) has argued, Fronto and his contemporaries should be termed 'mannerists' rather than 'archaists', because they did not write entirely in old Latin, bur rather used archaic vocabulary selectively in their works. The use of archaic language was a significant change from the previous century, when the rhetorician Quintilian warned against excessive use of old forms (*Principles of Oratory* 2.5.21). For reasons of space, it is possible to give only very brief biographies of these authors: for further details, readers should consult the entries in the *Oxford Classical Dictionary.*

M. Porcius: Marcus Porcius Cato (234–149 BC) was a prominent statesman and general of the Republican era. His most famous works were *The Origins*, a history of Rome from its foundation, and *On Agriculture*, a handbook for the elite on estate farming. Fragments of approximately eighty speeches survive today, though Cicero (*Brutus* 65) is said to have read more than one hundred and fifty of them (Sciarrino 2007: 54–60). **Letters: 3, 5, 6, 15, 46** and **49.**

C. Sallustius: Gaius Sallustius Crispus, better known today as Sallust, was a senator and historian of the late Republic. He wrote *The Jugurthine War* and *The War of Catiline*, as well as an annalistic account of Roman history from 78 BC, known as *The Histories* (now fragmentary). These works were famous in antiquity, influencing later historians such as Tacitus, and Sallust was one of the most popular authors studied at school (Morgan 1998: 97–9; O'Gorman 2007). **Letters: 46** and **47**.

Plautus: T. Maccius Plautus, who lived in the mid-third to early second century BC, was a Roman comic playwright, and an especial favourite of Fronto. Many of his plays were based on Greek originals but adapted for the Roman audience. Plautus wrote at least twenty-one plays, including *The Bacchises, The Merchant, The Little Carthaginian*, and *The Boastful Soldier* (Manuwald 2011: 225–34). **Letters: 13, 41, 46** and **48**.

Q. Ennius: Quintus Ennius (239–169 BC), one of the earliest poets to write in Latin, is best remembered for his eighteen-book work, *Annals*, an epic chronicling the history of Rome from Aeneas until the second century BC. Ennius also wrote more than twenty tragedies in Latin, based on Greek originals (Manuwald 2011: 204–9). **Letters: 3** and **41**

L. Coelius: L. Coelius Antipater, who lived in the late second century BC, was the author of an account of the Second Punic War, said to be the first history in Latin written in an ornate style (Mellor 1999: 20–1). His work was well known in literary circles of Antonine Rome: not only was it quoted by Aulus Gellius

(*Attic Nights* 10.24.6–7), but the emperor Hadrian, with his taste for the archaic, is said to have preferred it to Sallust (*HA Hadrian* 16.6). See also **Letter 2**.

Naevius: Cn. Naevius was a Roman author of the third century BC, who wrote comedy, tragedy, and the epic poem *The Punic War* (Manuwald 2011: 194–5). See also **Letter 13**.

Lucretius: T. Lucretius Carus was a follower of Epicurus who lived in the first century BC. He wrote the six-book poem *On the Nature of Things*. See also **Letter 41**.

Accius: L. Accius, who flourished in the second century BC, was a Roman playwright and author of over forty tragedies. The majority of these were based on Greek myths. In addition to his dramatic works, Accius was also the author of several works on rhetoric and literature (Manuwald 2011: 216–25). See also **Letter 41**.

Caecilius: Caecilius Statius, another comic poet of the late third and early second century BC, was a former slave from the tribe of the Insubrian Gauls in north Italy. He wrote some forty-two comic plays, which were predominantly derived from Greek models (Manuwald 2011: 234–42). See also **Letter 15**.

Laberius: Decimus Laberius (106–43 BC) was an author of more than forty mimes, which were produced in Rome in the first century BC. Mimes were plays performed by barefoot actors without masks, and the cast included women as well as men. There was no set form of mime, and they ranged from more serious affairs to bawdy farces, usually comprising elements of political satire (Manuwald 2011: 178–83). See also **Letter 15**.

Novius: Novius was a first-century BC playwright whose works were in the bawdy style of Atellan farce, which originated at Atella in Campania, and was first performed at Rome in the third century BC. The plays generally featured stock characters such as clowns and hunchbacks in rural settings (Manuwald 2011: 169–77). **Letters: 3** and **6**.

Pomponius: L. Pomponius was the other principal author of Atellan farce in the first century BC, writing around seventy plays (Manuwald 2011: 267–70).

Atta: T. Quinctius Atta, a comic playwright of the first century BC, wrote *fabulae togatae*, plays which focused on Roman daily life. He was one of three men renowned for writing such plays, the other two being his predecessors Titinius and L. Afranius. Fronto's remark refers to the female characters in his plays, many of which dealt with domestic affairs (Manuwald 2011: 266–7)

Sisenna: L. Cornelius Sisenna was a senator, historian, and orator of the late Republic. His *Histories* covered political events of the 90s and 80s BC, including the Social War and Sulla's dictatorship. The 'bawdy words' refers to the *Milesian Tales* of Aristides, which Sisenna translated from Greek into Latin, and which were known for their sexually explicit content (Harrison 1998).

Lucilius: The poet C. Lucilius, who lived in the second century BC, was a wealthy member of the equestrian order. He gained fame for his thirty books of satires, a genre in which he was the acknowledged master, with his targets including several contemporary politicians. Lucilius was a champion of the Latin language, and was opposed to the unnecessary use of Greek (Von Albrecht 1997: 250–66).

M. Tullius: This is the great statesman and orator of the late Republic, M. Tullius Cicero, whose works exercised a profound influence on subsequent generations of Roman authors. Fronto would later write to Marcus that 'nothing is more perfect' than Cicero's letters, even his speeches (*Ad Ant. Imp.* 3.8, VdH^2 p. 104 = *Ad Ant. Imp.* 2.5, Haines II, pp. 156–8). This passage is one of the rare occasions on which Fronto does not express unstinting admiration for Cicero. The criticism that he did not seek out rare words is specific to Fronto's message here: such a task is so difficult, and requires such a depth of reading, that even Cicero could fall short.

seeking out appropriate words: In his *Attic Nights* (19.8), Aulus Gellius recounts an incident at Fronto's house which illustrates the orator's fondness for obscure words. A debate had broken out concerning the proper use of the singular and plural forms of *quadriga* ('chariot') and *harena* ('sand'). Fronto suggested his friends consult a range of Latin authors to try to solve the problem, but he also hoped it would encourage them to search for rare and unusual words in the future.

when you have been reading your exercises aloud to me: This statement makes clear that Fronto's letters to Marcus are a supplement to face-to-face teaching. Fronto contrasted this method of proactive instruction in rhetoric, involving composition, memorisation, and recitation, with what he saw as the more silent and passive study of philosophy (*De Eloquentia* 5.4, VdH^2 pp. 151–2 = *De Eloquentia* 4.3, Haines II, pp. 82–3).

someone who will ask: The introduction of a historical or imaginary figure into a speech or piece of writing is known as *prosopopoeia*, a technique used by Cicero (Anderson 2000: 106–7). This allows the author to speak as another person in order to emphasise their point, or to introduce a form of dialogue.

the offspring of free parents: Fronto presents three definitions of Marcus' public standing, each more important than the next. Free birth was a legal status, and a prerequisite for membership of the both the equestrian and senatorial orders. All equestrians had to have property worth 400,000 sesterces in order to qualify; they also had to be formally admitted by the emperor (Duncan-Jones 2006: 185–6, 219–21, cf. Millar 1977: 279–90). Hadrian had granted Marcus equestrian rank when he was six years old (*HA Marcus* 4.1). Marcus had subsequently entered the senate as quaestor, the most junior magistracy, in 139, the year this letter was written. For further discussion, see **Letter 2.**

devoted our lives to servicing the ears of learned men: Fronto uses the metaphor of servitude to contrast his status with Marcus' 'freedom' (Fleury 2001: 120–1), a somewhat disingenuous comment that reminds us of the unequal relationship between master and pupil. Fronto here uses a Latin phrase (*servituti serviendae*), which is a typical formulation of the playwright Plautus, one of his favourite authors (van den Hout 1999: 159).

'three-headed' came before the name Geryon: Geryon was a three-headed giant who lived on the island of Erytheia beyond the pillars of Heracles (Hesiod, *Theogony* 979–80). He owned the red cattle that Heracles was assigned to capture as his tenth labour. It was better Latin to put 'three-headed' (*triceps*) before 'Geryon' since adjectives of size or quantity usually preceded the noun they describe (Mountford 1938: 19).

it would be unnecessary to add the word 'ship' to 'trireme' (*triremis navis*): *Triremis* is a Latin adjective meaning 'having three banks of oars', as in Fronto's first formulation (*navis triremis*). However, it can also be used on its own as a noun to mean 'a ship with three banks of oars', as in Fronto's second formulation. The use of the word *triremis* in this manner makes the noun *navis* ('ship') redundant. For adjectives used as nouns in Latin, see Mountford (1938: 50–2).

how was the heat 'suspended'? Marcus used the verb *suspendo*, which means 'to hang, suspend' as well as 'to be uncertain', much as suspended is used in English. However, as van den Hout (1999: 161) points out, the prince's use of *suspendo* in this context was not entirely unprecedented.

'sent out' . . . 'sent through', or 'sent down': Fronto launches into a display of erudition, establishing that in this aspect of their relationship, he has the upper hand. His knowledge is emphasised by the alliteration of the suggested words: ***d**epelli* ('sent out'), ***d**egi* ('sent through'), and ***d**emeare* ('sent down').

a work of history: In the Roman world, there was no such thing as a 'professional historian'. Historians were generally, though not always, elite men who were accomplished in fields such as politics, warfare, law, or oratory. The writing of history was heavily influenced by rhetorical theory and the idea that the facts could be marshalled to suit the arguments of the historian. Speeches were also an integral part of Roman historical writing, allowing the author to bring his characters to life while displaying his own rhetorical prowess (Woodman 1988; Marincola 2007). Fronto's expertise in rhetoric therefore made him a suitable person to provide advice on the writing of history. He would later be commissioned to write a history of the Parthian Wars waged by Lucius Verus, though he never finished it (**Letters 47, 49**; Kemezis 2010). Many

Roman emperors wrote memoirs or autobiographies, most notably Augustus' famous *Res Gestae*, but also Tiberius, Claudius, his wife Agrippina the Younger, Vespasian, and Hadrian. The emperor Claudius was also famous for writing histories of Rome, the Etruscans, and the Carthaginians (Suetonius, *Claudius* 41.1–2). Marcus is not known to have produced a historical work.

what is appropriate for a letter: Roman writers often noted that there was a certain length appropriate for a letter, usually when they felt they had exceeded it, and this is especially evident in Pliny the Younger (e.g. *Letters* 2.5, 4.17, 8.6, with Gibson and Morello 2012: 244–8, 254–5). Brevity was one of the key attributes of a letter, according to ancient epistolary theorists (Demetrius, *On Style* 228 = Trapp 2003: no. 73). Letters composed of numerous papyrus rolls transgressed the limits of the genre, as they appeared more like a book (White 2010: 64–5).

Letter 2. Marcus to Fronto (139)

Ad M. Caes. 3.9, VdH^2 p. 42 = *Epist. Graec.* 6, Haines I, pp. 18–21.

Hello, my wonderful teacher,

1. If you've been able to get some sleep after the bouts of insomnia that you've been complaining about, I'd hope you'd write to me. And I'd tell you that your first priority is to look after your health. Then, make sure you hide and bury somewhere that axe of Tenes* that you're threatening to use. Now don't stop your practice of pleading cases, or everyone else might as well do the same.

2. You say that you have made a rough draft of something in Greek* that makes you happier than almost anything else you have written. Wasn't it you recently giving me an earful about why I was writing in Greek?* But now it is really very important that I write in Greek. Why? Well, I want to test myself, to see whether I can more easily pick up those things that I've not yet learnt, since those things that I *have* learnt fail me. Now if you did really care for me, you'd have sent me this new something that makes you so happy. Anyway, I do read

your work, even if you are reluctant for me to do so, and that's what makes life worth living.

3. You've sent me a grisly subject this time. I've not read the piece of Coelius that you sent, and I won't, until I've worked out the right sentiments to use. But the speech I have to give as Caesar* has me gripped within its vicious vice. Now finally I realise how much work it actually is to write something for a long time, producing and then polishing only a few lines a day.

4. Goodbye, my inspiration. Shouldn't I be blazing with love for you since you wrote to me? What should I do? I can't stop it. But I can say that at the same time and place last year I was consumed with longing for my mother. This year, it's you who arouses this same longing.* My mother sends her best wishes.

Commentary

axe of Tenes: Tenes was the son of Cycnus, king of Colonae in the Troad. After Tenes was falsely accused of rape, Cycnus locked him and his sister in a chest and set them adrift at sea. The chest made landfall at the island of Leucophrye, and the inhabitants made Tenes their king. When Cycnus discovered the truth, he sailed to the island to beg forgiveness from his children. Cycnus moored his boat by tying it to a rock on the mainland, but Tenes refused to meet with him and cut the rope with an axe (Pausanias 10.14.2). The reference to the 'axe of Tenes' is thus to a hasty action which cannot be undone.

something in Greek: This appears to be the so-called *Treatise on Love*, which Fronto would soon send to Marcus (*Addit.* 8, VdH[2] pp. 250–5 = *Epist. Graec.* 8, Haines I, pp. 20–31). The work was written in Attic Greek in the style of the speech of Lysias in Plato's *Phaedrus*, a philosophical work of the fourth-century BC that examined education, rhetoric, and love, particularly towards young men. The work enjoyed a particular revival in the second century AD as part of the Greek 'Second Sophistic', and would have been familiar to all educated men of the period (Trapp 1990). In an extended form of rhetorical role-play, Fronto addresses Marcus as if he were one such Greek youth. Richlin (2006a: 36–9) translates the *Treatise* in the style of eighteenth century English, capturing the tenor of Fronto's expression perfectly. Marcus replied in effusive terms expressing his love and devotion to his teacher (*Addit.* 7, VdH[2] pp. 249–50 = *Epist. Graec.* 7, Haines I, pp. 30–3). The exchange is as much about Greek rhetoric and education as it is about love – a literary game, if you will – for the two were inextricably linked in Plato's world (Swain 2004: 20–1; Richlin 2006b: 116–7).

why I was writing in Greek? Fronto was perfectly capable of writing in good Greek, and does so on several occasions in the corpus of letters, especially when social or cultural reasons dictated use of the language (Swain 2004: 17–28). Marcus had been trained to read and write in both Greek and Latin, but he may have only just begun intensive study in Greek rhetoric at this time. However, as Marcus' tutor in Latin rhetoric, Fronto preferred his pupil to write in that language.

the speech I have to give as Caesar: In 139 Marcus was appointed quaestor, co-opted into the major priestly colleges, and made a leader of one of the six equestrian squadrons (*HA Marcus* 6.3), although he is not attested with the title of 'prince of the youth' (*princeps iuventutis*) as was the case with many previous sons of emperors (Horster 2011: 97–8). The most important development was that he was also formally granted the name 'Caesar', becoming M. Aelius Aurelius Verus Caesar (Birley 1993: 56). The mint of Rome began to produce coins of Pius bearing Marcus' portrait and titles on the reverse, and, in 140, minted coins in Marcus' own name (Börner 2012: 279).

The second century witnessed the transformation of 'Caesar' from a name to a title that effectively designated the heir to the throne (Horster 2011: 97–103). The Latin term used by Marcus in this letter is *Caesaris oratio*, which could be translated as 'speech of Caesar' or 'speech as a Caesar'. Some scholars have preferred the first option, arguing that Marcus was writing a speech in the style of Julius Caesar (Champlin 1974: 143; Richlin 2006a: 34–5). We think the second option is more likely, as does van den Hout (1999: 112), since Marcus draws an explicit contrast between the homework assignment set by Fronto, and the speech that is occupying the rest of his time. This interpretation of *Caesaris oratio* is supported by a fragmentary letter of the early 140s, in which

Fronto offers some thoughts on public speaking (*Ad M. Caes.* 3.1, VdH^2 p. 35 = Haines I, pp. 52–3).

> For instance, when it was necessary for you to speak in the senate or before a meeting of the populace, you used no inappropriate word, no obscure or unfashionable figure of speech, since you know that a Caesar's eloquence should be like a trumpet, not a flute, since flutes are quieter and trickier to play.

In late 139, Marcus would have been preparing his speech of thanks (*gratiarum actio*) for the consulship, a post that he would formally assume on 1 January 140. In a letter sent in 161/2, shortly after Marcus became emperor, Fronto reminded him of a speech he had delivered in the senate 'when he was barely beyond youth' (*Ad Ant. Imp.* 1.2.5, VdH^2 p. 88 = Haines II, pp. 38–9), which may be identical with the oration mentioned here.

This year, it's you who arouses this same longing: The language in this last passage firmly establishes the depth of Marcus' feelings, which seem to derive at least partially from his admiration for his tutor's intellectual abilities, hence the description of Fronto as 'my inspiration' (*spiritus meus*). It is telling that Marcus uses the same word, *desiderium*, to refer to his feelings for both Domitia and Fronto; it can mean 'longing' or 'desire' in both sexual and non-sexual ways (for the former, see Catullus *Poem* 2.5; for the latter Livy 21.4). Richlin (2011: 170) points out that Marcus is growing up, and his mother is no longer the centre of his world. But it is clear the young prince is also rather self-consciously using the amorous language of Latin love poetry to impress and flatter his tutor.

Letter 3. Fronto to Marcus (early 140s)

Ad M. Caes. 3.17, VdH^2 pp. 49–50 = *Ad M. Caes.* 3.16, Haines I, pp. 104–7.

To my lord,

1. Just in case you think I got some sleep, I was actually up almost all night going over in my mind whether I had inadvertently been too relaxed and kind

in my criticism of some defect in your work, all because of my affection for you. I considered whether you ought to be more skilled and proficient in eloquence at this stage, and whether your natural talents were being inhibited by idleness or carelessness. As I was worrying about these things, I realised that you've advanced further in your study of eloquence than could be expected given your age and the time since you've started your studies. You have exceeded my expectations about your progress, even though they were very high.

2. But what does this mean? In the middle of the night it struck me what type of speech you are actually writing. It's an epideictic one, and nothing is more difficult than that. Why? Because, although there are three accepted types of oratory – epideictic, symbouleutic, and forensic* – and the others are much less of an uphill struggle, being in their various ways like a downhill slope or level plain, the epideictic speech is a difficult slog. Likewise, although there are roughly three stylistic forms used in speeches – simple, standard, and grand* – there is almost no place in epideictic oratory for the simple style, which is essential for legal speeches. In epideictic oratory, everything must be written in the grand style, embellished and decked out with all the rhetorical trimmings, while there is little use for such flourishes in the standard style.

3. You will remember, of course, the great range of works that you have engaged with up to this point in time. There have been comedies, Atellan farces,* and the great orators of old, of which few – apart from Cato and Gracchus* – really resound like a trumpet: most of them bellow or whistle instead. Now tell me, what did you take away from Ennius when you read his work? How did tragedies help you in writing elevated verse? Indeed, verse helps greatly with the composition of oratory, just as oratory helps with the writing of verse. Now you have recently begun to read ornate and bombastic speeches: don't force yourself to try and imitate them at once. But, as I've said, we shall devote ourselves to the task and do our best. Acting as your guarantor, bondsman, and benefactor, I will quickly lift you to the heights of eloquence: the gods will see to it, and they will be favourable.

4. Farewell, my lord, be of good heart and good spirit, and place your trust in time and practice. Give my best wishes to my lady, your mother. When you referred to the training of the Persians, *battunt* was a good word to use.*

Commentary

epideictic, symbouleutic, and forensic: These three types of rhetorical speech were outlined by Aristotle (*Rhetoric* 1.3), and they were subsequently applied to Latin oratory (Cicero, *On Rhetorical Invention* 1.7; Quintilian, *Principles of Oratory* 3.4.1–16). An epideictic speech was an example of 'display' oratory, designed to showcase the speaker's talents, rather than to argue a specific point. Funeral orations and panegyrics in praise of individuals, places, or things were usually classed as examples of epideictic rhetoric (Menander Rhetor 332, 418–22). In contrast, symbouleutic rhetoric was the oratory of the political world, and might be performed in the Greek assembly or the Roman senate, while forensic oratory was the genre of the law court speech. The three genres are discussed by Carey (2010), Cooper (2010) and Usher (2010), respectively.

simple, standard, and grand: Fronto's contemporary Aulus Gellius (*Attic Nights* 6.14.1–2) outlines the same stylistic divisions, which were initially derived from Greek rhetoric (Demetrius, *On Style* 190).

Atellan farces: Comic playwrights number among those cited favourably by Fronto in **Letter 1**. The plays of Terence were a common part of any school curriculum, but Fronto probably exposed his pupil to a wider range of works owing to his love for archaic language (Von Albrecht 1997: 1,436–7; Claassen 2009: 58–61). Marcus clearly did his reading in this area, as **Letters 5** and **6** reveal.

Cato and Gracchus: For Cato, see **Letter 1**. 'Gracchus' is probably C. Sempronius Gracchus, tribune of the plebs in 123–121 BC, rather than his elder brother Tiberius, based on his citations by other authors of the Antonine age (Gellius, *Attic Nights* 1.11.15, 10.3.4; Gunderson 2009: 67–8).

***battunt* was a good word to use:** *Battunt* means 'they strike', deriving from the verb *battuo*, which was used colloquially in the second century to refer to fighting between soldiers and gladiators (Holford-Strevens 2010: 337–8). It was therefore appropriate for a discussion of military training.

Letter 4. Fronto to Marcus (early 140s)

Ad M. Caes. 3.21, VdH^2 pp. 51–2 = Haines I, pp. 172–3.

To my lord,

1. I'm staying in bed. If I'm ready for the journey when you go to Centumcellae,* I will see you at Lorium* on the seventh day before the Ides, if the gods favour me. Please give my apologies to our lord, your father, whom – and I wish good health and safety to you both – I love and cherish rather earnestly and deeply, and with great affection, since there was such a sound judgement passed in the senate,* which preserved the safety of the provinces and punished the guilty parties fairly.

2. When you open your game park,* you must remember that if you hit an animal, you must spur on your horse.

3. You will, of course, bring your Galba* to Centumcellae. Or can you be at Lorium on the eighth day before the Ides? Farewell, lord, and make sure you please your father, greet your mother, and long for me.

4. What Cato says about Galba's acquittal, you know better than me; I recall that he was acquitted on account of his brother's sons. Find out yourself whether this is accurate. Cato advised that no one should bring either their own or another's children for the purpose of gaining sympathy, nor their wives, relatives, or any women full stop. Give my best wishes to your mother, my lord.

Commentary

Centumcellae: Centumcellae (modern day Civitavecchia) was situated in Latium, some 62 km north west of Rome along the Via Aurelia. Trajan had constructed a villa when he was building his new harbour (Pliny the Younger, *Letters* 6.31), and the residence remained imperial property throughout the Antonine period. For details on the archaeological record, see Marzano (2007: 164–5, 353–8).

Lorium: Lorium was the site of another imperial villa on the Via Aurelia, and it was where Antoninus Pius died in 161 (Marcus, *Meditations* 1.16.8; *HA Pius*

1.8, 12.6). The site may be identified with the remains of a villa discovered at Castel di Guido, at the ninth milestone of the Via Aurelia (Marzano 2007: 311). Fronto himself owned a residence nearby, close enough for regular visits to Marcus. It is probably the same villa as the one in **Letter 48**.

sound judgement passed in the senate: The sentence is very enigmatic, as we do not know the full context of the case heard in the senate. It is tempting to see it as a reference to the condemnation of Cornelius Priscianus (*PIR*^{2} C 1418), governor of Hispania Citerior in 145, who was arraigned before the senate 'because he had disturbed the province of Hispania in a hostile fashion' (*Inscr. It.* 13.1 p. 205). Alternatively, Fronto could be referring to a case of provincial misgovernment, since such matters were regularly heard in the senate (Brunt 1961: 200–1; Talbert 1984: 464–6). A reference to provincial misgovernment would also fit in with the rest of the letter, which discusses the prosecution of the Republican senator Servius Sulpicius Galba. However, it was customary for the consuls, rather than the emperor, to preside over cases of maladministration in the senate (Talbert 1984: 481). This is one of many enigmatic historical references in the correspondence.

game park: The word *vivarium* can mean either a zoo, or a game reserve for the hunting of animals, as here. Game parks for the hunting of wild beasts had been attached to Roman villas since the late Republican period (Marzano 2007: 100). Hunting had long been a component of the aristocratic ideal, as shown by the treatises by Xenophon and Arrian on the subject. Game parks provided Roman aristocrats with an arena in which to display their manly excellence and courage (*virtus*) in peacetime (Edwards 2008: 42–5). Cassius Dio (72.36.2) mentions Marcus' hunting ability, despite his weak constitution. Even the decidedly unmilitary Pliny the Younger boasted of catching three boars on one occasion, though he treated the hunting expedition as an opportunity to clear his mind for further intellectual pursuits (*Letters* 1.6; Marchesi 2008: 118–20). Fronto is unlikely to have had much experience of hunting himself, making his instructions more than a little patronising.

your Galba: This does not refer to a living person, but a speech given by Cato the Elder against Servius Sulpicius Galba in 149 BC. Galba was indicted for massacring Lusitanians whom he had promised to treat fairly if they laid down their arms. Galba appealed to the sympathies of the Roman people by bringing his sons to the trial. Cato included his speech in his history, *The Origins*.

Letter 5. Marcus to Fronto (early 140s)

Ad M. Caes. 4.4, VdH[2] pp. 60–1 = Haines I, pp. 174–7.

Marcus Caesar greets his teacher Marcus Fronto,

1. After we'd got into the carriage, and I'd said goodbye to you, our journey wasn't too bad, apart from the odd sprinkling of rain. But before we came to the villa, we turned aside to Anagnia,* nearly a mile down the road. Then we saw that ancient town* – it's very small, of course, but has lots of antiquities, with more temples and religious objects than you could count. There was no part of the town where there wasn't some sanctuary, shrine, or temple.* There were also lots of linen books* dealing with religious subjects. Then when we were on our way out, we saw written twice in the gateway: '*Flamen*, put on your *samentum*'.* I asked someone who lived there what that last word meant. He said it was the Hernician word for the hide of the sacrificial victim, which the priest places on top of his cap when he enters into the city. We learnt lots of other things that we wanted to know too. But there's one thing we really don't want, and that's the fact that you're not here, and it really worries us.

2. Now, after you set out, did you go to the Aurelian region, or to Campania? Be sure to write and let me know, and tell me whether you've begun harvesting the grapes* too, and whether you brought a multitude of books to your villa, and also whether you miss me, which I know it's stupid to ask, since you do that of your own accord. Now if you *do* miss me and care for me, send me lots of letters, since they soothe and comfort me. For I'd really, really rather have the pick of your letters* than all the Massican and Gauran vines. For the Signian wines* are rank and rancid and have bitter berries, which means I'd prefer to drink them as wine rather than juice. Besides, it's much more enjoyable to munch on the grapes when they're past it rather than in their prime: I prefer to crush them with my feet rather than crunch them with my teeth. But let

them be favourable and forgiving to me, and may they verily pardon me* for these jokes. Farewell, my dearest, most charming, and most learned fellow, most delightful teacher.

3. When you see the juice fermenting in the jar, I hope it reminds you that that's the way my longing for you gushes, overflows and foams in my chest. Take care always.

Commentary

Anagnia: Anagnia is in the Sacco valley, south east of Rome. The imperial villa (*Villa Magna*) has been excavated at the site of the monastery of S. Pietro di Villamagna (Fentress et al. 2007; Fentress and Maiuro 2011). The extant remains stretch across some eleven hectares, from the main residence in the north to the bath-house and winery in the south. The dating of the brickstamps indicate that the complex was originally built by Hadrian on the site of an earlier villa or villas dating back to the Republican period (Fentress and Maiuro 2011: 338–42).

that ancient town: Anagina was occupied by the tribe of the Hernici from the period of the Iron Age, before being conquered by Rome and made a *civitas sine suffragio* ('state without the vote') in 306 BC (Livy 9.43.23–4). Cicero owned a villa there (*Ad Att.* 12.1).

sanctuary, shrine, or temple: Archaeological investigations have revealed votive deposits of the sixth/fifth centuries BC on the site of the church of S. Cecilia in Anagnia (Gatti 1996).

linen books: Key religious and political texts had been written on linen since the Etruscan period. The linen books containing the names of Roman magistrates were kept in the Temple of Juno Moneta on the Capitoline (Livy 4.20.8; Pliny, *Natural History* 13.69).

'*Flamen*, put on your *samentum*': A *flamen* was a type of Roman priest devoted to specific gods, such as the *flamen Dialis* (Jupiter) and *flamen*

Martialis (Mars). The title of *flamen* was later given to other priests, including priests of the imperial cult in the provinces. The word *samentum* is elsewhere unattested, and must have been a word used by the Hernician tribe (Adams 2007: 178–9).

cap: The *flamines* at Rome wore a skullcap which was topped with a sharp point of olive wood, and tied around the chin with strings. This style of cap was used by priests both in Rome and the provinces (Fishwick 1990: 476).

harvesting the grapes: Wine was an integral part of the Roman villa economy in both coastal and country regions (Purcell 1985; Marzano 2007: 44–6, 102–24). This is the beginning of an extended discussion of winemaking, prompted by Marcus' stay at the *Villa Magna*, which featured a significant winery (Fentress and Maiuro 2011: 344–53).

the pick of your letters: Marcus is making a pun here, since the Latin verb *legere* can mean 'to read' or 'to pick out', and by extension 'to harvest'. The wines he mentions come from Mount Massicus and Gaurus in central Italy, and were both highly regarded in antiquity (Pliny, *Natural History* 14.64).

Signian wines: Marcus is referring to the wines produced at the *Villa Magna*, since it lay in the territory of Signia (Fentress and Maiuro 2011: 340–1). The 'juice' refers to the must or unfermented wine, produced during the crushing process. In our translation, the alliteration of '**rank** and **rancid**' and '**bitter berries**' replicates Marcus' own Latin (*isti nimis* ***rancidos racemos*** *et* ***acidos acinos*** *habent*). This stylistic quirk continues throughout the rest of the letter: (i) 'to munch on the grapes when they're **past it** rather than in their **prime**'; (ii) 'prefer to **crush** them with my feet rather than **crunch** them with my teeth'; (iii) 'but let them be **favourable** and **forgiving** to me'.

may they verily pardon me: The series of jests culminates in a rather over the top request for the wines to excuse Marcus for what he has said. Marcus uses archaic Latin (*duint*, an early present subjunctive) to make this mock apology, which we have tried to convey in this translation by using 'verily'. The overall effect is of a young man who is rather too pleased with his literary affectations.

Letter 6. Marcus to Fronto (early 140s)

Ad M. Caes. 4.6, VdH[2] pp. 62–3 = Haines I, pp. 180–3.

Greetings, dearest teacher,

1. We are doing fine. I slept in a bit because of a little cold, which seems to have settled down. So from five until nine in the morning I read from Cato's *On Agriculture*,* and wrote a little bit (less horribly, by Hercules, than yesterday). Then, after paying my respects to my father,* 'I tended my throat'.* I prefer to say this rather than 'I gargled', since the expression is found in Novius and elsewhere. I swallowed a mixture of honeyed wine and water, letting it pass down my throat, then spat it out again. After looking after my throat I went to my father and stood by while he made a sacrifice.* Then we went for our morning meal. What do you think I ate?* A little bread, though I saw others devouring beans and onions and little fish still stuffed with their eggs. Then we set to work gathering the grapes,* and sweated profusely and shouted and, as our author says, 'we left a few hanging high as witnesses to the harvest'.

2. After midday we returned home. I studied a little and it was fruitless. Then I had a long chat with my mummy as she sat on the bed. It went like this: 'What do you think my Fronto is doing now?' She said: 'But what do you think my Cratia is doing?' Then I said: 'But what do you think our little sparrow, baby Cratia, is doing?' While we were nattering in this way and arguing about which of us loved you all more, the gong sounded to announce that my father had gone to the baths.* And then we bathed and dined in the pressing room* – oh, I mean, we didn't bathe in the pressing room, but only ate there – and listened happily to the country folk bantering away. Then after I've returned, before I turn onto my side and snore, I do my day's work* and give my completely delightful teacher an account of the day. If I could miss you even more, I would gladly waste away some more.

3. Take care, my Fronto, wherever you are, you're truly as sweet as honey, my love, my joy. How do you feel about me? I love you in your absence.

Commentary

I read from Cato's *On Agriculture*: Marcus worked in the early morning quite often. In a previous letter, he tells Fronto that he studied from 3am to 8am (*Ad M. Caes.* 4.5 VdH[2] pp. 61–2 = Haines I, pp. 178–81). Cato the Elder's *On Agriculture* provided advice to wealthy Romans on how to run their estates and their workers. It was not just a practical handbook, but had a political agenda that stressed the importance of landed wealth and estate management to Roman aristocratic identity (Reay 2005).

paying my respects to my father: The morning *salutatio*, or reception, was a formal ceremony in which Roman aristocrats were visited by their clients. The *salutationes* of a Roman emperor were especially stage-managed affairs presided over by freedmen who supervised the entrance of the emperor's subjects in strict order of hierarchy (Millar 1977: 20–1, 110–1). The funerary monument of L. Plotius Sabinus recorded that he was among the second group admitted to see Antoninus Pius (*CIL* VI 41111 = *ILS* 1078). There may not have been such an elaborate ceremony at the *Villa Magna*, since Pius did not order his courtiers to accompany him on journeys outside Rome (Marcus, *Meditations* 1.16.2). The emperor apparently liked to spend the vintage time in the manner of a private citizen (*HA Pius* 11.2).

'I tended my throat': The quotation is from Novius, another alliterative turn of phrase (*fauces fovi* in the original Latin). Marcus prefers this to 'I gargled' (*gargarissavi*), which originally came from Greek. The reference to Novius, whose plays were often set in rural locations, is especially fitting.

made a sacrifice: The sacrifice marked the beginning of the harvesting of the grapes and the production of the wine. Fentress and Maiuro (2011: 356–7) suggest that the sacrifice could have been either a lamb dedicated to Jupiter, or a goat to Liber Pater, the god of wine and fertility.

What do you think I ate: Bread was a very typical morning meal for Romans of all status groups, as it is today in the Mediterranean world. The 'little fish' are *maenae*, which were traditionally kept in jars of brine and eaten by the poor.

gathering the grapes: Pius and Marcus participated in the harvesting of the grapes, dedicating the first bunch to Jupiter (Fentress and Maiuro 2011: 358). Marcus quotes a line of Novius from his play *The Grape Gatherers.*

my father had gone to the baths: The excavations at the *Villa Magna* show that Pius would have been carried on his litter downhill from the main villa to the bath complex next to the winery, a distance of half a kilometre (Fentress and Maurio 2011: 358). The emperor probably kept to a strict routine: according to Marcus' *Meditations* (1.16.8), 'he was not fond of bathing at untimely hours'. It would presumably have been very inconvenient for the staff if he had done so.

dined in the pressing room: Dinner (*cena*), the main meal of the day, was held in the late afternoon or early evening (Donahue 2004: 8–9, 70–1). Fentress and Maurio (2011: 359) argue that Pius would have performed a sacrifice of the 'first must' (the juice extracted from the grapes) to Liber Pater before the dinner. Marcus' words make it clear that the crushing of the grapes continued throughout the meal. The remains of the villa reveal that the imperial party dined in a semi-circular *exedra* through which it would be possible to view the *calcatorium*, the room in which the crushing took place. This gave the event the sense of a theatrical performance that recalled traditional Italic harvest rituals (Fentress and Maurio 2011: 345–8, 359–60).

I do my day's work: The Latin is *pensum explico*, which literally means to 'unroll the wool', with the *pensum* being the allocation of wool which weavers were expected to get through in a day. Marcus thus ends the letter by writing of his own studies as if he was a humble wool-spinner, continuing his highly romanticised allusions to hard labour and country work. There is also a rather appropriate double meaning here, as weaving was a standard metaphor for literary composition in the ancient world (Plant 2004: 48).

2

Fronto and Herodes

Introduction

Fronto was not only Marcus Aurelius' tutor, he was also one of the most prominent legal advocates in Rome. The letters in this chapter revolve around a particularly inflammatory case in which Fronto served as a prosecutor. In **Letter 7**, Marcus asks him to withdraw from the trial, since the defendant was none other than Herodes Atticus, the infamous Athenian millionaire, politician, and orator. Since little else is known about the trial outside of the correspondence between Marcus and Fronto, the circumstances are somewhat controversial.

The date of the letters is probably the 140s, before Herodes' consulship in 143 and his appointment as Marcus' tutor in Greek rhetoric. In **Letter 8**, Fronto writes that he was unaware Herodes was a friend of Marcus, something that surely could not have been true after Herodes was employed by the imperial household (van den Hout 1999: 95). Bowersock (1969: 99) and Champlin (1974: 142) argue that Fronto either did not know of the relationship between Herodes and Marcus, or at least underestimated its extent. But this hardly seems plausible, given the level of intimacy between the prince and his tutor.

The trial seems to have been prompted by Herodes' failure to uphold the wishes of his father's will and his subsequent brutality towards Athenian citizens. The will specified that each Athenian citizen should be given one *mina* (the equivalent of one hundred *drachmae*) per year from his estate. Unwilling to be indebted to the Athenians for life, Herodes negotiated a one-off payment of five *minae* to each citizen. However, when they came to collect their payment, many of the citizens were handed a list of debts that they owed to Herodes' family, often dating back generations. These sums were deducted from their five *minae*, which meant that some received very little, while others were now in debt to Herodes (Philostratus, *Lives of the Sophists* 549). **Letter 8**, in which Fronto says that he will have to discuss people 'beaten and robbed' and 'a disloyal son who disregarded his father's wishes', imply that Herodes was brought to trial in Rome in connection with these events.

Some scholars have argued that Herodes himself was not the defendant, but the opposing counsel (Bowersock 1969: 95–9; Champlin 1974: 142; 1980: 63–4). On this reading of the evidence, Fronto intended to mention Herodes' unsavoury actions in order to discredit his opponent. Marcus and Fronto both refer to Herodes as the 'opponent' (*adversarius*) in **Letters 7** and **8**, which may indeed suggest he was the opposing counsel, but the word can also mean 'defendant' (Mousourakis 2003: 130). We regard it as more likely that Herodes himself was on trial, as do van den Hout (1999: 96) and Richlin (2006a: 55). In **Letter 8**, Fronto lists the crimes that he will have to discuss in relation to Herodes – including the beating and robbing of free men, the disregarding of a will, greed, and murder – and says that these are the charges 'on which the case rests'. This implies that Herodes was the defendant. However, the exact circumstances remain uncertain: was this a 'class action' brought by the Athenians, or was Herodes charged by a handful of citizens who had suffered? It may even have been the case that one of Herodes' freedmen was the perpetrator, as was the case with the murder of his wife Regilla.

This group of letters illustrates the many layers to Fronto and Marcus' relationship. After Marcus asks Fronto not to prosecute the case, and reveals his friendship with Herodes (**Letter 7**), his tutor replies in a manner that is deferential, but firm in its refusal (**Letters 8** and **9**). The correspondence is replete with the vocabulary of friendship, which masks the unequal power dynamics: as a member of the imperial family, Marcus clearly has the upper hand. When his tutor declines to withdraw, Marcus then reasserts his request more firmly, and Fronto writes a more conciliatory letter in return (**Letters 10** and **11**). The outcome of the case cannot be determined from the manuscript, but Herodes must have been acquitted, since Antoninus Pius made him consul in 143. Herodes and Fronto eventually reconciled, at Marcus' urging, and their relationship is explored further in **Letters 18, 19**, and **50**.

Letter 7. Marcus to Fronto (*c.* 140–142)

Ad M. Caes. 3.2,VdH^{2} p. 36 = Haines I, pp. 58–63.

Aurelius Caesar sends greetings to his Fronto,

1. I recall that you've often told me that you're keen to discover what you could do that would make me truly happy. That time is now at hand, and you have the opportunity to increase my love for you (if that's at all possible). For the trial draws near, in which I think men will listen favourably to your speech, but they will also be watching you with a certain degree of malice as you try to arouse their indignation.* Nor do I think there is any man who would dare to offer you advice in this matter. For people who are not really your friends* want to see you behaving unpredictably. On the other hand, those whose friendship you can count on are afraid that they will actually seem to be closer to your opponent, if they deter you from conducting your prosecution in the proper manner. However, if you've come up with a particularly elegant turn of phrase that suits the subject matter, they can't bear to deprive you of its delivery through their silence. And so, even if you think that I'm an imprudent counsellor or a presumptuous little boy or that I'm too well disposed towards your opponent, these reasons won't stop me from advising you as to what I think is the best course of action. But why do I say 'advise'? It is actually something that I *request* from you* – and request very earnestly – and, if I succeed, I promise in return that I'll be indebted to you.

And you will say: 'What? If I'm attacked, shouldn't I pay him back in kind?' But you will gain greater praise for yourself if you don't retaliate. It's true, that if he makes the first move, you will be forgiven for responding however you wish, but I have asked him not to start anything, and I believe that I've got my way. For I love both of you according to your own merits, and I know that he was educated in the house of my grandfather P. Calvisius,* whereas I was trained by you. So, for this reason, I'm really very keen in my heart of hearts that this truly odious business you are involved in will be settled in the most honourable way.

2. I hope that you'll approve of my plan, for then you'll be approving my wish. For, to be sure, it's better that I've acted less wisely in writing, rather than being less of a friend and saying nothing. Farewell, my dearest Fronto, my truest friend.

Commentary

arouse their indignation: This is a translation of the Latin rhetorical term *indignatio*, which represented an attempt on the part of the prosecution to generate resentment against an individual or action. It formed part of the conclusion of the prosecuting lawyer's speech (Cicero, *On Rhetorical Invention* 1.98, 100).

not really your friends: The theme of friendship operates on several levels: the friendship between Marcus and Herodes prompts him to write the letter in the first place, then the friendship between Marcus and Fronto enables the prince to make such a request. Marcus then deploys imaginary 'friends' of Fronto to help him persuade his tutor.

I request from you: We know from the end of **Letter 8** that Marcus did not write this letter himself, since Fronto complains that it was not in his handwriting. It was plainly dictated, as befitting an emperor writing to a subject, rather than a pupil to his tutor.

my grandfather P. Calvisius: P. Calvisius Tullus Ruso, ordinary consul in 109, was the father of Marcus' mother Domitia Lucilla. It was once thought that Herodes stayed with Calvisius *c.* 108, when his father, Ti. Claudius Atticus Herodes, was consul. But this consulship has been re-dated to *c.* 132 on the basis of a military diploma (Birley 1997b: 209–10, 229). Herodes probably visited Rome in the 110s.

Letter 8. Fronto to Marcus (*c.* 140–142)

Ad M. Caes. 3.3, VdH^2 pp. 36–8 = Haines I, pp. 62–7.

Fronto to my lord Caesar,

1. It is right that I have devoted myself to you, and it is right that all the rewards of my life derive from my investment in you and your father.* What could be

more friendly, more pleasing, more true?* But, I beg you, do away with the 'presumptuous little boy' and the 'imprudent counsellor'. There is plainly no risk of you persuading me to do anything boyishly or rashly. Believe me, if you wish – if you don't, I'll believe myself – that your prudence surpasses even that of old men.

2. Therefore, I understand that in this matter, your advice is venerable and serious, whereas mine is truly puerile. For what need is there to stage a spectacle for all sorts of audiences? If your man Herodes were decent and virtuous,* it wouldn't be right for him to be harried by my insults; but if he is dissolute and morally bankrupt, then it isn't a fair contest between us and we won't suffer the same damage. For all intercourse with an impure person ends up defiling you,* even if you emerge the victor. But the former argument is more believable, that a man you consider worthy of your protection is in fact honourable. If I had known about this at all, then verily may all the gods cast me down* if I have dared to injure with a single word anyone who was your friend.

3. Now I do want you to help me out by giving me advice on this point as well, because of your love for me, which makes me a most fortunate man. Indeed, I know that I should not say anything injurious to Herodes that doesn't pertain to the case. But how should I treat those matters that *are* relevant to the case (and they are most frightful)? This is what I am very uncertain about and on which I seek your advice. I must speak of free men who have been beaten and robbed; one of them was even killed. I must speak of a disloyal son who disregarded his father's wishes. I will need to examine savageness and greed, and I will need to establish a certain individual – Herodes – as a murderer in this trial. Regarding these charges, on which the case rests:* if you think that I ought to bear down and press hard on my opponent with all the resources at my disposal, give me your advice, my excellent lord, you who are most generous to me.

And if you think that I should be somewhat lenient, I will follow your advice as to the best course of action. You can be certain, however, about what I have said: I will mention nothing extraneous to the case at hand about his character and the other aspects of his life. But if you think that I ought to serve my own argument, I warn you now that I will not be making exaggerated use of the opportunity provided by this case. For they are frightful crimes and they must be addressed in a frightful fashion. Everything that happened to those men who were injured and robbed has the flavour of gall and bile, so if I call him an uneducated little Greek* at any time, it won't be totally out of proportion.

4. Farewell, Caesar, and love me very greatly, as you do. I truly love your little letters twice as much. For that reason, I'd prefer that when you write to me, you do it in your own hand.

Commentary

in you and your father: Fronto's opening note reinforces the status dynamics at work in these letters: his owes his public position – and his continued maintenance of that position – to the imperial family. It may even have been that Pius urged Marcus to write the previous letter (van den Hout 1999: 98).

more true: Fronto picks up on the theme of friendship from Marcus' letter. The Latin term for 'more true' (*verius*) is a play on words, since Marcus' original name was M. Annius Verus, and Hadrian frequently called him 'most truthful' (*verissimus*) (Dio 69.21.1–2; *HA Marcus* 1.10). As Richlin (2006a: 257) points out, Fronto uses the word *verus* in various different forms throughout the letter, in a manner that is difficult to replicate in English translation.

If your man Herodes were decent and virtuous: The Latin is very important here. Firstly, Herodes is described as *iste*, which literally means 'that one of yours', but is also used for a defendant in a trial. Secondly, in the first part of the sentence – 'if your man Herodes were decent and virtuous' – Fronto uses the subjunctive mood, often used to express doubt or possibility, whereas in the second part – 'if he is dissolute and morally bankrupt' – the verb is in the indicative mood, which indicates a fact.

For all intercourse with an impure person ends up defiling you: The word *complexus* ranges in meaning from 'connection' to 'embrace' and 'sexual intercourse'. This was a deliberate choice of words on Fronto's part (Richlin 2006a: 58). The verb *commaculare* does not simply mean 'to stain', but to make someone ritually impure, unfit for religious practices.

then verily may all the gods cast me down: Fronto uses archaic Latin here, hence the somewhat grandiose translation.

these charges, on which the case rests: Fronto says it will be necessary to attack Herodes in detail, because he deprived the 'free men' of Athens of their inheritance by disregarding his father's will. Philostratus (*Lives of the Sophists* 449) records that some Athenians were arrested for being in debt, though he does not mention murder. However, it would be plausible if one of Herodes' freedmen had killed Athenian citizens. The freedman Alcimedon would later kill Herodes' wife Regilla, allegedly on his master's orders. Herodes himself was brought to trial in Rome as a consequence (Pomeroy 2007: 119–29). We may be dealing with a similar state of affairs here, hence Fronto's cryptic remark that 'a certain individual' (*quidam*) was to be accused of murder. The manuscript actually has Herodes' name at this point, as in our translation above, but it is suspected of being a later gloss (Richlin 2006a: 58, cf. van den Hout 1999: 101).

uneducated little Greek: The diminutive *Graeculus* ('little Greek'), popularised by Cicero, could be patronising or affectionate, depending on the context (Swain 1996: 405). However, when coupled with *indoctus* ('uneducated'), it appears that Fronto is trying to be deliberately insulting. This is evidence that Herodes was not yet in imperial employment, for Fronto could not have made such a vituperative attack on another of Marcus' tutors.

Letter 9. Fronto to Marcus (*c.* 140–142)

Ad M. Caes. 3.4, VdH² p. 38 = Haines I, pp. 66–7.

Greetings, my lord,

1. When I had already closed and sealed my previous letter* it occurred to me that the men who will plead this case (and it appears that a number will be involved) will speak of Herodes rather harshly; take notice of this, as you consider the extent to which it is only me involved in this affair.

2. Farewell master, and take care, so that I can be happy. It seems that Capreolus (who is currently out of town), and my friend Marcianus, will plead the case; even Iulianus,* I think.

Commentary

closed and sealed my previous letter: It was standard practice to fold and seal the papyrus on which the letter was written, and place the address on the outside (Trapp 2003: 8). Similar habits can be observed in the writing tablets found at Vindolanda in northern England. The wooden leaves of the tablets were punched and tied together with cord, and the address was written on the exterior (Bowman 1994b: 112–14).

Capreolus . . . Marcianus . . . Iulianus: Capreolus and Iulianus are not known from other sources. In the latter case, the manuscript reads Villianus or Lullianus, neither of which are known Roman names (van den Hout 1999: 104). Marcianus may refer to P. Iulius Geminius Marcianus (*PIR*[2] I 340), from Fronto's hometown of Cirta; if this is true, he would have been very young at the time. Birley (1993: 79) suggests he may be that Marcianus' father.

Letter 10. Marcus to Fronto (*c.* 140–142)

Ad M. Caes. 3.5, VdH[2] p. 38 = Haines I, pp. 66–9.

Greetings, my dearest Fronto,*

Now I'm thankful and grateful to you, dearest Fronto, since you did not reject my advice, and you actually approved of it. As for those issues that you raised in your truly friendly letters, here is what I think. Everything that is relevant to the case that you're overseeing must obviously be offered up in court, but those issues that are really your own personal feelings – regardless of whether they are justified or are a result of provocation – must be suppressed.* And so that you won't damage your credibility in this drawn-out affair, or diminish your own self-respect by airing these opinions... *[Two fragmentary lines.]* ... this is the one worry that truly bothers me, that you should say something that seems to be unworthy of your character, unhelpful for your case, or open to criticism by those in attendance. Goodbye, dearest Fronto, most delightful to me.

Commentary

my dearest Fronto: Throughout this letter, Marcus emphasises the strength of the relationship between him and his tutor. Fronto is called 'dearest' (*carissime*) no fewer than three times, and his two replies to the Caesar are styled 'truly friendly letters' (*litteras amicissimas*). Finally, at the end of the letter, Fronto is 'most delightful' (*iucundissime*).

must be suppressed: Despite Marcus' protestations of friendship, the tone is actually quite firm: Fronto must not let his personal animosity towards Herodes influence his judgement, or he risks damaging his reputation.

Letter 11. Fronto to Marcus (*c.* 140–142)

Ad M. Caes. 3.6, VdH[2] p. 39 = Haines I, pp. 68–71.

To my lord,

I will do this, lord,* since in all things, which ... *[A few illegible letters.]* ... as I understand your wishes. I act the same way in all other respects, and I beg and implore you never to be silent about what you want me to do. Advise me in the most appropriate way, as you have done on this occasion. *[The opening of this line is fragmentary.]* ... will I start anything against your wishes. I should even prefer... *[Several words missing.]* ... in a case, to go through point by point, so that we deliver it in a Ciceronian manner.* For when they compress their deliberation into such a small line, I desire particularly ... *[Several words missing.]* ... cannot be accomplished in this manner. But if we plead our case in continuous speeches, which permits me to say nothing beyond the constraints of the present matter, I must make use of a steely gaze, vehement voice, and serious words. But now I should prefer ... *[A word missing.]* ... with a finger raised in anger which ... *[A word or two missing.]* ... injured your man, but it is difficult to ask him to do anything like this: for it is said he burns with a desire to plead his case. But I don't criticise him for this; but I do advise you to be careful so that those matters, which are relevant to the case, don't get dredged up in a manner that's a little too hostile. However, you do offer good advice – I should uphold my professional reputation: and yet, if we were practising with weapons or wrestling, we could not engage in these sports without an element of competition ... *[Two fragmentary lines follow.]* ... I have happily praised your Opician.*

Commentary

I will do this, lord: Fronto's tone is more conciliatory than in his previous two letters on the subject, which were full of hostile invective towards Herodes. Despite the fragmentary state of the manuscript, the meaning is clear: Fronto will do as Marcus asks, as long as it is consistent with his professional conduct.

in a Ciceronian manner: Fronto discusses two possible approaches to his prosecution of Herodes (van den Hout 1999: 106). The first method would involve a dispassionate treatment of the evidence, broken down into its constituent parts. The second option is to give one continuous speech, a different technique, also practised by Cicero, which would involve a certain degree of theatre: 'a steely gaze, vehement voice, and serious words'.

your Opician: *Opikoi* was the Greek word for the Oscans, a prehistoric tribe based in the region of Campania. The term 'Opician' is thus used as a derogatory term, meaning 'barbarian' (Dench 1995: 29–66).

3

Fronto the Consul

Introduction

In July and August 142, Fronto served as suffect consul with C. Etrilius Regillus Laberius Priscus (Eck and Roxan 1995; Eck 1998). **Letters 12–17** can all be dated to this two-month period, in which Fronto, residing in Rome while consul, writes to members of the imperial family in Naples. Several of the letters deal with Fronto's speech of thanks (*gratiarum actio*) to the emperor for granting him the consulship, a custom since the Augustan period (Talbert 1984: 227–8). He would eventually deliver the speech, somewhat late in his term, on 13 August (**Letter 12**). It elicited an obliging reply from the emperor Antoninus Pius, who praised Fronto's ability to find something new to say in a genre that had become formulaic (**Letter 14**). Marcus' remarks about Greek panegyrists performing in the theatre at Naples (**Letter 15**) act as a thematic complement to Fronto's own speech.

This collection of correspondence also sheds light on the wider world of the imperial court and its connections with Fronto's family. In **Letter 13**, Marcus suggests that Fronto's wife Cratia is nothing less than his rival, indicating the depth of his affection for his tutor. Fronto reveals in **Letter 16** that Cratia has been sent ahead to Naples, to join the imperial family for the birthday celebrations of Marcus' mother, Domitia Lucilla. Fronto then writes to Domitia herself (in Greek) to apologise for his absence, detailing the sort of birthday party he imagined she deserved (**Letter 17**).

The final two letters deal with Fronto's career after his elevation to the consulship. **Letter 18** examines a legal case involving an unopened will, and although very fragmentary, it is valuable because it contains the largest extant fragment of Fronto's speeches. At the end of this letter, Marcus reveals that Herodes Atticus' baby son has died, and asks Fronto to write to him. Part of

Fronto's letter of consolation is still preserved (**Letter 19**), and although it is supposed to be sympathetic towards Herodes, it strikes several discordant notes, suggesting that their rivalry has not been entirely buried.

Letter 12. Fronto to Marcus (between 16 July and 13 August 142)

Ad M. Caes. 2.4, VdH[2] pp. 24–5 = *Ad. M. Caes.* 2.1, Haines I, pp. 108–12.

The consul to his Caesar,

1. In your most recent letter, you asked why I was yet to give my speech in the senate.* I must also issue an edict of thanks to my lord your father, but the edict will be circulated on the occasion of our games.* It will start like this:

> I considered that this day, on which I shall give – thanks to the indulgence of our greatest emperor – a spectacle which everyone will enjoy and will be immensely popular, was a suitable opportunity to give *my* thanks, so that the same day . . .

And this would be followed with some conclusion worthy of Cicero. I will deliver my speech in the senate on 13 August. Maybe you will ask, why so late? I am never in a hurry to carry out my official duties with undue haste. But, since I should act without any pretence towards you, I'll tell you what is on my mind.

I praised the deified Hadrian,* your grandfather, in the senate on a number of occasions with great enthusiasm, and I did this willingly, too. And these speeches are always in everyone's hands. But, if it can be said – respectfully acknowledging your devotion towards your grandfather – I wanted to appease and assuage Hadrian as I would Mars Gradivus or Father Dis,* rather than to love him. Why? Because the act of love requires a degree of confidence and intimacy. Since I possessed no such confidence myself, it stands to reason that although I showed Hadrian great reverence, I could not love him.

I do actually love and esteem Antoninus,* as I do the sun, the day, my life and very breath, and I feel that I am loved by him in return. I must praise him in such a way that my praise does not lie concealed in the acts of the senate,* but so that it is circulated widely and read, and so that I am not ungrateful to you. Then, as the saying goes, in the words of the fugitive courier, 'I ran sixty miles for my master, but I will run one hundred for myself, so that I can escape'. In the same way I too ran for my master when I used to praise Hadrian, but today I run for myself – that's right, for myself – and I will compose this speech of my own accord.* Therefore I will write it at my own convenience, slowly, leisurely, and gradually.

2. If you are truly in a hurry for it, find some other way to entertain yourself. Kiss your father, embrace him, and finally, praise him yourself. Otherwise, you should expect to hear on 13 August everything as you would like to hear it.

3. Farewell, Caesar, and show yourself worthy of your father. And if you feel like writing something, write it slowly.

Commentary

my speech in the senate: In the Antonine period, there were usually ten to twelve consuls per year, with each pair of consuls holding office for approximately two months. The first pair, who took office in January, were known as ordinary consuls and gave their name to their year. The substitute pairs, like Fronto and Priscus, were called suffect consuls. Only one member of the consular pair gave the speech of thanks to the emperor, and obviously in this case the duty was given to Fronto. The most famous example of a *gratiarum actio* is the speech delivered by Pliny the Younger in 100, which was later published as the *Panegyricus* (Roche 2011).

our games: Each pair of consuls was expected to stage games celebrating their appointment (Talbert 1984: 59–60). Roman magistrates issued edicts from the days of the Republic onwards (*Digest* 1.2.2.10, 12). They were written on wooden boards painted white, which were easy to erase and use again (Millar 1977: 254). Fronto's own edict did not deal with administration or legal matters, but was solely designed to flatter the emperor, an indication of the political realities of the imperial period (van den Hout 1999: 61).

I praised the deified Hadrian: Fronto published these speeches as a way of enhancing his reputation as an orator, and his own personal position, in much the same way as Pliny the Younger had done with his *Panegyricus* for Trajan (Champlin 1980: 83; Rees 2011: 176). Outside the senate, panegyrics of Hadrian were delivered by Aspasius of Byblos, Aelius Sarapion of Alexandria, Zenobius, and Orion of Alexandria, probably when the emperor visited the eastern provinces (Birley 1997a: 82).

Mars Gradivus or Father Dis: Mars Gradivus was the god of war and the army, while Father Dis was the Roman equivalent of Hades, the god of the underworld. These comparisons conjure up an image of a stern and autocratic emperor, somewhat different from the ideology of the *civilis princeps* – the emperor who behaved as if he were a citizen (Wallace-Hadrill 1982). They enable Fronto to show his respect for Hadrian – a respect due to gods and emperors alike – but emphasise the difference between his regime and that of Pius. Hadrian's hostility towards some members of the senate was well known: he executed four senators of consular rank upon coming to the throne, and at the end of his reign, two relatives were put to death for allegedly plotting against him (Birley 1997a: 86–8, 290–2).

I do actually love and esteem Antoninus: After Hadrian's death, the senate refused to deify him and proposed to annul all his acts. Antoninus reminded the august body that these acts included his own adoption, and they relented, bestowing the title of Pius (dutiful) on their new emperor (Dio 69.23.3, 70.1–2, cf. *HA Pius* 5.1). Fronto benefited personally from the new regime: in a letter to Pius, he declared that his accession was 'the birthday of my welfare, my reputation and my safety' (*Ad Ant. Pium* 5, VdH[2] pp. 164 = Haines I, pp. 226–9). That he could write like this in letters to Antoninus and Marcus suggests that the new regime acknowledged the problems of Hadrian's principate and was determined not to repeat them. Upon his accession, Pius refused to execute any senators, even those who had been informers (Dio 70.2.1).

acts of the senate: The acts of the senate (*acta senatus*) were formally compiled by a junior senator known as the *ab actis senatus*. They were collected and published on the orders of Julius Caesar during his first consulship in 59 BC, but Augustus forbade their circulation (Suetonius, *Augustus* 36). The *acta senatus* are unlikely to have preserved all senatorial proceedings verbatim, but instead provided a summary or edited account (Talbert 1984: 308–22).

of my own accord: Fronto states that he delivered a speech in honour of Hadrian because he was required to do so, but that his oration for Antoninus Pius will be of his own free will. He is being slightly disingenuous here, since the *gratiarum actio* for the consulship was an obligation, not a choice, and served to reinforce the fact that a senator became consul only at the emperor's pleasure.

Letter 13. Marcus to Fronto (between 16 July and 13 August 142)

Ad M. Caes. 2.5, VdH^2 pp. 25–6 = *Ad. M. Caes.* 2.2, Haines I, pp. 112–15

To Fronto, the most esteemed consul,

1. I surrender: you have won.* Through your loving, you have obviously beaten all those who have ever lived and loved. Take your crown, and let the herald proclaim openly from your tribunal this famous victory of yours: 'The consul M. Cornelius Fronto is the winner,* and receives the crown in the contest of the Great Friendship Games.' But even though I've been beaten, I'll not desist or discontinue my eagerness. So you'll love me more than any man loves another man, and I'll love you more than any man loves you – although I possess less vigour in my loving – and more than you love yourself. Now, Cratia will also be a competitor in this contest, and I'm uncertain whether I can better her. For I'll say of her, as Plautus says,* 'the tempest of love has not only soaked her clothes with great raindrops but has flooded the marrow of her bones.'

2. Do you realize what a letter you have written to me? I'd even be so bold to say that even the woman who gave birth to me* and raised me never wrote

anything to me that was so charming and honey-sweet. And this wasn't because of your way with words or eloquence, for on that score not only my mother, but all living people would have to surrender to you (and they most certainly do). But I can't go on enough about your letter, which wasn't just lucid and learned, but actually bubbled over with such friendliness, abounded with so much affection, and sparkled with such love, that it has carried my spirit to the heavens with joy, stirred it up with the most ardent longing, and finally, as Naevius* says, 'filled my heart with a dangerous love'.

3. About that other letter of yours,* the one in which you indicated why the speech that you're going to deliver in the senate in praise of my lord would be deferred to a later date. It gave me such delight that I couldn't resist – and it's up to you to decide whether this was rash – reading it out to my father himself. But I don't need to go on about how pleased he was by your words, since you are aware of his great benevolence and the superb style of your own letter. This gave rise to a long conversation between us about you, which was much, much longer than that between you and your quaestor* concerning me. So I have no doubt that your ears were burning* for quite some time in the forum. So my lord approves and understands the reasons why you have delayed the delivery of the speech to a later date . . . *[The letter breaks off here.]*

Commentary

I surrender: you have won: Marcus is replying, first of all, to a letter from Fronto that no longer survives, but we can ascertain from this one that it dealt with the close relationship between master and pupil. Unable to match Fronto's way with words in expressing his fondness for his teacher, Marcus adopts a tone of mock defeat, undoubtedly inspired by the fact that he was currently in Naples watching the festival being held there (**Letter 15**). The metaphor of the *agon* ('competition') is developed throughout the letter; this was a standard rhetorical technique of the period (König 2005: 254–300; Mattern 2008: 69–97).

The consul M. Cornelius Fronto is the winner: In the original letter, this line is in Greek, as a way of evoking a victory proclamation such as might be heard at the Olympic Games or similar competitions.

as Plautus says: The quotation actually appears to be a paraphrase of several lines from his play *The Haunted House* (*Mostellaria* lines 138–43).

even the woman who gave birth to me: Marcus has introduced two rivals to his mock contest, Fronto's wife Cratia, and his own mother, Domitia Lucilla. Richlin (2011: 168–9) argues that these women 'serve as indices of love' for Marcus. Since a mother is naturally given to praising her children, the fact that Fronto can outstrip her 'honey-sweet' words is a telling indication of his talent, which the prince so admires and perhaps even hopes to emulate.

Naevius: See **Letter 1**.

That other letter of yours: Marcus now turns from his initial subject to reply to **Letter 12**, and tells Fronto that he has read it out to Antoninus Pius. He was evidently not put off by Fronto's remarks about Hadrian.

quaestor: The identity of Fronto's quaestor is unknown: there were twenty such junior magistrates elected each year, four of whom were assigned to the consuls in office (Talbert 1984: 17).

your ears were burning: This is a modern English translation of the Latin expression 'your ears were ringing'.

Letter 14. Antoninus Pius to Fronto (soon after 13 August 142)

Ad Ant. Pium 2, VdH[2] pp. 161–2 = Haines I, pp. 126–9.

Antoninus Caesar* to Marcus Fronto,

1. *[The opening of this letter is fragmentary.]* ... by Hercules, [I am amazed] that you are able to find [new perspectives] in subjects that are well-trodden and expected.* But clearly, the desire to accomplish something effectively means that one can do it superbly. There is nothing more powerful than those sentiments of yours, nothing more courteous than your manner of

delivery, all accomplished in good taste. Nor will I be so remiss as to deprive you of the praise you so richly deserve out of fear that I might seem arrogant in praising praise directed at me.* And so, you have accomplished your task well,* most properly in fact, and – apart from the actual content – you are clearly due all the credit. It certainly hasn't given me much new insight into your thoughts, since I already knew that you were the most obliging supporter of my policies and proclamations.* Goodbye, my dearest Fronto.

2. Also, that section of your speech, which I was most pleased to see dedicated to the honour of my Faustina, was even truer than it was eloquent. For the fact of the matter, by Hercules, is that I would prefer to live with her on Gyara than in the palace without her.*

Commentary

Antoninus Caesar: Fronto had sent Pius a copy of the speech that he delivered in the senate, together with a covering letter, which now only survives in a few fragments (*Ad Ant. Pium* 1, VdH[2] p. 161 = Haines I, pp. 126–7). The emperor's reply, which we have here, was conveyed with a letter from Marcus to Fronto in which the prince lavished praise on his teacher's rhetorical prowess (*Ad M. Caes.* 2.3, VdH[2] p. 27 = Haines I, pp. 128–31). Neither Pius nor Marcus heard the speech being delivered, as they were in Campania, but the ceremonies of imperial government continued regardless of whether the emperor was present. Many consuls must have been fated to deliver their speeches to an absent honorand.

well-trodden and expected: As Champlin (1980: 88) notes, this letter is exceptional in providing the honorand's reaction to a panegyric. Fronto himself felt that his speech was well received, telling Marcus that it was greeted with applause and acclamation (*Ad M. Caes* 2.2, VdH[2] pp. 17–21 = *Ad M. Caes.* 1.8, Haines I, pp. 118–25).

praising praise directed at me: This slightly unattractive expression may seem strange in English, but preserves the tone of the Latin original. Pius uses both the verb *laudo* ('I praise') and the noun *laus* ('praise'), a construction known as an etymological figure.

you have accomplished your task well: The speech does not survive, but Champlin (1980: 83–9) reconstructs some of the contents from references in the letters.

Fronto includes some details in a letter, written in Greek, which he sent to Marcus' mother (*Ad M. Caes.* 2.3, VdH² pp. 21–4 = *Epist. Graec.* 1, Haines I, pp. 130–7). Fronto tells Domitia that he mentioned her and Marcus by name, and that the speech included references to the character (τρόπος) and virtue (ἀρετή) of both Pius and Marcus. In the letter, he embarks on an extended simile, comparing himself to Protogenes, the painter of Ialysus. While Protogenes had only one subject, Fronto had two:

> the first is the great king, ruler of all the land and sea, and the other is the son of the great king, who is not only his child just as Athena is of Zeus, but also – since he's your son – as Hephaestus is of Hera. (*Ad M. Caes.* 2.3.4)

The speech probably had a section on the imperial dynasty, discussing Marcus' natural mother (Domitia), his adoptive father (Pius), and the connection between the families in the forthcoming marriage to the emperor's daughter, Faustina the Younger.

In a letter to Marcus, Fronto describes the reaction to two statements he made regarding the nobility of senators (*Ad M. Caes.* 2.2.1, VdH² p. 17 = *Ad M. Caes.* 1.8.1, Haines I, pp. 118–19):

> what a symphony of praise rang out in response to 'back then all representations of family members were decked out with patrician insignia'. But when I made a comparison between noble and obscure families with the statement, 'as if anyone would think that the flames kindled on a funeral pyre and on altars were identical, because they both give light', it was received with some murmuring.

Fronto made a distinction between the past glories of the senate, and the decline in standing of its members, which seems to have been controversial (Champlin 1980: 88–90). It was a strange sentiment coming from a new man.

Fronto may have praised Pius' completion of the British War in 142 in this same speech (Champlin 1980: 85; van den Hout 1999: 608). The emperor's governor in Britain, Q. Lollius Urbicus, won a victory against the British tribes for which Pius was hailed *imperator* (*HA Pius* 5.4). Since Urbicus' success has been dated to the summer of 142, it would have been appropriate for Fronto to mention it in his speech (Birley 2005: 136–9). Fronto's oration is cited by an anonymous orator in his panegyric for Constantius I delivered in 297 (*Pan. Lat.* VIII(V).14.2):

> Thus, when Fronto, not the second, but the other ornament of Roman eloquence, was praising the ruler Antoninus for having brought the war in Britain to completion, although he had remained behind in the City in the palace itself, and had delegated the command of the war to others, he averred that the Emperor deserved the glory of its whole launching and course, as if he had actually presided at the helm of a warship. (trans. Nixon and Rodgers 1994: 132–3).

Shortly after he became emperor in 161, Marcus apparently re-read Fronto's speech, which gave his former tutor great pleasure (*Ad. Ant. Imp.* 4.2, VdH[2] pp. 105–6 = *Ad Ant. Imp.* 2.2, Haines I, pp. 302–4).

most obliging supporter of my policies and proclamations: Champlin (1980: 88) describes the letter as 'delightfully tart', and it is certainly reminiscent of some of the weary-sounding letters written by Trajan to Pliny the Younger in Bithynia.

I would prefer to live with her on Gyara than in the palace without her: Since Pius' wife, Faustina the Elder, had died in 140, this must be his daughter, Faustina the Younger, who would have been about twelve years old at the time. Gyara was an island in the Cyclades to which exiles were regularly sent. The sentiment is quite touching: Antoninus had lost his wife, to whom he was devoted, only two years before, and Faustina was the only one of his four children still living (Birley 1993: 242–3).

Letter 15. Marcus to Fronto (late August 142)

Ad M. Caes. 2.11, VdH^2 pp. 30–1 = Haines I, pp. 140–5.

M. Aurelius Caesar greets his consul and teacher,

1. Since I wrote to you last absolutely nothing has happened that'd be worth telling you about, or which would interest you when you did hear about it. For we have spent our days engaged in virtually the same activities – the same theatre, the same *odeum*,* the same wish that you were here too. Why do I call it the 'same' wish? It's really a wish that is renewed and grows on a daily basis, in the same way that Laberius speaks of love, as he was accustomed to do, in his own inimitable fashion: 'Your love grows as quickly as a leek, as firmly as the palm tree.'* So I'm applying his feelings about love to my longing for you.

2. I want to write more, but I've nothing to hand. Wait, something comes to mind: we've been hearing panegyrists here:* Greeks, naturally, but brilliant beings. Even I, who am about as far away from Greek literature as my Caelian hill is from the land of Greece itself,* could hope to equal Theopompus when compared with them. Therefore, these 'men of unimpaired knowledge', as Caecilius* wrote, have almost forced me, a modern-day Opician,* to write in Greek.

3. The Neapolitan climate is generally fine, but really very variable. One minute it's cold, the next it's warm, the next it's bone-dry. First, in the middle of the night, it's warm (as at Laurentum),* then it's freezing first thing in the morning (like Lanuvium).* Then during the night, early morning and dawn, up until the rising of the sun, it's cold (just like Algidus),* then before midday the sun shines (as at Tusculum);* but then at midday there's a burning sun worthy of Puteoli;* and when the sun sets out to bathe in the ocean, the temperature at last becomes more bearable, like the climate at Tibur.* This stays the same in the evening and our sleep time, 'until the dead of night strikes us', as Marcus Porcius says.

4. But why do I, who promised to write only a few things, keep going on with these Masurian absurdities?* And so, goodbye, my very kind master, most distinguished consul. Long for me as much as you love me.

Commentary

the same theatre, the same *odeum*: Naples had both a traditional Greek uncovered theatre, as well as a covered theatre, or *odeum*. They stood directly next to each other, a common pattern in the former Greek colonies of southern Italy (Sear 2006: 126–7). Here Marcus spells the name of the covered theatre as *odium* rather than *odeum*. *Odium* also means 'hatred' or 'dislike', and Marcus could be being deliberately ambiguous here (cf. van den Hout 1999: 80). Marcus was probably watching the dramatic and musical performances at the *Sebasta*, a festival established in honour of Augustus in Naples in AD 2 (Geer 1935). The four-year cycle on which these games operated means that they would have been held in 142. A letter of Hadrian records that the Neapolitan *Sebasta* was to begin nine days before the Kalends of October (*AE* 2006, 1403 a–c; Jones 2007). This means the *Sebasta* would have been held in the late summer, which fits the chronology of this letter. In another letter, Marcus tells Fronto that he can only work on his hexameter poetry at night, because his days 'are consumed' by attendance at the theatre, one of the duties of the heir apparent (*Ad M. Caes.* 2.8, VdH^2, pp. 28–9 = *Ad M. Caes.* 2.10, Haines I, pp. 136–41). As emperor, Marcus (*Meditations* 6.46) described the entertainments offered by the theatre and amphitheatre as offensive and boring (see also Dio 71.29.3–4; *HA Marcus* 4.8).

'Your love grows as quickly as a leek, as firmly as the palm tree': Laberius is discussed in **Letter 1**. This was a humorous line in its original context (Panayotakis 2010: 408–9), and seems to be used tongue-in-cheek here.

we have been hearing panegyrists here: 'Panegyrists' is a translation of the word *encomiographi*, unattested elsewhere in Latin literature. An *encomium* was a Greek term meaning 'song of praise' used to denote a panegyric delivered in honour of a ruler. Panegyrics were commonly performed at the *Sebasta* in Naples (*IG* XIV, 755e, Addenda = *I.Napoli* 63). The genre of the prose panegyric flourished in the Antonine period. Its practitioners included Dio Chrysostom from Prusa, who delivered orations *On Kingship* to the emperor Trajan, and Aelius Aristides of Smyrna, who gave the speech *On Rome* in the presence of Pius in 155. In an earlier letter, sent to Fronto from the same sojourn in Naples,

Marcus said that he had heard a declamation by M. Antonius Polemon, one of the foremost rhetoricians of the age, but was unimpressed (*Ad M. Caes.* 2.10, VdH[2] pp. 29–30 = *Ad M. Caes.* 2.5, Haines I, pp. 116–9). Nor was Marcus greatly taken with the performances of the panegyrists: 'brilliant beings' is one of many sarcastic turns of phrase in this letter.

as my Caelian hill is from the land of Greece itself: Marcus was born in a house on the Caelian hill in Rome in 121 (*HA Marcus* 1.5–7).

Theopompus: Theopompus of Chios was a Greek historian who lived in the fourth century BC and wrote a historical work called the *Philippica*. Theopompus was also a highly regarded orator, with his works including the *Encomium of Philip* and *Advice to Alexander*.

Caecilius: See **Letter 1**.

a modern-day Opician: In **Letter 11**, Fronto called Herodes Atticus an 'Opician', and here Marcus uses it sarcastically to describe himself. His point is that even an ill-educated Roman – 'a modern-day Opician' – could reach the rhetorical heights of Theopompus in comparison with the efforts of the Greek panegyrists he heard declaiming in Naples. Marcus' mocking tone is underscored by the fact he was himself well educated in Greek language and literature.

Laurentum: Laurentum was south east of Rome, close to Ostia. The imperial family had a villa there, as did many Roman aristocrats, such as Pliny the Younger (*Letters* 2.17). The imperial villa has been identified with the site of Tor Paterno at Castelporziano (Marzano 2007: 317).

Lanuvium: Lanuvium was located to the south east of Rome in the Alban hills, and was the birthplace of Antoninus Pius and Commodus (*HA Pius* 1.8; *HA Commodus* 1.2).

Algidus: Algidus, also located in the Alban hills, was popular with Roman aristocrats because of its cooler temperatures in the summer (Statius, *Silvae*

4.4.16; Martial, *Epigrams* 10.30.6). Marcus' description of Algidus as *gelidus* ('cold') indicates a direct allusion to Horace (*Odes* 1.21.6) who uses the same adjective to describe the place.

Tusculum: Tusculum was on the northern side of the Alban hills, and was an enormously popular summer retreat: Cicero and Maecenas both had villas there, as did the imperial family (Martial, *Epigrams* 5.1).

Puteoli: Located on the northern shore of the bay of Naples, close to Baiae, Puteoli was home to popular hot springs and many aristocratic villas (D'Arms 1970: 116–64).

Tibur: Tibur was a town in Latium to the east of Rome, and home to Hadrian's massive villa complex, encompassing some 120 hectares (Opper 2008: 130–65). The overall effect of this list of resorts and retreats suggests that Marcus – far from being genuinely interested in the climatic variation in different Italic regions – was thinking about all the places he would rather be than in Naples.

Masurian absurdities: Masurius Sabinus was a famous lawyer of the Julio-Claudian period. He wrote three books on civil law, as well as several treatises, including *Memorable Events* and *On the Indigenous Population.*

Letter 16. Fronto to Marcus (late August 142)

Ad M. Caes. 2.13, VdH^2 p. 32 = Haines I, pp. 144–7.

To my lord,

I've sent Cratia* to celebrate your mother's birthday with her, and I have instructed her to stay there until I myself arrive. And so the very minute that I lay down the consular office,* I'll board my carriage and wing my way to you. In the meantime, I've told my Cratia, upon my word of honour, that she would be in no danger of starvation: I'm sure your mother will share those nibbles that you sent with her dependant.* My Cratia isn't a big eater, either, as the wives of common lawyers are reported to be.* She could even live happily on just your mother's kisses. But what will happen to me? There aren't any kisses left anywhere in Rome.* All my fortunes, all my delights, are at Naples. Tell me, what is the custom of resigning a magistracy on the day before it ends?* Aren't I prepared to swear by all the gods to resign early? And what is this about – swearing that I'm about to give up my consulship? Indeed I swear that I've long wanted to resign my consulship, so that I may embrace Marcus Aurelius.

Commentary

I've sent Cratia: The imperial family is still away from Rome, either in Naples or at one of their Campanian residences.

I lay down the consular office: When a senator came to the end of their consulship, they had to swear an oath stating that they had not contravened any laws (Pliny, *Panegyricus* 65.2).

her dependant: Fronto refers to his wife Cratia as Domitia Lucilla's *clienta*, which literally means 'female client'. It is difficult to translate, since we have no equivalent term in English to denote a social inferior who benefits from the patronage and support of a social superior. Hence we have rendered it as 'dependant', in preference to 'protégé', recommended by van den Hout (1999: 86). The masculine form, *cliens*, is very common, but the feminine version less so: it occurs a number of times in the plays of Plautus, which may have inspired Fronto (*TLL* 1,346–7, s.v. *clienta*). Fronto's patronising choice of words shows his lack of understanding of female friendships. Cratia was much younger than Domitia Lucilla, perhaps as much as twenty years her junior (Richlin 2011: 177–91). She probably formed part of Domitia's circle when she was in Rome, or at least visited her frequently: there is no indication that her journey to join the imperial family was an exceptional circumstance.

as the wives of common lawyers are reported to be: The term *causidicus* referred to a lawyer who received pay for their services, and was thus the subject of some condescension from aristocratic advocates such as Fronto who were independently wealthy and took no fee (Quintilian, *Principles of Oratory* 12.7.7–8).

There aren't any kisses left anywhere in Rome: This final passage emphasises how isolated Fronto feels in Rome, while the imperial court is elsewhere. The kisses to which he refers are not those of romantic love, but of court ceremonial. In a letter from the 160s sent to Lucius Verus, Fronto refers to the privilege of receiving a kiss from the emperor (*Ad Verum Imp.* 1.7, VdH^2 pp. 111–12 = *Ad Verum Imp.* 2.8, Haines II, pp. 238–41).

resigning a magistracy on the day before it ends: There are two examples of senators who became consul for a single day: the first was Caninius Rebilus in 45 BC, who took office when Q. Fabius Maximus died on the last day of the consular year (Cicero, *Ad Fam.* 7.30.1). The second incident took place in 69, after the incumbent A. Caecina Alienus defected to the Flavians. Rosius Regulus took up the office for 31 October, the last remaining day of Alienus' tenure (Tacitus, *Histories* 3.37). Richlin (2006a: 107) notes that Cicero would never have resigned his consulship on such grounds, but the world had changed in the intervening centuries. The suffect consulship was an honour for Fronto, but his world revolved around the emperor and his court much more than the senate house.

Letter 17. Fronto to Domitia Lucilla (late August 142)

Ad M. Caes. 2.15, VdH^2 pp. 32–3 = *Epist. Graec.* 2, Haines I, pp. 146–51.

To the mother of Caesar,*

1. I have happily sent my Cratia to you with great enthusiasm, by the gods, to celebrate your birthday: I would have come myself if I could. But my consulship is a ball and chain* around my feet at the moment. For there are but few days of my tenure remaining, and these are especially busy on account of my responsibilities. When I have been set free, I plan to run to you with greater

enthusiasm than even those who race the *stadion*.* For they wait just a moment at the starting mechanism before they are allowed to race, whereas I have been prevented from running my race and joining you for two months now.

2. I imagine that it should have been like this, with all the women, all from different places, coming together for the occasion and celebrating your birthday. Firstly, those women who love their husbands, are devoted to their children, and behave as becoming a true woman;* secondly, those who are genuine and faithful; and thirdly, those who are considerate, affable, and unassuming should have joined in the festivities. And many other kinds of women should have been there to have their share of your praise and virtue, since you possess all the virtues and have command of all the abilities that define a woman, just as Athena possesses and wields each one of her skills. As for other women, they possess only the one virtue that has been allotted to them, and they are praised for it, just like the Muses, who are each commended for their art on an individual basis.

3. But if I had stood at your doors, having won the honour of introducing the women worthy of attending this celebration,* I would have taken my cue from Homer and excluded those false friends who only pretend to like you, since they say one thing to your face, but suppress what they are really thinking.* Everything they do is an affectation, from their laughter to their tears. Laughter was originally created by nature as a genuine act, which would show people's teeth as they laughed. But now it has been transformed into an act of trickery and deceit, so that those who are trying to cause trouble actually keep their lips closed. Indeed, it is the goddess Deception,* who is certainly a woman, who receives the greatest attention from female worshippers: she is truly the child (?) of Aphrodite, created from the many and different female qualities . . . *[The remainder of the letter is lost.]*

Commentary

To the mother of Caesar: This is one of two extant letters that Fronto wrote to Domitia during his consulship. In the first letter, probably sent in July 142, he apologises for not having written recently, implying that there was an ongoing correspondence between the two (*Ad M. Caes.* 2.3, VdH[2] pp. 21–4 = *Epist.*

Graec. 1, Haines I, pp. 130–7). Both letters are written in Greek, in which Domitia Lucilla must have been proficient, though we do not have her replies.

a ball and chain: It was common for senators of the imperial period to complain about their public offices, while at the same time enjoying the prestige they brought. When appointed curator of the sewers of Rome and the Tiber, Pliny the Younger (*Letters* 3.1) famously complained that he was 'crushed by a thousand tasks', and similar sentiments are found throughout the letters of the fourth-century senator Symmachus (Matthews 1975: 9).

those who race the *stadion*: Fronto employs the athletic metaphor because the imperial family has been attending the *Sebasta* at Naples, perhaps taking a cue from his protégé Marcus (**Letter 13**). The *stadion* race was from one end of the stadium to the other, a distance of nearly two hundred metres. Fronto uses the correct terminology, including the word for 'starting mechanism' (ὕσπληξ), which was a rope or barrier released to signal the start of the race (*LSJ*[9] s.v. ὕσπληξ).

becoming a true woman: This is a translation of the Greek adjective *sôphrôn* (σώφρων), derived from the noun *sôphrosyne* (σωφροσύνη), which meant soundness of mind and self-control, but gradually came to mean control over one's sexual desires. This was a prime attribute of a good woman in the Greek and Roman worlds, though it was not exclusively a female virtue (North 1966; **Letter 19**). Leading aristocratic women of the age were praised for their *sôphrosyne*, as we can see in Augustus' catalogue of female virtues (Dio 56.3.3) and an inscription honouring Regilla, wife of Herodes Atticus (*IG* IV 1599).

introducing those worthy of attending this celebration: Fronto uses the word *eisagôgeus* (εἰσαγωγεύς), which is a technical term for the Athenian magistrate who introduced cases into a law court (*LSJ*[9] s.v. εἰσαγωγεύς). He probably chose such formal language to explain the role he envisaged for himself at this female gathering: not a participant, but a guardian.

suppress what they are really thinking: The sentiment is spoken by Achilles in Homer's *Iliad* (9.313).

Deception: *Apate* (Ἀπάτη) was the personification of deception. The manuscript breaks off mid-sentence, and the text itself is deficient, so the reading 'child' (τόκος) is very uncertain. Van den Hout (1999: 89) points out that Hesiod (*Theogony* 224) actually lists Deception as the daughter of Night. But deceit was a quality intimately associated with Aphrodite, as seen elsewhere in the *Theogony* (205–6), where Hesiod refers to the whispers, smiles, and deceits that are the goddess' preserve.

Letter 18. Marcus to Fronto (late 142 or early 143)

Ad M. Caes. 1.6, VdH² pp. 10–13 = Haines I, pp. 154–63.

Marcus Aurelius Caesar sends greetings to his teacher Fronto,*

1. Wasn't I impudent to send some of my writings to be read by such an intelligent and judicious man! The passage from your speech,* which my dear father asked me to choose,* I declaimed in a reasonable fashion. The words, it's true, ought to have been spoken by their own author: in this case, they could hardly be greeted with the exclamation that they were 'Worthy of the writer himself!' But I won't put off any longer what you really want to hear about: my lord was so moved by what he heard that he regarded it as a nuisance that he was occupied with public business elsewhere when you were due to give your speech.* He was truly astonished by the range of ideas, the various virtues of the expression, the evident originality of the argumentation, and the skilful structure of the speech. Now I think you're going to ask me which bit I enjoyed the most. Here we go, I'll start with this:

2. 'In those legal cases which are decided by non-imperial judges,* there is no inherent danger, because the decisions they make are valid only for those particular cases. But the precedents that come into effect by your rulings,* emperor, prevail in perpetuity. Your power and authority are so much greater than that attributed to the Fates. The Fates determine what will happen to each of us individually, but when you make a ruling that pertains to individuals, you create a universal precedent.

3. For this reason, if you approve the verdict of the proconsul,* you will give all the magistrates of every province a ruling to follow when they decide cases

of this kind. What, then, will happen? Surely it will be the case that all wills from provinces distant and beyond the sea will be referred back to Rome for a hearing before you.* A son will become suspicious that he has been disinherited: he will demand that his father's testament not be opened.* A daughter will demand the same thing, then a grandson, a great-great grandson, a brother, a cousin, a paternal uncle, a maternal uncle, a paternal aunt, a maternal aunt. All kinds of relatives will take advantage of this privilege, so that they might forbid the will to be opened and enjoy possession by the rights assigned to relatives by blood.* What will happen once the case is finally referred back to Rome? The assigned heirs will set sail, but the disinherited will remain in possession, dragging things out day by day, begging for adjournments, and extending their time with various excuses: "It is winter and the sea is rough in winter: he can't be here." Then, when winter is over: "The unpredictable and dangerous spring storms delay him." When spring has finished: "Summer is hot, the sun burns travellers and the man could get sea-sick." Autumn follows: the harvest will be blamed* and he'll say he's exhausted.

4. Am I making these things up, fabricating a story? Isn't this what has happened in this very case? Where is the other party, who should have been here for some time already to plead his case? "He's on the road." What point in the journey is he at? "He's coming from Asia." And yet he's still in Asia! "It's a long journey, even if he hurries." Is it by ship, by horse, or by the diplomatic fast-track* that he speeds along so slowly? And in the meantime, as soon as you announce the hearing for the first time, Caesar, an adjournment is requested and granted;* when you fix the date of the hearing a second time, a two-month delay is requested. The two months ran out on the last Ides, and a fair few days have passed by since then. Has he arrived at last? If he hasn't arrived, is he at least close by? If he isn't yet close by, has he at least left Asia? If he hasn't yet left, is he at least thinking about it? What is that man thinking about except coveting another's property, stealing their crops, laying waste to their fields, and bringing the whole estate to ruin? He is not so foolish that he would prefer to come before Caesar and be defeated than to remain in Asia and keep hold of the estate.

5. If a custom were introduced that the wills of the deceased should be sent to Rome from the overseas provinces,* these wills would be placed in a peril more undeserving and painful [than] if the bodies of those who had died were

shipped off overseas and [mal]treated.* *[The next line is uncertain.]* There are opportunities for the disposal of corpses in the injuries that are done to them: sometimes the seas devour them in a shipwreck, rivers drag them away headfirst, sands cover them over, wild beasts tear them to shreds, and the birds pick at them. The human body is buried sufficiently whenever it is destroyed in these ways. But when a will is submerged by a shipwreck, it is also the case that the property, the family, and the household founder and remain unburied. Once upon a time, wills were brought out from the safest temples of the gods,* from the registries, vaults, archives, or storerooms; but now wills are crammed in then tossed about with the merchants' cargo and the crew's belongings. The next thing we know, everyone's last will and testament will be thrown overboard with the vegetables if there's a need to jettison some cargo. Instead, perhaps we should set up a customs tax to be exacted on wills. This never needed to be established before, because wills did not sail on the high seas ... *[The text now becomes very uncertain for the following two sections, and is omitted here.]*

8. We shall add something about the funeral. The members of the household* would know how they should grieve: the slave who has been freed mourns in one way, the client bound to deliver praise mourns in a different way, and the friend honoured with a bequest in another. Why introduce uncertainty and suspense to the funeral rites? The inheritance of all animals is decided upon immediately after death: the wool is stripped from sheep straightaway, just like the ivory from elephants, claws from lions, and feathers and plumage from birds: is it our true inheritance to lie neglected in this limbo as though we are left for robbers?'*

9. I think I have ended up writing it all out. Well, what should I have done, when I admired the whole passage, when I loved the whole author so much? Goodbye, most eloquent, most learned, dearest, sweetest, most longed-for master, and my most missed friend.

10. The son born to Herodes has died today.* Herodes is not taking it well. I'd like you to write* a few words to him about this, as befits the situation. Take care always.

Commentary

to his teacher Fronto: In Fronto's reply to this letter he refers to his consulship in the past tense, which means that it must be dated after 1 September 142 (*Ad M. Caes.* 1.7, VdH[2] pp. 13–16 = Haines I, pp. 162–9). Fronto was planning to join the imperial family in Naples immediately after his consulship expired, so this letter should be placed at least a month or two later, since he has had time to return to Rome and resume his legal affairs. It probably dates from late 142 or early 143 (van den Hout 1999: 24–5, 35–6).

The passage from your speech: Fronto was involved in a case concerning an unopened will, which some relatives of the deceased were trying to ensure remained sealed so they could retain control of the estate. Fronto represented the legitimate heirs who would not receive their rightful inheritance unless the will was opened. The case was originally considered by the provincial governor, but then referred to Rome for imperial judgement (Champlin 1980: 61–2).

which my dear father asked me to choose: This is one of several instances in the correspondence which demonstrates how the relationship between Pius and Fronto was not especially close, but was mediated through Marcus. His cloying praise of Pius in his consular speech was very much the fawning act of a courtier (**Letter 14**).

when you were due to give your speech: Roman emperors could hear cases in a variety of locations, such as the tribunal in the *forum Romanum* or one of the imperial fora, as well as in various temples or the imperial palace itself (Millar 1977: 229–30; Bablitz 2007: 34–9).

In those legal cases which are decided by non-imperial judges: The majority of legal hearings in Rome took place before the urban praetor, the urban prefect, or the praetorian prefect. The emperor's court was usually only convened for appeals, on which he was the final arbiter in both criminal and civil cases, and matters referred to him by governors and other officials (Crook 1967: 70–7). There were also a vast number of petitions (*libelli*) sent to the emperor by provincials who asked for advice or intervention in legal cases (Millar 1977: 240–52, 507–49).

But the precedents that come into effect by your rulings: The rulings (*decreta*) to which Fronto refers were the decisions announced by the emperor after he had heard the case, though they were usually transcribed later into written form (Millar 1977: 239). The jurist Gaius (*Institutes* 1.5) classified these rulings as a form of imperial regulation (*constitutio*), along with edicts and letters. Jurists also commonly referred to the emperors' replies to petitions, known as rescripts (*rescripta*), as legal precedents (Riggsby 2010: 90–1).

verdict of the proconsul: Since Fronto refers to his opponent travelling from Asia in section 4, the governor must either be the proconsul of Asia (at the western end of Turkey) or Bithynia and Pontus (on the northern shore of Turkey).

for a hearing before you: A hearing (*cognitio*) denotes a formal investigation by a judge (Riggsby 2010: 118–19). In this case the judge was the emperor himself, who was advised by leading senators and equestrians who made up his council (Millar 1977: 228–40). It is uncertain whether the proconsul of Asia himself referred the case to Pius, or whether one of the parties appealed the proconsul's ruling (Millar 1977: 532–3).

he will demand that his father's testament not be opened: Roman wills were sealed in the presence of seven witnesses, with their contents only to be revealed after death. If the testator decided to revise their will, they were entitled to do so, but still required witnesses to attest to the amendments and the re-sealing of the document (Crook 1967: 127–8; Champlin 1991: 75–6).

enjoy possession by the rights assigned to relatives by blood: This is the crux of the issue: Fronto defends his client's right to have the will read so he can claim his inheritance. On the other side, his opponents are family members hoping to have the will declared invalid. If this were to happen, the estate would pass to the following relations, in order of preference: children, relatives on the father's side, then other blood relations, then the husband or wife (Champlin 1991: 106).

the harvest will be blamed: This was a legitimate excuse, as Marcus ruled (in a speech to the senate) that no one should be forced to appear in court at harvest or vintage time (*Digest* 2.12.1). However, this concession could be withdrawn in matters of urgency in which the property could be lost in the event of a delay (*Digest* 2.12.1.2, 2.12.3).

the diplomatic fast-track: Fronto is referring to the *cursus publicus*, a network of stations on roads throughout the empire which allowed those on official business to rest and change horses between legs of their journey. In order to use the *cursus publicus*, one had to present a certificate attesting to their eligibility (Suetonius, *Augustus* 49.3–50.1).

an adjournment is requested and granted: Adjournments (*dilationes*) were an accepted part of court procedure, but emperors did try to limit them. On one occasion, Pliny the Younger (*Letters* 1.18) remarks that it would be difficult to obtain an adjournment for a case, especially in the Centumviral Court, though these were not unprecedented (see Pliny, *Letters* 5.9). Marcus Aurelius himself allowed no more than two delays (*Digest* 2.12.17), while Diocletian and Maximian ruled that the maximum time for postponement in the case of a province across the seas would be nine months (*Digest* 3.11.1.1).

overseas provinces: The term 'overseas provinces' (*provinciae transmarinae*) refers to the regions between Rome (and Italy) and the eastern Mediterranean that were usually reached by ship (Arnaud 1994). The term was used to describe the commands of Gaius Caesar and Germanicus, who were both sent to the east to arrange transmarine affairs (*AE* 1980: 214; *Tabula Siarensis* l. 15; *Senatus Consultum de Cn. Pisone patre* ll. 29–30). The adjective could also be used in a less technical sense, as in one of the Vindolanda Tablets (II.344) from northern Britain, in which the writer described himself as 'a man from overseas' (*homo transmarinus*).

if the bodies of those who had died were shipped off overseas and [mal] treated: The Romans placed great store on ensuring that bodies of the deceased were given proper treatment. After a family member had died, their relatives would close their eyes, wash the body and prepare it for viewing before the formal funeral procession. Cremation was the standard Roman practice until the mid-second century, when it was eclipsed by inhumation. Even the poorest members of society went to great lengths to ensure that their ashes or bodies would have a proper resting place after death, joining funeral associations that would help to pay for their burial. Cicero (*On Duties* 1.55) wrote of the importance of family members sharing tombs; these often included the extended household, such as slaves and freedmen and their families. The purpose of Fronto's argument is to show that if the maltreatment of a corpse is a bad thing – as his audience would agree – then maltreatment of the deceased's will is even worse. For an overview of Roman funerary practices, see Toynbee (1971) and Hope (2007).

the safest temples of the gods: Augustus deposited his will in the Temple of Vesta in Rome (Suetonius, *Augustus* 101), and we also have evidence of less distinguished Romans placing their documents in temples (*Digest* 43.5.3.3). Such formalities were not a legal requirement, and wills could also be entrusted to friends, relatives, or slaves (Champlin 1991: 76–7; *Digest* 43.5.1.1, 43.5.4). The jurist Ulpian advised that after a will had been read, it should either be given to the principal heir, or placed in a temple for safekeeping (*Digest* 10.2.4.3).

The members of the household: The Romans had no word for 'family' in the modern sense. *Familia*, as here, more properly means household, and included not only relatives, but also clients, freedmen, and slaves.

left for robbers? This is where the passage from the speech quoted by Marcus ends. The outcome of the case is not known, though van den Hout (1999: 28) points to a rescript of Pius preserved by Gaius (*Institutes* 2.120). The rescript stated that those who gained possession of an estate through a will that was not drawn up in accordance with the law were still able to maintain their claim against any rivals alleging that the deceased was intestate.

The son born to Herodes has died today: Herodes Atticus and his wife Regilla were probably living at their estate on the outskirts of Rome on the Via Appia (for which see Tobin 1997: 355–71; Pomeroy 2007: 149–56). We have no firm date for the marriage of Herodes and Regilla, though the baby referred to in this letter is usually thought to have been their first child. Most estimates place their marriage in the early 140s, while Herodes was still in Rome (Tobin 1997: 32; cf. Pomeroy 2007: xii, who prefers 138/139).

Marcus' statement is a little more complicated than it might as first appear. The Latin, as it appears in van den Hout's edition, reads: *Herodi filius natus <hodi>e mortuus est.* This could be translated as either, 'The son born to Herodes today has died', or 'The son born to Herodes has died today'. The first implies the baby died on the same day it was born. The latter is not quite so precise, though the child was undoubtedly still very young. Moreover, we should be wary of placing too much emphasis on the time, since *hodie*, the Latin word for today, is merely a reasonable supplement to the lacuna in the manuscript, which only has the letter *e*.

I'd like you to write: This final request, though couched in familiarity, is really more of an order, and once again highlights the power imbalance between Fronto and Marcus. Sufficient time, at least a year or so, has passed since the court case featured in **Letters 7–11** for Herodes and Fronto to reach a sort of détente. A letter from Marcus, which is probably dated to the intervening period, suggests that the prince had encouraged their reconciliation (*Ad M. Caes.* 4.2, VdH[2] pp. 54–6 = Haines I, pp. 74–9).

Letter 19. Fronto to Herodes Atticus (late 142 or early 143)

Ad M. Caes. 2.1, VdH[2] pp. 16–17 = *Epist. Graec.* 3, Haines I, pp. 168–71.

[Fronto to Herodes]

1. *[The opening of this letter is missing.]* ... it is not hard to maintain one's composure in less trying times. For, in all circumstances, it is not becoming for a man of good culture* to wail and cry over everything beyond acceptable

limits . . . . *[There is a small lacuna here.]* . . . for my part, I would rather overstep the bounds of joy than grief. For unreasonable pleasure is to be reckoned better than unreasonable mourning.

2. But you are not yet beyond the proper age for raising other children.* Every loss is difficult to deal with when hope is torn away, but becomes easier if hope of recovery remains. And the man who does not await this is himself ill-born* and causes more harm to himself than does Fortune. For while it is true that Fortune takes away the present, such a man deprives himself of hope as well.

3. I will teach you where you can easily find consolation,* since I have learned it myself from experience rather than through the study of philosophy. It has always happened that I have suffered whenever I felt deeply about something. Once I was besotted with the philosopher Athenodotus, then with Dionysius* the orator. And when I considered that I would still remember, deep down, the man whom I had come to love, I was less prone to grief and happenstance. But if you, as I do, love this well-born young man,* known for his virtue and education and fortune and self-control, you will not fail if you join yourself to him and place all your hope of a good future in him. For as long as he is with us – for I declare myself to be your rival for his affections,* and I don't make a secret of it – all other things can be dealt with, and should be relegated to second place.

Commentary

a man of good culture: The Greek word *paideia* (παιδεία) means both 'upbringing' and 'education', but also by extension, the culture and intellectual ability fostered by such an education in philosophy, rhetoric, music, and geometry, what we would term the 'liberal arts'. In the high Roman empire, the age of the 'Second Sophistic', *paideia* was a specifically Hellenic quality that articulated the cultural supremacy of the Greeks over the Romans (Whitmarsh 2005: 13–14). It is thus rather patronising for Fronto to be telling Herodes – one of the foremost Greek orators of his day – what is appropriate for a man of *paideia*. According to Aulus Gellius (*Attic Nights* 13.17), *humanitas* was the Latin equivalent of *paideia*.

the proper age for raising other children: Herodes was still only in his early forties, and would subsequently have several other children with his wife Regilla. The Augustan marriage legislation specified that all men between the ages of 25 and 59 had to be married in order to produce children, though this did not preclude them fathering children in later years. Legislation of the emperor Claudius specified that men aged 60 and over could still marry women aged under 50 for the purposes of procreation (Parkin 2003: 193–9).

ill-born: Scholars have noted how inappropriate Fronto's language is here, since the Greek word *agennês* (ἀγεννής) not only means 'ill-born' or 'lowly', but also 'childless' (van den Hout 1999: 43; Richlin 2006a: 124).

you can easily find consolation: We discuss the genre of the 'letter of consolation' in Chapter 8.

Athenodotus . . . Dionysius: Fronto studied at Rome under Athenodotus, who was himself a pupil of the noted Stoic philosopher C. Musonius Rufus. Fronto called Athenodotus his 'teacher and father' (**Letter 21**). Little else is known about Dionysius, known as 'the Slim' (Champlin 1980: 20–1). The parallel does not really offer much consolation: it seems inappropriate to compare leaving one's teacher to the loss of a child.

love this well-born young man: The tone of this passage is both aggressive and sexually charged, as Fronto deliberately sets himself up as Herodes' rival. The orator employs the traditional virtues of personal excellence to paint Marcus as the paradigmatic Hellenic youth: he possesses virtue (*arête*), education (*paideia*), and self-control (*sôphrosyne*). In a way, this serves to elevate the prince above the competition between his tutors. Marcus is also 'well-born' (γενναίου), undoubtedly juxtaposed with Fronto's previous use of 'ill-born' (ἀγεννής) to describe a man who lacks appropriate self-control. It is worth noting that the rivalry which Fronto establishes in these letters is at odds with Marcus' own wishes: in **Letter 7** the prince states that he loves Fronto and Herodes on their own merits.

rival for his affections: The Greek word translated here as 'rival for his affections' is *anterastês* (ἀντεραστής). It is one of several key terms explored in

Greek erotic and pedagogical discourse, along with *erastês*, the older lover/teacher, and the *erômenos*, the younger beloved/pupil (Dover 1989: 16). Fronto and Marcus had themselves used this language to refer to their relationship in their correspondence, most notably the *Treatise on Love*, and Marcus' reply (Richlin 2006b: 115–17). By employing such terms here, Fronto is not only delineating his relationship with the young prince, but also articulating the extent of his own familiarity with Greek literature and culture, which was Herodes' professed area of expertise.

4

Family Affairs

Introduction

This chapter focuses on Fronto's relationship with Marcus Aurelius and his family in the 140s and 150s. In 145, Marcus married Faustina the Younger, the daughter of Antoninus Pius. Their first child, Domitia Faustina, was born in 147, and thirteen more children followed over the next twenty years, though most of them died in infancy. Through these letters, we observe Marcus coming of age, a development that seems to have unsettled Fronto to a certain degree.

Many of these letters concern illness, which was a common topic in Roman letters. Such discussions were a form of social bonding between friends and associates, enabling them to express concern and offer consolation or advice. But even by these standards, Fronto and Marcus devoted significant time to discussing their symptoms and ailments, often in excruciating detail. These letters can be interpreted as a different manifestation of their teacher–pupil relationship and the affection that it engendered (Freisenbruch 2007). This chapter opens with one of Fronto's most dramatic accounts of his ill-health as he describes a crippling bout of gastroenteritis (**Letter 20**) and Marcus' own reports of medical dramas in his family (**Letter 21**).

Fronto continued to tutor Marcus after his marriage in 145, but probably not for too much longer. In a letter of 146/147, Marcus confessed that he had been losing interest in his exercises, and thoughts of philosophy and ethics had occupied his mind instead (**Letter 22**). Some of Fronto's letters written after this period appear to be especially anxious about changes in their relationship. For example, **Letter 23** is a short note from Marcus concerning the illness of Domitia Faustina. It was dashed off in a hurry, and gives the impression that Marcus was truly worried about whether she would survive. Fronto's response (**Letter 24**) briefly disposes of the issue of Faustina's sickness, as he expresses relief that it is not Marcus himself who is seriously ill (only his baby daughter!). The rest of the letter is a fulsome account of his own feelings for Marcus, and has doubtless contributed to the view of Fronto as self-absorbed and insensitive (Whitehorne 1977b: 416–17; McLynn 2009: 49). However, it could also be interpreted as an expression of anxiety on the part of a teacher whose pupil has now grown up and may not need him any more (Freisenbruch 2007: 247–51).

Discussion of Marcus' family, however superficial, gives Fronto opportunities to continue to integrate himself into the prince's life. **Letters 25–27** are short missives concerning the children's birthdays, the health of family members, and apologies on Fronto's part for not being able to present himself at the morning *salutatio*. The letters give the impression that he visited the imperial palace almost daily when in Rome, paying his respects to Marcus, while Cratia visited the women of the family (**Letter 26**). Neither Fronto nor Marcus seem interested in the lives of the women beyond a paternalistic concern for their well-being. This is made abundantly clear in the final letter in which Marcus praises his wife for her obedience to his orders (**Letter 27**). These letters can only offer us a glimpse into the world of elite women through the eyes of men.

Letter 20. Fronto to Marcus (*c*. 139–156)

Ad M. Caes. 5.55, VdH[2] pp. 80–1 = *Ad M. Caes.* 5.40, Haines I, pp. 240–3.

My lord,

I've been brought low by a disease of my bowels* that was so terrible that I lost my voice and was wracked by a bout of retching, then I was choked by a tightness of breath, and finally, my circulation stopped. Without the blood flowing through my veins I fainted away. And then my nearest and dearest let out cries of grief, and I didn't come round for quite a while. There wasn't a moment or opportunity for the doctors to revive or treat me with a warm bath,* cold water, or food, and it was only in the evening that I swallowed some little bits of bread sprinkled with wine. And so I was brought back to life. I didn't recover my voice for three whole days. But now, thanks to the favour of the gods, I'm doing very well indeed – I can walk more easily, and I can converse more clearly. Then – if the gods allow it – I intend to be taken out in the carriage tomorrow. If I can put up with the flint paving, I'll rush to you as fast as I can. I'll know I'm really alive when I can see you. I'll be leaving Rome on the seventh day before the Kalends, if the gods are favourable. Farewell, my sweetest master, whom I desperately long for, who is my entire reason for living. Give my best to your lady.

Commentary

a disease of my bowels: This is our translation of the Latin word *cholera*, which usually refers to any kind of profuse diarrheal disease. This includes cholera (*Vibrio cholerae*), but also typhoid fever, food poisoning, and various other less serious illnesses. According to Aberth (2011: 102), cholera can cause 'complete prostration due to a sudden drop in blood pressure and shock can occur within hours, so that it was said a man healthy in the morning could be dead by evening, or a person could simply collapse in the street lying in his own excrement.' Though Fronto's illness was clearly serious, we hesitate to identify it as cholera, since he does not mention anyone else suffering from the same illness, and cholera is an epidemic disease. Fronto may have come down with an infectious illness that triggered something more serious, such as a heart attack or stroke (Whitehorne 1977b: 415; van den Hout 1999: 212–3).

treat me with a warm bath: In discussing treatments for suffers of *cholera*, Celsus (*On Medicine* 4.18.5) recommends they should take a bath on the third day. For bathing as a health treatment in the Roman world, see Fagan (2006).

Letter 21. Marcus to Fronto (*c.* 139–152)

Ad M. Caes. 5.23, VdH[2] pp. 72–3 = *Ad M. Caes.* 5.8, Haines I, pp. 196–7.

To my teacher,

Here's an account of how I've been passing my time. My sister* was seized with pain in her female parts* suddenly and so badly that it was awful to see how she looked. Then my mother, alarmed and not thinking of herself, dashed her side against the corner of the wall, causing herself (and us) much pain with the blow. Then when I went to lie down, I found a scorpion in my bed;* but I caught it and killed it before I lay down on top of it. If you are feeling better, that's a relief. My mother is a little better now, thanks to the favour of the gods.

Farewell, my best and sweetest teacher. My lady wishes you well.

Commentary

my sister: Annia Cornificia Faustina, Marcus' younger sister, was married to the senator M. Ummidius Quadratus. She died in 152, so the letter must have been written before this date (Birley 1993: 108).

pain in her female parts: The euphemism 'female parts' (*muliebres partes*), though often translated 'private parts', is not necessarily specific to any particular part of the female anatomy.

I found a scorpion in my bed: It was evidently quite a day *chez* Marcus! While the Elder Pliny (*Natural History* 5.7.7) associated the scorpion with Africa, scorpions of one species or another are found in most parts of the world. Though all possess some form of venom to kill their prey, only a very small proportion of species are dangerous to humans. Those that are, however, can deliver a lethal sting (Williams 2009: 904–9). Pliny recommended wearing an amulet to prevent scorpion stings, and included in his text the recipe for a potion to treat those who had already been stung (*Natural History* 25.72). Marcus' visitor may have been hiding under his bedclothes to escape the daylight.

Letter 22. Marcus to Fronto (between 26 April 146 and 26 April 147)

Ad M. Caes. 4.13, VdH² pp. 67–8 = Haines I, pp. 214–19.

To my teacher,

1. Gaius Aufidius is completely full of himself,* praises his own judgement to high heaven, and proclaims that there has never been a more upright man than he – yes, I'm not exaggerating – who has emerged from Umbria* and come to Rome. What more can I tell you? He prefers to be acknowledged as a judge rather than an orator. When I smile,* he eyes me condescendingly: he says that it's easy to sit idly next to the judge, but actually to be the judge – that's a noble calling. He's talking about me! But the matter turned out fine in the end, so it's all good, and I'm happy.

2. I'm pleased, but also worried, at the prospect of your arrival. As to why I might be happy, no one needs to ask. But as to why I'm worried, I'll confess to you (may the gods help me). You know that task you set me to write* – well, I've put hardly any effort into it, even though I've had lots of time. The works of Ariston do me good at this point of time, but they have me worried. When they teach me better things, they do me good, but when they reveal to me truly how far distant my own nature is from these ideals, your pupil all too often gets ashamed and angry with himself. He's now twenty-five years old and has taken to heart no ethical beliefs or idealistic principles. So I punish myself, I get angry with myself, I'm sad, I get jealous, I deprive myself of food.

3. Since I'm now held captive by these thoughts, each day I've put off the duty of writing until the next. But I'll come up with something, and as some Attic orator* warned an assembly of the Athenians, 'We must sometimes allow the laws to rest'. So I'll make peace with the books of Ariston,* and let them rest, and I'll give my full attention to your poet of the stage,* but not before reading through some of the shorter speeches of Cicero. But I'll write about only one of the two subjects,* because Ariston will never rest so quietly as to allow me to have anything to do with the other side as well.

4. Goodbye, my best and most respected teacher.* My lady sends her best wishes.

Commentary

Gaius Aufidius: C. Aufidius Victorinus, who studied with Marcus, and would also have been in his mid-twenties when this letter was written.

from Umbria: Victorinus' family came from the Umbrian town of Pisaurum, located on the eastern coast of Italy. It was quite a boast he made, since the family of the emperor Nerva came from Umbria, as incidentally, did the poet Propertius.

When I smile: Victorinus was arguing a case before a judge in his capacity as an advocate. Marcus was acting as an advisor (*assessor*), presumably as part of his training for imperial rule (van den Hout 1999: 186–7). The anecdote implies there was some friendly banter between the two friends concerning Victorinus' appearance in court.

You know that task which you set me to write: Fronto has still been setting exercises for Marcus, though the prince has grown lax in completing them. This letter shows Marcus at a crucial transitional point in his life – he obviously still thinks he should do what Fronto has asked, and is guilty for not doing so, but at the same time, he feels able to explore new avenues.

some Attic orator: Their identity is uncertain, especially since the line Marcus quotes is in Latin, rather than Greek.

Ariston: Ariston was a Stoic philosopher of the third century BC, though his views did not always agree with those of more mainstream Stoics. His particular focus was on ethical principles. Champlin (1974: 144), followed by Birley (1993: 226), argues that the reference is actually to the legal expert Titius Ariston, which would give a certain thematic unity to the letter. However, we are inclined to regard him as the philosopher, given Marcus' concern for ethics and self-improvement.

your poet of the stage: Possibly Plautus, but no certainty is possible.

But I'll write about only one of the two subjects: This line is somewhat controversial. It is usually regarded as a clear statement by Marcus that he cannot study both rhetoric and philosophy, and therefore marks a turning point in his relationship with Fronto (van den Hout 1999: 186; Richlin 2006a: 141). Champlin (1974: 144; 1980: 121–2) argues that the letter is more concerned with jurisprudence than philosophy, but this does not seem convincing. It is surely no coincidence that the ancient editor placed this letter at the end of *Ad M. Caes.* book 4, as if to delineate a significant transition (van den Hout 1999: 186). It is clear that Marcus is undergoing 'some inner crisis' (Birley 1993: 226).

most respected teacher: Marcus uses this expression only twice in the extant correspondence to characterise Fronto, and its employment here in preference to a more fulsome expression of love is an indication of the prince's mind-set.

Letter 23. Marcus to Fronto (*c.* 147–151)

Ad M. Caes. 4.11, VdH^2 p. 65 = Haines I, pp. 202–3.

Caesar to Fronto,

If the gods favour us, I think we've some hope of recovery:* the diarrhoea has stopped, the feverishness has gone,* but the wasting has left her very thin and her little cough remains. Of course you realise I'm writing to you about our tiny little Faustina:* we've been completely occupied looking after her.* Make sure you tell me if your own health is on the mend, as I hope you'll do, my teacher.

Commentary

I think we've some hope of recovery: Childhood illnesses of the kind that are considered minor in Western societies today would have claimed the lives of a significant proportion of children born in the Roman world. The infant mortality rate was likely to have been quite high, and perhaps comparable to that in developing nations of the modern world (Parkin 1992: 67–90). In 2012, according to the World Health Organisation, 'In developing countries, about half of all childhood deaths – 4.9 million – are caused by no more than four conditions: pneumonia, diarrhoeal diseases, malaria, and measles' (World Health Organisation n.d.). The situation would probably have been similar in Rome, especially for the poor, with the absence of adequate hygiene, vaccination, and antibiotics. Malnutrition reduces the likelihood that the sufferer will survive infectious diseases, even with modern medical intervention (Pelletier et al. 1995: 443–8).

the feverishness has gone: Faustina may have been suffering from a childhood illness that would be regarded as relatively minor today. If Romans actually did follow the advice of medical writers such as Soranus (which is doubtful) it is possible that the care they gave their children actually made them weaker and more likely to succumb to infectious disease. For example, Soranus recommended that newborn babies not be fed for 'up to as long as two days,' and that they not be allowed to consume the mother's first milk (*colostrum*), which is now known to be full of antibodies that protect the infant from infection (*Gynecology* 2.17–18).

tiny little Faustina: Marcus uses the diminutive forms of many of the words in this letter – *febriculae* ('feverishness'), *tussiculae* ('little cough'), *parvola* ('little one') – emphasising the fragility of his baby girl.

we've been completely occupied looking after her: Children were surrounded by a large network of people who could care for them in times of need. Pliny's account of the illness of Minicia Marcella shows that children sometimes received treatment from doctors, as well as care from other siblings, nurses, and teachers and, of course, from their parents (*Letters* 5.16, 6.16.3–4). Fathers could overrule the decisions of the physicians, sometimes with fatal consequences (Gourevitch 2010: 284).

Letter 24. Fronto to Marcus (*c*. 147–151)

Ad M. Caes. 4.12, VdH[2] pp. 65–7 = Haines I, pp. 202–9.

Fronto to Caesar,

1. Good gods, how alarmed I was when I read the opening of your letter! It was written in such a way that I imagined some danger to *your* health. But then, when you explained that the danger I'd thought was yours at the beginning was actually your daughter Faustina's, how my sense of panic changed! Not only changed, but – to be frank – somewhat assuaged. In response, you may well say, 'Did my daughter's peril seem to you less serious than my own? Did it seem like that to you, though you proclaim that Faustina is like a bright light to you, like a holiday, like the protection of hope, like a promise fulfilled, like complete joy, like praise that is noble and enduring?' It's true, I know what came over me while reading your letter, but for what reason it came over me in this way, I don't know. I don't know, I say, why I was more dismayed at your peril than that of your daughter, unless perhaps, all else being equal, it's those things we think of first that seem worse to us.

2. In fact *you* may know better than me what caused this feeling, since you know more about the nature and feelings of men than I do,* and have learned more about them. I was moderately well prepared by my teacher and father Athenodotus* in the study of concepts and ideas, which he called 'images'. These should not only be understood but actually applied in reality. And this particular idea has struck me, which might explain why my fears seemed to diminish when they were transferred: the same thing often happens to a man carrying a heavy weight on his shoulders – when he transfers the weight from his left to his right shoulder, even though the weight itself has not reduced one little bit, transferring the weight seems to lighten it.

3. Now, since in the last part of your letter you've reported that Faustina is feeling a little bit better, and have banished all my fear and concern, it seems that it's not a bad time to turn to a free and frank discussion of my affection for you. For it's perhaps acceptable for those who have been relieved of great fear and anxiety to play around a little and act like a fool. I hold you so dear, and I feel this way during the serious and important times we have spent together as

much as in the many frivolous ones. As to what these frivolities are, I'll point them out to you.

4. If I ever see you in my sleep, 'held fast in a sweet and peaceful dream',* as the poet says, there is never a moment I'm not embracing and kissing you.* Then, according to the theme of each dream, either I burst into tears or jump for joy and delight. This is one token of my love, taken from the *Annals*, and it is a poetic and quite sleep-inducing one.

5. Listen to another one, this time an argumentative and contentious one. Sometimes, I have railed against you behind your back, making serious complaints in front of a few of my closest friends. I've done this when you made an appearance at a meeting in a rather grumpy mood, or when you came into the theatre with your head buried in a book, or kept on reading during a dinner party (at that time I wasn't yet staying away from the theatre or dinner parties). At those times I certainly used to call you a hard and unreasonable man, tiresome even, when occasionally anger had stirred me up against you. But if anyone else disparaged you at a dinner party within my hearing, I couldn't listen to it and keep my temper. And so it was easier for me to say these things about you than to put up with anyone else saying them, just as I could more easily strike my daughter Cratia than see anyone else strike her.

6. I'll add a third of these frivolous remarks. You know how at all the money-changers' tables,* and in booths, shops, colonnades, entrance-courts, and windows, anywhere and anytime, there are your images on display* to the crowds. They are quite badly painted, and many of them are sculpted and carved by heavy-handed (or more probably, talentless) artists. But even though I think your visage never looks more unlike you as I pass by, it still never fails to force a kiss from my mouth.

7. Now I shall stop these silly things and turn to serious matters. This letter to you is an indication of how much I love you, since I was more disturbed by *your* danger than that of your daughter, even though in general I'd hope for your sake that your daughter would outlive you, as you'd outlive me. But see that you do not accuse me in front of your daughter, as if I really did care more for you than for her. The danger is that your daughter would be greatly disturbed by this, since she is a serious and old-fashioned lass. She might get angry and snatch her hands and feet away from me when I try to kiss them, or extend them only reluctantly. Good gods, then I'll kiss her cute little hands and

chubby little feet more willingly than your regal neck and your courteous and proper face.

Commentary

you know more about the nature and feelings of men than I do: Fronto is referring to Marcus Aurelius' interest in philosophy, of which he would have been especially aware after receiving **Letter 22**.

my teacher and father Athenodotus: First mentioned in **Letter 19**, the philosopher Athenodotus taught Fronto about *eikones* (εἰκόνες), a Greek word which literally means 'images' or 'figures'. In rhetorical discourse, its meaning encompasses both metaphors and similes.

'held fast in a sweet and peaceful dream': This is a quotation from Ennius' *Annals* (see **Letter 1**).

embracing and kissing you: The language is intense and passionate, indicative of the depth of feeling Fronto has for his pupil, as Richlin (2006b: 123–4) has noted. However, it must be remembered that the ancient Romans were openly affectionate in public, much more so than many people in modern-day Britain, Australia, or America. Kissing was an integral part of friendship, and of court ritual (Paterson 2007: 147–8; Williams 2012: 256–7). Pliny the Younger (*Panegyricus* 22–3) commented that Trajan would only kiss senators, while Tiberius tried to place a ban on people kissing, possibly in an attempt to prevent the spread of a disease (Suetonius, *Tiberius* 34). Elsewhere in the letters, Fronto refers to a crowd of courtiers kissing Marcus farewell as he got into his carriage (*Ad M. Caes.* 3.14, VdH^2 pp. 45–7 = *Ad M. Caes.* 3.13, Haines I, pp. 218–23). Lucius Verus also expressed his desire to have Fronto embrace and kiss him, and Fronto wrote of the privilege of receiving his kiss (*Ad Verum Imp.* 1.4, 1.7, VdH^2 pp. 109, 111–12 = *Ad Verum Imp.* 2.5, 2.8, Haines II, pp. 236–7, 238–41). We can perhaps read this sentiment as an expression of Fronto's anxiety about his position now that Marcus is married and has children of his own.

money-changers' tables: The first references to 'money-changers' or 'bankers' appear in the fourth century BC (Andreau 1999: 30). These men facilitated trade in the marketplace and may have exchanged bullion for minted coinage. They were responsible for checking and changing money, and probably provided credit when auctions were taking place (Andreau 1999: 133).

your images on display: Busts of the Roman emperor would be placed in conspicuous spots around the streets of Rome and the provincial towns. These images were probably reproductions of a master version produced by an artisan directly associated with the imperial household, though the imitations could be very poor (Stewart 2003: 157–84).

Letter 25. Fronto to Marcus (early 150s)

Ad M. Caes. 5.57, VdH[2] p. 81 = *Ad M. Caes.* 5.42, Haines I, pp. 244–5.

To my lord,

1. May you rejoice and celebrate many of your children's birthdays* for a long time to come! You're dear to your parents, popular with the people, esteemed by your friends, and entirely worthy of your success, family, and public standing! I'd ransom my whole life to pay the debt I owe to you and your children, and not just the little of my life that is left to me, but also the portion that I've already lived, if only it could all be restored to me whole again. If I could walk easily,* this would be the day on which I'd want to be amongst the first to embrace you, but of course I must yield to my feet, since they cannot take too much walking. I'm considering making use of the waters.* If I think of anything better, I'll make a note of it for you.

2. Farewell, my sweetest lord. Give your Faustina my best wishes, and congratulate her and kiss our ladies in my name, and, as I am accustomed to do, kiss their feet and hands. Please give my regards to your mother.

Commentary

your children's birthdays: After the death of Domitia Faustina, Marcus had two girls, Annia Aurelia Galeria Lucilla, born in 150, and Annia Galeria Aurelia Faustina, born in 151. A son, T. Aelius Antoninus, was born and died in 152 (Birley 1993: 247). Fronto and his wife attended birthdays of members of the imperial family when they could (**Letters 16–17**).

If I could walk easily: Aulus Gellius (*Attic Nights* 2.26.1) says Fronto suffered from gout, though rheumatism has been suggested as a possibility (Whitehorne 1977b: 415).

I'm considering making use of the waters: The Romans considered bathing to be an important treatment for several kinds of illnesses, and 'healing spas' were popular (Fagan 2006: 190–207). This may be what Fronto is referring to, as he uses the term 'the waters' (*aquae*), rather than stating that he would use a bath (*balneum*), or go to bathe (*lavare*).

Letter 26. Fronto to Marcus (*c.* 145–161)

Ad M. Caes. 5.25, VdH[2] p. 73 = *Ad M. Caes.* 5.10, Haines I, pp. 194–5.

To my lord,

Victorinus has only told me just now that your lady* has more of a fever* than yesterday. Cratia reported* that she had been recovering. It's for this reason I haven't been to see you, because I've been feeling fragile with a bit of a cold.* But tomorrow morning I'll come and see you at home;* at the same time, if it is convenient, I'll pay a visit to your lady.

Commentary

your lady: This is probably Marcus' wife Faustina, rather than his mother (van den Hout 1999: 195).

more of a fever: Graeco-Roman physicians of this era understood fever to be driven by the hot and cold 'humours' of the body (Hippocrates, *Crises* 45–50). If Faustina had a common cold or similar illness, she could have expected to be treated with plant-based remedies such as powdered mustard, onion, or radish, or with a concoction based on honey (Dioscorides, *On Medical Materials* 3, 83; Galen, *On the Natural Faculties* 2, 9; Hippocrates, *On the Nature of Man* 7). Faustina may have been attended by the coterie of physicians who served the imperial household (Galen, *On Prognosis* 11).

Cratia reported: Fronto's wife had evidently paid a visit to the women at the imperial residence.

a bit of a cold: The noun *gravedo* is quite rare in Latin literature, and can mean both a cold (as here and in Celsus, *On Medicine* 1.2) and a hangover (Pliny, *Natural History* 20.136).

I'll come and see you at home: This letter is both an apology for Fronto's absence from the daily *salutatio* (he did not want to infect Faustina), and also a promise to attend the next day. Since Fronto clearly expected Marcus to receive his letter the day it was sent, both men would have been in Rome at the same time, with 'home' (*domum*) referring to the imperial palace.

Letter 27. Marcus to Fronto (*c.* 145–161)

Ad M. Caes. 5.26, VdH^2 p. 73 = *Ad M. Caes.* 5.11, Haines I, pp. 194–5.

To my teacher,

Faustina has had a fever* today too, and I feel I've actually noticed it more today. But, gods willing, she puts my mind at rest, since she follows my wishes so obediently.* Of course you would've come if you could. I'm delighted that you now *are* able to, my teacher, and promise to set out soon. Farewell, my most delightful teacher.

Commentary

Faustina has had a fever: Physicians in the Roman household were not given carte blanche in treating their patients. The most senior man in the household was always in control, so Marcus would have overseen his wife's care and convalescence. If Faustina were treated by physicians, it would be up to Marcus to decide which treatment was best for her and who would carry it out (Flemming 2000: 67–74, 265). Physicians had to actively compete – often at the bedside of their patient – for their suggested cures to be the ones chosen (Mattern 1999a: 7–9; Gourevitch 2010). This happened to the imperial physician Galen when the treatment he offered to Marcus Aurelius was at odds with that of the other doctors (*On Prognosis* 11.1–8).

follows my wishes so obediently: Similar sentiments are found in Marcus' *Meditations* (1.17.8), where he praises Faustina for her submissiveness. Roman husbands, sons, and fathers depicted their women as conforming to idealised standards of virtue and behaviour, which reflected favourably upon the men themselves. Carlon (2009: 138–85) shows how Pliny's depictions of his wife, and other women in his social circle, help him to depict himself as the model of the perfect Roman man.

5

Politics and Patronage

Introduction

This chapter brings together letters illuminating the political and social life of the Roman elite in the age of the Antonines. Most of the letters can be dated to the reign of Antoninus Pius, when Marcus Aurelius was still Caesar (except **Letter 28**, of uncertain date). They illustrate Fronto's relationship with his wider social network, as he writes letters on behalf of his friends and acquaintances, sometimes lavishing praise on them, at other times apologising on their behalf.

Patronage is a consistent theme throughout these letters. Many 'letters of recommendation' (*litterae commendaticiae*) appear in the writings of Fronto, Pliny the Younger, and Cicero (collected in *Ad Familiares* Book Thirteen). They were written by patrons on behalf of their protégés, clients, and friends to influential individuals, such as senators and emperors, who were able to grant favours, honours, or official posts (Saller 1982: 108–10, 127–38; Wilcox 2012: 79–96). The letters usually praised the subject's personal qualities and virtues, their family background and level of education, and their achievements in literature and rhetoric (Cotton 1985; Rees 2007). This formula was fairly consistent across the genre: for example, letters requesting army posts do not usually contain discussion of military aptitude, but focus on cultural attainment instead (Birley 2003). The conventional nature of these letters meant that patrons might have had difficulty in determining whether the endorsement was really genuine: in one letter Cicero (*Ad Fam.* 13.6) writes of using a special mark to draw attention to candidates who really did merit proper consideration. **Letter 28** is a letter of recommendation written by Fronto for a friend who will shortly appear in a law court, while **Letter 29** concerns an imperial freedman. The tone of these letters is generally quite formal.

Fronto put his talents of persuasion to a somewhat different test when plunged into an embarrassing scandal at court. His friend Censorius Niger died sometime between 146 and 158 and made Fronto heir to five-twelfths of his estate. Unfortunately, he also used his will to settle a personal grudge against Antoninus Pius' praetorian prefect, Gavius Maximus. This placed Fronto in the delicate position of having to apologise to the emperor for abuse levelled at one of his most trusted officials, as well as to Maximus himself (**Letters 30–31**). The language of these letters is very stilted and formal, reflecting Fronto's unease. His embarrassment is made patently clear in a revealing letter to Marcus (**Letter 32**).

The last years of Pius' reign brought Fronto a series of honours, which he was forced to decline on the grounds of ill-health. Firstly, he turned down the position of patron of Cirta, instead recommending three younger senators, including his future son-in-law C. Aufidius Victorinus, who married his daughter Cratia in 157 (**Letter 33**). Secondly, Fronto, as befitting his status as a senior ex-consul, was selected for the proconsular governorship of Asia, one of the most prestigious posts in the senatorial career. However, he did not feel up to the challenge, and wrote to Pius asking to be excused (**Letter 34**). Fronto continued to play a role in court life, however, petitioning Pius for procuratorships for his friends Calpurnius Iulianus and the historian Appian (**Letter 35**). It is interesting that Iulianus also twice declined positions offered to him by the emperor. In the eyes of Fronto and some of his circle, the honour came in the offer of an appointment rather than in carrying out the administrative tasks it entailed.

Letter 28. Fronto to Claudius Severus (prior to *c.* 166)

Ad Amicos 1.1, VdH[2] p. 170 = Haines I, pp. 282–7.

Fronto sends his greetings to Claudius Severus,*

1. They say that the custom of recommendation originally stemmed from human kindness, when a man wanted to introduce and acquaint one of his friends with another. And then the custom gradually developed to the point

that it did not seem an improper act to give recommendations for men involved in public or private suits,* either to the judges themselves or their assessors who were present.* This was not, in my opinion, done to undermine the impartiality of the judges or to divert them from pronouncing a just verdict. But there was a long-standing practice in these courts of summoning character witnesses once the official arguments had been made. These individuals would provide a personal assessment of the defendant, giving their opinion in good faith. Our customary letters of recommendation seem to perform the same function of providing a favourable character testimony.

2. Why did my introduction go into the topic in such depth?* I did not want you to think that I had given too little consideration to your own importance and public standing in commending my dearest friend Sulpicius Cornelianus* to you. He will soon be pleading a case before you and your court, but I venture to praise my friend's character in accordance with the established practice, as I have described it. He is an industrious and hard-working man with a generous and genial character; he is truly devoted to our state; he relies on his integrity, rather than being too bold; he is [dear] to me because of his enthusiasm for literature and accomplishment in the liberal arts ... *[The text breaks off here, and the next two pages of the manuscript are illegible. We begin again mid-sentence.]* ... we were not joined together in this friendship casually or at random, nor, I confess, did I seek out Cornelianus' friendship on a whim. For compliments about his character had already made their way to me, and I have ascertained the veracity of those remarks which reached my ears through my own personal experience of him, and I have confirmed this on many occasions. We lived together, studied together,* shared jokes and confidences, we have put each other's loyalty and counsel to the test: our friendship has been a source of pleasure and mutual benefit in every way.

3. So therefore, I beg and beseech you, as much as I possibly can ... *[A few illegible words.]* ... for this man who is the dearest to me in the case ... *[The next line is fragmentary.]* ... encouraged a man of our order to bring a complaint, but when the records of the court have been read ... *[The remainder of the sentence is fragmentary.]* The devotion that exists in my heart impels me to commend him to you in such great detail, but he replies that your love for me is a guarantee ... *[A missing word or two.]* ... whatever I ask, one word of mine will seem to you to be the equivalent of a speech.

Commentary

Claudius Severus: This could be Cn. Claudius Severus Arabianus (*PIR*^{2} C 1023), ordinary consul in 146, or his son, Cn. Claudius Severus (*PIR*^{2} C 1024), ordinary consul for the second time in 173, and the husband of Marcus' daughter Annia Galeria Aurelia Faustina.

in public or private suits: Roman public law was concerned with state affairs, while private law dealt with contracts, property law and criminal matters that did not pertain to the state. A party to a dispute could compel his opponent to appear firstly before a magistrate, who arbitrated the dispute and offered legal options. The case would then go before a judge or panel of judges, who would decide the outcome (Crook 1967: 68–80).

the judges themselves or their assessors who were present: Judges were not necessarily especially qualified in Roman law: they could simply be men of high status who were distinguished in some way and were approved by both parties to the dispute (Crook 1967: 79–82).

Why did my introduction go into the topic in such depth? Far from being deliberately verbose, Fronto is emphasising that it is entirely appropriate for him to write to the presiding judge of a case involving his friend (Champlin 1980: 69). Nevertheless, the original letter must have been quite long, since two pages of the manuscript are missing.

Sulpicius Cornelianus: Cornelianus features in a second letter of recommendation from Fronto to Appius Apollonides, in which he is praised for his eloquence (*Ad Amicos* 1.2, VdH^2 p. 171 = Haines II, pp. 286–9). Champlin (1980: 30) suggests he could be the same Cornelianus who later held the post of imperial secretary of Greek letters (*ab epistulis Graecis*), though this is uncertain.

We lived together, studied together: Cornelianus was one of the scholars who stayed at Fronto's house on the Esquiline, along with the historian Appian (**Letter 35**) and the senator Gavius Clarus (**Letter 45**).

Letter 29. Fronto to Marcus (*c.* 139–156)

Ad M. Caes. 5.52, VdH² pp. 79–80 = *Ad M. Caes.* 5.37, Haines I, pp. 238–9.

To my lord,

This Aridelus* of yours, who returns my letter to you,* looked after me when he himself was still a boy,* from the time when I was mad about partridges* until I embarked on more serious pursuits. He is your freedman, and he has administered your affairs* diligently: for he is an honest, measured, keen, and attentive man.* He now seeks the position of an administrator* in the proper way, given his status, and since this is an appropriate time. Give him your support, lord, as much as you can. If you do not recognise this man's face, when you come to the name of Aridelus,* remember that it is Aridelus who has been commended to you by me.

Farewell, my sweetest lord. My best wishes to your lady.*

Commentary

Aridelus: Aridelus was a freedman of the imperial household, who at one stage had been Fronto's own child-minder (*paedogogus*). The imperial household had many hundreds of freedmen associated with it, performing different roles across the broad spectrum of domestic and administrative duties (Weaver 1972: 58–70). Fronto mentions other imperial freedmen in **Letters 37** and **42**.

who returns my letter to you: Roman aristocrats usually relied upon their slaves, freedmen, or other associates to carry letters to each other. These couriers often arrived at all hours, especially if the sender lived nearby (Cicero, *Ad Att.* 12.1.2).

was still a boy: It was common for writers of letters of recommendation to attest that they had known the subject since birth (Wiedemann 1989: 96). Aridelus was probably in his early teens when he acted as Fronto's *paedogogus*, accompanying him to school, the baths, or other journeys about town. The fact that he later entered the imperial service means that he probably travelled with Fronto from Cirta to Rome.

mad about partridges: Wealthy Romans sometimes kept aviaries in which they housed a wide variety of birds (Cicero, *Ad Q. Fr.* 3.1.1; Ovid, *Amores* 2.6.12–16; Pliny, *Natural History* 22.19.40–1). A number of different kinds of partridges are found across the region: the grey partridge (*Perdix perdix*), and various partridges of the genus *Alectoris*. A subspecies of the grey partridge, the native Italian partridge (*Perdix perdix italica*), is now extinct as a result of habitat loss, hunting, and outcrossing with other subspecies (Liukkonen-Anttila et al. 2002: 979). The red-legged partridge (*Alectoris rufa*) is also found in southern Europe and North Africa. Fronto mentions his continuing enthusiasm for partridges in **Letter 39**.

he has administered your affairs: There is a play on words here, as noticed by Champlin (1980: 170). Fronto writes that Aridelus has 'administered' (*procuravit*) Marcus' affairs, and he now seeks to become an 'administrator' (*procurator*).

he is an honest, measured, keen, and attentive man: Fronto is not as fulsome in his praise of Aridelus as he is of his higher status associates such as Gavius Clarus (**Letter 44**). Indeed, Mouritsen (2011: 62–3) has pointed out that the vocabulary of praise for freedmen was somewhat different from that featured in senatorial and equestrian recommendations: they were lauded for hard work and loyalty rather than their learning or literary accomplishments (cf. **Letter 28**).

the position of an administrator: The Latin term is *procurator*. Freedmen procurators must be distinguished from men of equestrian status who held senior financial procuratorships in the provinces, or those called 'praesidial' procurators who served as independent governors (Eck 2000: 261–3). The freedmen procurators held office in Rome or the provinces, supervising activities such as gladiatorial games (*procurator a muneribus*) and mining operations (*procurator metallorum*) or administering imperial estates (*procurator patrimonii*) (Weaver 1965; 1972: 267–81). On the basis of the evidence (which is limited), it appears that there were no fixed rules for the promotion of imperial freedmen (cf. van den Hout 1999: 211). Fronto writes in general terms, suggesting that Aridelus had probably seen sufficient service to justify a promotion, but does not mention any specific post (Eck 2002: 148–9). It is testament to Marcus' status as Caesar that Fronto could write to him directly, rather than having to approach the emperor.

when you come to the name of Aridelus: Presumably Fronto is referring to an official list of freedmen to be examined when promotions were considered.

your lady: Either Marcus' mother Domitia Lucilla, in which case the letter would be dated prior to her death *c.* 156, or his wife Faustina, thus placing it in the years 145–161.

Letter 30. Fronto to Antoninus Pius (between 146 and *c.* 158)

Ad Ant. Pium 3, VdH^2 pp. 162–4 = Haines I, pp. 254–9.

Fronto to Antoninus Pius Augustus,

1. If I had my way, emperor, I would sincerely wish that our friends and relatives would always conduct themselves in accordance with our own standards. And if they were not to adopt our standards, I would want them at least to take our advice. But since it is a man's character that guides him through life, I confess that I find it difficult to accept that my friend Censorius Niger* did not moderate his language in his will in which he made me his heir. The fact of the matter is that I would be acting shamelessly if I tried to clear his name by defending him, but I would dishonour our friendship if I did not at least mitigate his offence by making apologies for it.

2. There is no question that Censorius Niger lacked control of his words and wrote in an inconsiderate manner, but he was a man who was steadfast, blameless, and virtuous in many areas of his life. It would befit your clemency, emperor, to weigh up this one single offence of the pen against his other excellent deeds.

3. When I first entered his circle of friends, his ready actions in the civil and military spheres had earned him significant glory. I will not mention all his friends, but he was especially close to Marcius Turbo* and Erucius Clarus,* two outstanding men – the former the most distinguished of the equestrian order, the latter of the senatorial order. After this came a plethora of honours, and an increase in his personal standing as a result of your approval. This was the type of man whose friendship I sought.

4. Someone might say that I ought to have suspended our friendship after I had discovered that his favour with you had diminished.* It was never my practice, emperor, to abandon friendships formed in good times the moment some trouble arose. And certainly – for why should I not explain my personal feelings? – I count someone who does not love you as an enemy, but I consider a man for whom you have little affection to be worthy of pity, rather than my enemy. *[The end of section 4 is unintelligible, as are several lines at the beginning of section 5.]*

5. . . . and I dearly wish that Niger had followed my advice, as he did in most matters, and thus asked for my counsel before writing his will. He would never have left such a mark on his own memory with these unthinking words, which have done more damage to himself than to anyone else. *[Several lines are lost here.]* . . . this man at that very time at which he had caused offence; but he causes this offence through an act of love. In just the same way, many animals who are bereft of skill and interest in rearing their young mishandle their eggs and offspring with their teeth and talons, crushing them not out of hatred, but because of their inexperience in child-rearing.

6. I now call as my witnesses the gods and goddesses of heaven and the underworld and the sacred loyalty of human friendship,* that I have always been the originator . . . *[This final section is particularly badly damaged, with at least five further fragmentary lines, probably more.]* But we should always pursue those matters which we do not wish [to be silent about] nor want [to deny] and – if the gods are fair – are true and consistent with the basis of our friendship.

Commentary

Censorius Niger: His career is briefly discussed in the *Dramatis Personae* section on pp. 16–17.

It would befit your clemency: Fronto appeals to one of the standard virtues of a 'good' Roman emperor, his clemency (*clementia*) (Wallace-Hadrill 1981). The virtue encapsulated the emperor's sense of forgiveness and leniency towards his subjects, and towards foreign peoples.

Marcius Turbo: Q. Marcius Turbo Fronto Publicius Severus (*PIR*^{2} M 249) was appointed praetorian prefect in 121 by Hadrian. Cassius Dio (69.18.1–4) records that Turbo was extremely devoted to his position, spending most of his time at the palace attending to his duties. Even Fronto himself once found Turbo judging cases late into the night. In 138, Turbo was replaced by Gavius Maximus, possibly a victim of Hadrian's capriciousness in the last years of his life (Syme 1980: 67–75; *HA Hadrian* 24.9). He died before this letter was written.

Erucius Clarus: Sex. Erucius Clarus (*PIR*^{2} E 96) entered the senatorial order thanks to the patronage of Pliny the Younger (*Letters* 2.9). Clarus served in Trajan's Parthian campaigns and captured Seleucia on the Tigris (Dio 68.30.2). He was subsequently made consul in 117. Clarus' uncle, C. Septicius Clarus, was the colleague of Marcius Turbo as praetorian prefect during Hadrian's reign until he was dismissed for excessive familiarity with the empress Sabina (*HA Hadrian* 9.5, 11.3). Pius showed Clarus high honour by appointing him urban prefect, and consul for the second time in 146. Clarus took a keen interest in the customs and literary works of Rome's past (Aulus Gellius, *Attic Nights* 7.6.12, 13.18.2–3). Since Clarus is discussed in the past tense, the letter must postdate his death in 146 (Champlin 1974: 149; van den Hout 1999: 385–6).

his favour with you had diminished: Niger initially moved easily in court circles, winning a series of promotions from the emperor. **Letter 31** reveals that Niger and Gavius Maximus had a falling out, which understandably altered his standing with Pius. We do not know the ramifications of this fall from grace. As Rogers (1959) points out, there were a number of possible outcomes when one lost favour, but it rarely resulted in extreme punishment such as death or exile: exclusion from court was far more likely.

the sacred loyalty of human friendship: This letter offers an important insight into how subjects might approach the emperor to seek clemency for a friend or relative (Barden Dowling 2006: 249–50). It covers much of the same ground as a letter of recommendation, emphasising Censorius' virtues, his career and achievements for the Roman state, and the good company he keeps. But in other ways, the tone is quite different, as Fronto must walk the difficult path of defending a man who has offended the emperor.

Letter 31. Fronto to Gavius Maximus (between 146 and *c.* 158)

Ad Ant. Pium 7, VdH² pp. 165–6 = Haines I, pp. 258–61.

Fronto sends greetings to Gavius Maximus,*

[The first part of this letter is lost.]

4. Last of all, since my love for Niger did not begin because of you, it should not cease because of you either. Nor did you inherit your affection for me from Niger. For this reason, I beseech you,* don't let my friendship with him come between us, because it has no relevance to our own relationship.* Now, if it must be said – and I call the gods as my witnesses to this – I often saw Censorius Niger shedding many tears because he longed for you and he was saddened at your estrangement.

5. Perhaps there will be another opportunity when I might be able to conciliate and assuage your feelings regarding his memory. In the meantime, to ensure that your ears are not receptive to any remarks made by malicious men about me . . . *[A few words are missing.]* . . . that loyalty,* which I maintained steadfastly and sincerely with Censorius, I will try to maintain with you to an even greater degree, so that it is both long-lasting and genuine.

Commentary

Gavius Maximus: His career is briefly discussed in *Dramatis Personae* on p. 17.

I beseech you: The Latin verb *quaeso* was archaic and very formal, so we translate it as 'beseech' (van den Hout 1999: 392).

to our own relationship: Fronto emphasises that his closeness with Censorius Niger was entirely unrelated to his relationship with Gavius Maximus. This provides us with an interesting insight into the overlapping circles at the imperial court: Fronto probably interacted with the praetorian prefect on a professional basis (and undoubtedly needed to continue to do so), whereas Niger was a close personal friend.

loyalty: As with his letter to Pius above, Fronto justifies his actions by emphasising his friendship with Censorius.

Letter 32. Fronto to Marcus (between 146 and *c.* 158)

Ad Ant. Pium 4, VdH^2 p. 164 = Haines I, pp. 260–3.

To my lord Caesar,

1. Censorius Niger has breathed his last. He left me five-twelfths of his estate* in his will. The document was properly drawn up in most respects, except for the fact that it featured some poorly chosen words;* he had greater regard for his own indignation than what was really appropriate for himself in this situation. For he launched a particularly harsh attack on Gavius Maximus, a man of senatorial rank* to whom one really must show the proper respect.

2. Because of this it seemed necessary to me to write to our lord your father, and to Gavius Maximus himself, sending letters in which it was enormously difficult to strike the right tone. On the one hand, I could not refrain from criticizing the actions of my friend Niger, which I condemned, but on the other I wanted to do my duty as his friend and heir. I wanted you to know about

this,* as with all my other business, and I even tried to write to you a much longer letter on this subject, by Hercules. But, as I thought about it more, it seemed better not to bother you or to take you away from more important business.

Commentary

five-twelfths of his estate: Roman legal procedure traditionally divided the deceased's estate into twelve parts. The remainder of Niger's estate may have been distributed among his relatives, since at least one quarter of the estate was usually left to the deceased's children (if they had any). Once the will had been read, the heirs had to formally accept or decline the inheritance offered to them (Riggsby 2010: 154–7). This explains Fronto's desperate letters to Pius and Gavius Maximus – he wanted to accept his share of Niger's estate, but not to endorse his comments (Champlin 1980: 100–2).

some poorly chosen words: It was not unprecedented for Romans to abuse their enemies in their wills, even high-profile ones. Before he committed suicide, the senator Fulcinius Tiro composed a will that vilified the emperor Tiberius and the praetorian prefect Sutorius Macro (Tacitus, *Annals* 6.38.1–3; Champlin 1991: 16).

a man of senatorial rank: Gavius Maximus was a member of the equestrian order, but had been awarded 'consular decorations' (*consularia ornamenta*) by Antoninus Pius (*HA Pius* 10.6; *CIL* IX 5358 = *ILS* 1325). This granted him the status of an ex-consul and the right to wear the same dress without having ever held the office. It did not confer membership of the senate (Talbert 1984: 366–70). Maximus had a reputation as 'a most austere man' (*HA Pius* 8.7), and Fronto's standing at court no doubt depended on maintaining a good relationship with him.

I wanted you to know about this: Fronto evidently felt he was able to confide in Marcus: the tone is of a man releasing his anxiety after having written two difficult letters.

Letter 33. Fronto to the Magistrates and Councillors of Cirta (*c.* 156)

Ad Amicos 2.11, VdH² pp. 199–200 = Haines I, pp. 292–5.

To the magistrates and councillors of Cirta,*

1. *[The opening section of the letter is lost.]* ... I would prefer to see greater emphasis placed on the safeguarding of our community* rather than my own personal standing. For that reason I urge you to elect your patrons* from, and to communicate your decisions in this matter to, those men who have outstanding reputations in Rome's law courts. Firstly, there is Aufidius Victorinus, who will be enrolled on the list of our community's citizens, if the gods look favourably on my plans. For I have arranged my daughter's engagement to him, and I could not have made better provisions for my family's future, or for my daughter's life, when I chose a man of such outstanding character and eloquence* as my son-in-law. Then there is Servilius Silanus,* a truly admirable and most articulate man, whom you could have as a patron as if he were actually a citizen, since he is from the neighbouring town of Hippo Regius, with whom we have friendly relations. You would also be acting properly in selecting Postumius Festus,* on account of his character and eloquence, and because he is from our very own province and a nearby community at that. You will take pleasure in deriving benefits – which will not be insubstantial – from these patrons. Select these three men, because they are some of my closest associates, not on account of their association with the house of the Licinii ...* *[The end of the line is uncertain.]*

2. *[The next several lines of the text are fragmentary, but the sense is clear: Fronto served his hometown while his health was strong, but he now recommends younger men to take his place. There is another significant lacuna before the next section.]* ... for we should have a man who is acceptable to the people, and of consular rank,* and able to provide advice in matters of public law. For I too, I hope you will agree, played my part in the affairs of our community with some distinction when in the prime of my life. There are a great number of other Cirtensians who sit in the senate* as most distinguished men. The third and

final distinction is the greatest,* to support your own city . . . *[The remainder of the letter is virtually lost.]*

Commentary

Cirta: Fronto's hometown of Cirta was the chief city in the *IIII coloniae Cirtenses* – 'the four Cirtensian colonies' – which also included Rusicade, Chullu and Milev (Champlin 1980: 6–7). The colonies were administered by three magistrates (*triumviri*) and the councillors (*decuriones*) who sat on the local senate (*curia*).

the safeguarding of our community: Fronto was approached to serve as patron of Cirta, and now writes to the magistrates to decline the offer (Champlin 1980: 10–11). Fronto is known to have served as patron of Calama, another town to the west of Cirta, before his consulship (*CIL* VIII 5350 = *ILS* 2928). As Champlin suggests, Fronto may have been patron of Cirta in the past, and was now recommending younger men for the position. Alternatively, the councillors could have approached Fronto after the previous patron had died or resigned the post.

elect your patrons: From the late Republic onwards, municipal communities began to appoint individual Romans, usually senators or equestrians, to represent their interests. The selection of patrons was carefully controlled, as is shown by the regulations set out in municipal laws such as the *lex Vrsonensis* from Urso in Spain (*CIL* I^2 594 = *ILS* 6087, sections 97, 130, translated as Crawford 1996: no. 25). An inscription from Agbia in Africa Proconsularis records that Cincius Victor had been made patron 'to safeguard our community by the consensus of all the councillors' (*CIL* VIII 1548 = *ILS* 6827). The relationship was formalised through a document known as the *tabula patronatus*, a bronze tablet inscribed with the resolution of the municipal senate, with one copy remaining in the community, the other given to the patron (Nicols 1980). The patronage of these individuals allowed provincial cities to have a voice in the senate or at the imperial court: an unknown equestrian was honoured by Thugga in Africa Proconsularis as 'patron and most eloquent advocate' (*ILTun.* 1514). Beyond the arena of legal representation, patrons could assist in the maintenance of law and order, including resolving disputes at the local level, and often functioned as benefactors by paying for the construction or repair of public buildings (Nicols 1988).

outstanding character and eloquence: All three candidates proposed by Fronto are praised for their character and for their eloquence (either the noun *eloquentia* or the adjective *facundus*), qualities that would enable them to fulfil their role as advocates for Cirta (Champlin 1980: 10–11).

Servilius Silanus: M. Servilius Silanus (*PIR*[2] S 599) was suffect consul in 152, and later ordinary consul for the second time in 188. He came from Hippo Regius, an old Punic town to the north-east of Cirta.

Postumius Festus: Postumius Festus (*PIR*[2] P 886), suffect consul in 160, was a senator from a nearby (but unnamed) town in the province of Numidia. A monument in Festus' honour erected by his descendant T. Flavius Postumius calls him an 'orator and outstanding in his eloquence' (*CIL* VI 1416). Festus was part of Fronto's literary circle: the pair feature in a memorable scene from Aulus Gellius (*Attic Nights* 19.13) in which they discuss Latin and Greek words for 'dwarf'.

the Licinii: The Licinii were a powerful local family in Cirta (Champlin 1974: 154; van den Hout 1999: 459). Only one member of this clan is known: Licinius Montanus, who was a pupil of Fronto and stayed at his house in Rome (*Ad Amicos* 1.3, VdH[2] pp. 172–3 = Haines I, pp. 278–83).

consular rank: Aufidius Victorinus and Servilius Silanus had been consul in 155 and 152 respectively, while Postumius Festus would go on to hold the consulship in 160. City patrons could range widely in status from military veterans and local municipal worthies to equestrians and senators. In the second century, communities in Numidia turned increasingly to their own citizens who had gained prominence in the senatorial elite (Warmington 1954: 52).

Cirtensians who sit in the senate: The first senators from Cirta were Q. Aurelius Pactumeius Clemens and Q. Aurelius Pactumeius Fronto, who were adlected to praetorian rank by Vespasian and Titus in 73/74, with Pactumeius Fronto going on to hold the consulship in 80. By the mid-second century, the ranks of senatorial Cirtensians included Clemens' descendant P. Pactumeius Clemens, Sex. Calpurnius Agricola, P. Iulius Castus, and Q. Antistius Adventus Postumius, as well as Fronto and his brother Q. Cornelius Quadratus (van den Hout 1999: 460). The title of 'most distinguished man' (*vir clarissimus*) was held by all senators from the early second century.

The third and final distinction is the greatest: This line gives the impression that Fronto has been listing the honours to which residents of Cirta can aspire. Judging from the content of the preceding section, it appears that membership of the senate in Rome is the second highest honour, but the greatest is to serve as patron of Cirta.

Letter 34. Fronto to Antoninus Pius (late 150s)

Ad Ant. Pium 8, VdH^2 pp. 166–7 = Haines I, pp. 236–9.

Fronto to Antoninus Pius Augustus,

1. The facts themselves show that I made every effort – and desperately wished – to serve in the post of proconsul,* most sacred emperor. For I exercised my right to participate in the balloting process* while the matter was being decided. After it became apparent that another candidate had seniority under the terms of the law granting precedence to those with more children,* I regarded the magnificent province that was left to me as if it had been my original choice. I diligently made the necessary preparations for administering a province,* so that I could deal with this heavy burden more easily through the assistance of my friends.* From home, I summoned friends and relatives of whose loyalty and integrity I was certain. I wrote to colleagues in Alexandria,* so that they would to hurry to Athens and wait for me there,* and to these well-educated men I assigned oversight of my Greek correspondence.* I encouraged

prominent men from Cilicia* to come as well: I have a great number of friends in that province, since I have always championed the public and private interests of Cilicians before your court. From Mauretania I summoned to my side a man who respects me greatly – and the feeling is certainly mutual – Iulius Senex.* I required not only his supportive nature and industriousness, but also his military experience in hunting down and detaining brigands.

2. I did all these things relying on the hope that I could at least reduce the frequency and seriousness of the bouts of poor health* that afflicted me by following a restricted diet and drinking water, even if I was unable to keep them completely in check. As a result of this I was healthy and active for longer than usual, so that I was able to represent two friends of mine in your court, and on matters that required no little effort on my part. Then I was struck down by an episode of illness so powerful that it showed that all my hopes had been in vain ... *[The rest of the letter is very fragmentary.]*

Commentary

proconsul: The proconsulships of Asia and Africa were two of the most prestigious posts in the senatorial career, and Fronto had recently been appointed to the Asian governorship (*Ad M. Caes.* 5.51, VdH^2 p. 79 = *Ad M. Caes.* 5.36, Haines I, pp. 234–7). The post was usually held for twelve months, probably beginning in July, and Claudius is said to have encouraged proconsuls to leave Rome for their province by mid-April (Dio 60.17.3). However, by the third century, the proconsular year began in April, making it uncertain when Fronto's term actually commenced (Barnes 1986; Talbert 1984: 497–8). In the second century, appointment to these proconsulships occurred about fifteen years after a senator had been consul (Alföldy 1977: 110–24; Parkin 2003: 116–18, 296 fig. 2). Since Fronto was consul in 142, this letter should be dated to the late 150s.

the balloting process: The governors of Asia and Africa were selected by lot. The exact procedure is not explained in any detail in the ancient sources, but it seems that that all eligible ex-consuls would draw lots to see who would receive a proconsulship that year (Talbert 1984: 348–9). Cassius Dio (53.14.3–4) writes that the procedure was controlled by the emperors, who ensured that only their nominees were eligible to enter the ballot. On some inscriptions, senators specifically refer to the fact that they had been appointed proconsul by lot (*CIL* XIV 3609 = *ILS* 1104; *AE* 1940, 99).

the law granting precedence to those with more children: Senators who had three or more children were accorded special benefits under the terms of Augustus' marriage legislation, which was designed to encourage the aristocracy to produce more children. The Papian-Poppaean Law permitted senators with the 'right of three children' (*ius trium liberorum*) to stand for magistracies earlier, and gave them priority among their peers (Treggiari 1991: 66–7). The emperor could make exceptions and grant this privilege to those without three children, as in the case of Pliny the Younger and Suetonius (Pliny, *Letters* 10.2, 10.94, 10.95).

Cratia was Fronto's only living child, as the other five died young (**Letter 53**). Children who had died in war were taken into account when determining precedence amongst senators, but other deceased children did not count (Aulus Gellius, *Attic Nights* 2.15). The other senator who participated in the ballot had more children, and was therefore able to choose which province he desired first.

the necessary preparations for administering a province: As proconsul of Asia, Fronto would be assisted by three legates, usually of praetorian rank, whose duties were primarily judicial (Dio 53.14.7; *Digest* 1.16.4.6, 1.16.5–6). He would also have a quaestor, a more junior senator responsible for financial matters. The quaestor would be selected by lot, but the proconsul was entitled to choose his legates himself. The governor's administrative staff would also include equestrian and freedman procurators (Eck 2000: 284–8). Fronto's main responsibilities as proconsul were to tour the province and hear cases involving its inhabitants at fourteen key locations, known as assize-centres, and to oversee the financial management of the cities (Burton 1975; 2004: 318–22).

the assistance of my friends: In addition to the officials discussed above, it was customary for senatorial governors to assemble their own group of advisers to assist them in their province (Weaver 2002). These friends (*amici*) who served on governors' councils are often listed on inscriptions preserving their judicial and administrative decisions (Harris 1992).

Alexandria: Although Fronto never formally studied in Alexandria, the main intellectual centre of the Mediterranean world, he had friends and colleagues based there, including the historian Appian (**Letter 35**).

hurry to Athens and wait for me there: The proconsul of Asia was expected to arrive in the province by sea, disembarking at the city of Ephesus (*Digest* 1.16.4.5); Fronto would make this final stage of journey from Athens.

my Greek correspondence: Fronto was proficient in Greek, but would need assistance to handle the vast number of letters and petitions from provincials.

Cilicia: The province of Cilicia was located in southern Asia Minor (modern-day Turkey). Fronto states that he earned friends in Cilicia as a result of representing their interests at Rome. Senators could certainly act as patrons of entire provinces and defend their interest in court, as in the case of C. Iulius Asper, who was honoured as 'the most excellent orator and faithful defender of clients' by the Spanish and Mauretanian provinces (*CIL* XIV 2506 = *AE* 1997, 261). Fronto's interests in Cilicia are not unexpected, as he is known to have delivered the speech *For the Bithynians* on behalf of the nearby province of Bithynia, which lay in northern Asia Minor. For another legal case involving provincials from Asia, see **Letter 18**.

Iulius Senex: The detection and punishment of robbers and highwaymen was one of a governor's duties, according to Ulpian (*Digest* 1.18.13.pref). Antoninus Pius gave instructions on how to deal with brigands during his own term as proconsul of Asia in the 130s (*Digest* 48.3.6, pref.1 = Levick 2000: no. 47). Neighbouring Cilicia was also infamous as a haunt of brigands and pirates (Strabo, *Geography* 14.5.6), which provides an additional reason for Fronto's recruitment of his friends from the province. For the phenomenon of brigandage, see Shaw (1984).

the bouts of poor health: Fronto would have been at least sixty at the time this letter was written, and he had suffered from poor health throughout his life. It was not unprecedented to decline the post: an inscription recording the career of C. Salvius Liberalis Nonius Bassus states that 'having been made proconsul of Asia by lot, he excused himself' (*CIL* IX 5533 = *ILS* 1011).

Letter 35. Fronto to Antoninus Pius (late 150s)

Ad Ant. Pium 10, VdH[2] p. 168 = *Ad Ant. Pium* 9, Haines I, pp. 262–5.

Fronto to Antoninus Pius Augustus,

1. I accept, Caesar, that the modesty of my friends requires that I should not make improper requests on their behalf … *[A lacuna of uncertain length follows.]* … in response to my request you have already increased the public standing of one equestrian, my close companion Sextius Calpurnius,* by awarding him two procuratorships. These two procuratorships are favours that you have actually given four times: twice when you gave him the positions, and twice when you accepted his requests to be excused* from holding them.

2. For two years now I have entreated you on behalf of my friend Appian,* with whom I have shared both a long-standing friendship and the ritual of study* on a near-daily basis. And indeed, I am completely convinced, and – if I might be so bold – will state firmly that he possesses the same modesty as my friend Calpurnius Iulianus. For he wishes to acquire this position in order to increase his status in his old age,* not out of ambition or from a desire for the procuratorial salary.* When I first petitioned on behalf of Appian, you received my request so beneficently that I was obliged to have hope.

3. When I asked you again last year, you replied to me with very favourable words, and in a tone that was full of respect, that if you gave a procuratorship to Appian at my request, it would unleash a torrent of advocates asking for the same thing. You doubtless recall the man from Greece* whom you graciously and cheerfully named. There are many things that separate these two men, including their age and the condition of childlessness, which needs to be alleviated with some consolations.* I would venture to say that there is no

difference in the honesty and integrity of these two upstanding citizens, but nevertheless, I will speak freely and declare I would rank the man whom I have not named behind my friend.

4. Finally I will say, as my candour and honesty – not to mention my confidence in my love for you – compel me to do so, that it is surely fairer for the other man also to obtain a post on my account. Please remember, my lord emperor, that when he follows my example and makes his petition, that I have been making my requests of you for two years. Therefore, if you think it appropriate, grant him the position after two years as well. He will be following our own example,* if he also seeks your permission to be excused the post.

Commentary

Sextus Calpurnius: Nothing is known about Sextus Calpurnius Iulianus outside this letter. He is described as a 'close companion' (*contubernalis*), a term Fronto regularly uses to denote the younger men who lived and studied in his house in Rome (Champlin 1980: 64). Our Calpurnius could have been a relative of the senator Sextus Calpurnius Agricola (*PIR*^{2} C 249), who had a distinguished military career during the Marcomannic Wars.

his requests to be excused: There are some uncertain cases from the second century in which men received honorary procuratorships, but this does not seem to be what has happened in this case: Calpurnius was offered the posts, but declined them (Nutton 1971: 269–72).

Appian: Appian was the author of a *Roman History* from Rome's beginnings to the reign of Trajan, focusing on wars with foreign peoples and the expansion of Rome's domains. The work was made up of twenty-four books, five of which focused on the civil wars at the end of the Republic. In the preface to his history, Appian said he had held high office in Alexandria, served as an advocate in Rome, and was then appointed a procurator (pref. 15). This is the position for which Fronto petitions on his behalf in this letter. Fronto's correspondence includes two letters exchanged with Appian (*Add. Epit.* 4–5, VdH^2 pp. 242–8 =

Epist. Graec. 4–5, Haines I, pp. 264–79). The best English introduction to his work is Gowing (1992).

long-standing friendship and the ritual of study: Since we do not know if Fronto visited Alexandria, this would have occurred when Appian was at Rome pursuing his legal career (Champlin 1980: 42).

to increase his status in his old age: A letter from Marcus to Q. Domitius Marsianus, in which the emperor promoted Marsianus 'to the distinction of a procuratorship with a salary of two hundred thousand sesterces' confirms that procuratorships could confer such status (*AE* 1926, 183 = Levick 2000: no. 134). If Appian attained this position, he would cease to be merely a regular equestrian and instead have the higher status of *vir egregius*, a title given to equestrian procurators in the second century.

a desire for the procuratorial salary: There were several grades of equestrian administrative posts, carrying annual salaries of 60,000, 100,000, and 200,000 sesterces, respectively. In the reign of Marcus Aurelius, the salary level of 300,000 sesterces was introduced for officials such as the head of financial affairs (*a rationibus*) (Eck 2000: 261–2).

the man from Greece: The identity of this rival is unknown.

the condition of childlessness, which needs to be alleviated with some consolations: Childlessness carried something of a social stigma in ancient Roman society, despite being not uncommon amongst the upper class. To be elderly and childless was considered a sad fate, and although such people were not subject to the penalties of the Papian-Poppaean Law, Tiberius' senatorial decree on inheritance meant that the childless could lose much of their wealth to the state (Parkin 2003: 201–7).

He will be following our own example: This remark shows that this letter must come after **Letter 34**, in which Fronto declines the proconsulship of Asia.

6

The Reign of Marcus and Verus

Introduction

On 7 March 161, the emperor Antoninus Pius died in his villa at Lorium after a reign of over twenty years (*HA Pius* 12.6). Marcus Aurelius and Lucius Verus ascended to the throne as joint emperors. Marcus was the senior emperor because he had held the tribunician power (*tribunicia potestas*) since 147, and he alone became chief priest (*pontifex maximus*) (Birley 1993: 116–17). Their joint rule would last until Lucius Verus died of a stroke in early 169. The next three chapters each deal with different aspects of Fronto's correspondence between 161 and *c.* 166, when he is presumed to have died. In Chapter 6, we examine the developing relationship between Fronto and his former pupils, who are now in full command of the empire. Chapter 7 collects Fronto's correspondence dealing with the Parthian War, which required Lucius Verus to travel to Syria. In Chapter 8, we turn to examine Fronto's grief at the deaths of his wife and grandson.

Fronto appears to have been out of Rome when Pius died, returning to the city on 28 March. He wanted to visit his former pupils but was somewhat unsure of the protocol. When Fronto did come to the palace, he called only upon Marcus, a slight which caused Verus to write and complain (**Letter 36**). Fronto sent a masterful letter in return, excusing himself while flattering Verus (**Letter 37**). The letters of the 160s show that Fronto and Marcus' friendship remained undiminished, despite the latter's change of status. In **Letters 38–39** they discuss their mutual delight with Marcus' twin sons, who were born in August 161. This correspondence is complemented by **Letter 40**, from Fronto to his son-in-law Aufidius Victorinus, who had been appointed governor of Germania Superior. Victorinus and Cratia had left one of their sons in Fronto's care, and the senator hoped that the boy would grow up to take after his grandfather. In **Letter 41**, we return once again to the relationship between Fronto and Marcus, as he teases his former pupil about working while on holiday at Alsium, a pleasure resort. In a letter containing some effective, and some dubious, attempts at humour, he reminds Marcus that even emperors need to let off steam once in a while.

The next three letters concern the will of Matidia the Younger, Marcus' fabulously wealthy great-aunt, who died in the early 160s (**Letters 42–44**). Matidia had no biological children, and designated Marcus' wife Faustina as her heir. In this capacity, Faustina was to be in charge of an investment fund for some of Matidia's foster-children. Matidia had originally intended to bequeathe legacies to other foster-children in attachments to her will (known as codicils), but had subsequently decided to void the bequests by breaking the seals on the documents. However, as Matidia lay on her deathbed, these former beneficiaries had the codicils re-sealed, so that they would again appear valid. This led to a legal battle concerning the validity of both the will and the re-sealed documents, as well as the proportion of the estate that could be allocated to Faustina (Champlin 1980: 70–2). The judge in the case was none other than the emperor himself, who was forced to consider the ethics of ruling in favour of his own wife and daughters. Fronto, of course, was ready with some forthright advice for Marcus.

Shortly after Pius' death, Rome became embroiled in a war with its largest neighbour on the eastern frontier, the Parthian empire. In the summer of 162, Lucius Verus travelled to Syria in order to take charge of the campaign. He was already in the east when Marcus wrote to him to seek advice regarding the will (**Letter 42**). After an initial hiatus in their correspondence, Verus and Fronto began to write to each other again. Fronto in particular needed to ask Verus a favour on behalf of his protégé, Gavius Clarus (**Letter 45**). The letter is a carefully constructed literary artifice, praising Clarus in fulsome terms before making a request for a benefaction.

Letter 36. Verus to Fronto (*c.* April 161)

Ad Verum Imp. 1.11, VdH^2 pp. 114–15 = *Ad Verum Imp.* 1.3, Haines I, pp. 294–7.

To my teacher,

Yes, I've a serious complaint about you, my teacher, and yet my distress even surpasses this complaint, since I've not been able to embrace you, nor speak to you, for such a long time,* even though you came to the palace, and after I'd only just left my dear brother at that. You can be sure I gave him a good talking to, asking why he did not call me back, and he didn't dare to deny that he was at fault. Was it really that difficult, I ask you, to let me know in advance that you were coming to see my brother,* and would like to see me too, or even asking me to return, so that we might talk with each other? What would that have taken? If you summoned me to your house today, wouldn't I drop everything and run willingly to you? In fact I've been sick with the thought that I couldn't visit you every day. I believe it's the most burdensome thing about our position* that the occasions on which I can come and visit you are so rare. *[The next several lines are fragmentary. Verus appears to ask Fronto to give him some warning in the future as to his arrival in Rome.]* Farewell, my teacher, who is very dear to your Verus. Give my best wishes to Cratia.

Commentary

for such a long time: Letter 37 reveals that Fronto and Verus had not seen each other for four months because the orator had been at his estates in the country.

I'd only just left my dear brother: Given the size of the imperial complex on the Palatine in the Antonine period, it is hardly surprising that Fronto and Verus missed each other. The remodelling and expansion of the residence under Domitian meant the palace now had several courtyards, peristyles, reception areas, and a stadium (Coarelli 2007: 145–53). There was no official division between the 'public' and 'private' areas of the palace, as shown by Zanker (2002: 110–11), but the way in which Fronto and Verus missed each other implies that Fronto was in the imperial quarters rather than in the formal reception rooms.

coming to see my brother: Although Verus employs many of the same terms of endearment as Marcus to refer to Fronto, it appears that their relationship was not as close (Champlin 1980: 110–11; Birley 1993: 120). There are far fewer letters sent between the pair, and they became especially infrequent while Verus was in the east.

the most burdensome thing about our position: Verus uses the word *statio*, which appears to be a technical term used to refer to the position of emperor, as found in the 'Senatorial decree concerning Gnaeus Piso the Elder' (*Senatus Consultum de Cn. Pisone patre*, lines 129–30), Velleius Paterculus (2.124.1), and a letter of Augustus (Aulus Gellius, *Attic Nights* 15.7.3). Verus' comment provides a rare insight into the life of an emperor, for whom the burdens of official administration clearly constrained his private activities.

Letter 37. Fronto to Verus (April 161)

Ad Verum Imp. 1.12, VdH[2] pp. 115–16 = *Ad Verum Imp.* 1.4, Haines I, pp. 296–301.

To my lord Verus Augustus,

1. I will soon prove to you that it was not my fault that I did not see you yesterday – alas! – when I came to the palace to see both of you. But if I had willingly, seriously and consciously ... *[Two words missing.]* ... I would have discharged the obligation, and it would have by no means displeased me. For it was ... *[One line missing.]* ... in a courteous letter you remonstrated with me; nor would I have been as happy as I am now* that your longing for me has resulted in this rebuke if, when I had come to you, I had been received by you with the highest honour. For you address all men of our order respectfully and with your own particular brand of charm when they appear before you, but you do not go to great lengths to ask after them when they are not. This is really

the heart of the matter, since I would prefer you to be genuinely angry with me for this, rather than too willing to forgive me. For we tend to grow angry if we truly miss someone; but we are never angry with, or long for, those from whom we are estranged, since we have stopped loving them.

2. It is true that you and your brother have been elevated to positions of such great power, and you are surrounded by a congregation of men of all types, and of all classes, to whom you distribute shares of your affections. Since you also grant a share of your love to me, but my hopes and fortunes are entirely invested in both of you, what am I to do? *[The next three lines are fragmentary.]* . . . than I would place you before them. For in the same way, I would surely deserve you placing them before me.

3. But I do not wish to put off my own defence any longer. It was no fault of my own that I did not meet you, as I said. For I returned to Rome from my estate on the fifth day before the Kalends of April* so that, if I could manage it, I would be able to embrace you both on that very day after such a long time away. But your letter to me . . . *[The next three lines are fragmentary, part of which has been interpreted as reading 'the encroaching old age of your grandfather' (?)]** . . . unless I should have pressed on from the countryside: what then would I have done? Should I have asked, 'Is everything all right'? Or should I have kissed you? Or told you a story? After four months, should I have returned to the sight of your tears or to display my own? Therefore, what did I do the next day? I did not dare to write to your brother,* nor to you, to tell you that I would be coming to see you both. Instead, I wrote to your freedman Charilas* with these words, if I remember correctly: 'You will know if today is suitable* for me to come and see them; let me know, since you are a level-headed man and my friend. Write to me if there are new developments.' With his urging . . . *[The final pages of the letter are illegible.]*

Commentary

as happy as I am now: Fronto claims that Verus' reproach is a greater sign of his love than any reception at the palace would have been. This demonstrates the way in which Fronto adroitly plays the part of imperial courtier, as Champlin

(1980: 110–11) has argued. Despite his former status as Marcus and Verus' tutor, he must still observe court protocol and account for his failure to see Verus.

the fifth day before the Kalends of April: The Roman date is the equivalent of 28 March, that is, three weeks after the death of Antoninus Pius. We do not know exactly where Fronto was during his four-month absence from Rome: Birley (1993: 120) suggests he could have been visiting his hometown of Cirta in Numidia, explaining his inability to return earlier.

the encroaching old age of your grandfather: Van den Hout (1999: 282) has argued that this reference to a grandfather means that the deceased is not Antoninus Pius, but Verus' grandfather L. Ceionius Commodus. However, the manuscript is very fragmentary in this section, with many uncertain readings, and we have no evidence as to when Commodus died. On the other hand, the precise date of 28 March provided by Fronto fits very well with the death of Pius.

I did not dare to write to your brother: It is noteworthy that Fronto did not feel he could write directly to Marcus: as van den Hout (1999: 285) drily notes, 'such restraint is found nowhere else in Fronto's letters'. It may have been that he was uncertain of his position now that his former pupil was emperor, and unsure of how to proceed, hence his decision to consult an imperial freedman.

Charilas: Charilas' exact position is unknown: he was perhaps one of the imperial bedchamber attendants (*cubicularii*) or the *ab admissione*, the freedman who admitted visitors into the imperial presence, and effectively controlled access to the emperor (Champlin 1980: 111; van den Hout 1999: 285).

You will know if today is suitable: Fronto wrote to Charilas in Greek, which was undoubtedly the freedman's native language. Unfortunately, we do not know what Charilas advised, since the manuscript breaks off.

Letter 38. Marcus to Fronto (late 161)

Ad Anton. Imp. 1.1, VdH[2] p. 86 = Haines II, pp. 30–3.

To my teacher,

1. I ask the gods* for a good year, good health, and good fortune on the occasion of your birthday, an important day for me, and I am confident that my wish will be granted. For I commend to the favour of the gods a man whom they are already pleased to help of their own volition, and one whom they consider worthy of their assistance. When you consider your situation on this day of celebration, my teacher, you should take account of everyone whom you truly hold dear: among the first ranks of these, you should include your student, and also my dear brother, as we are both men whom you love with all your heart.

2. Goodbye, and may you maintain enduring good health for many years, my teacher, and be truly happy with the well-being of your daughter, grandchildren, and son-in-law.*

3. Our Faustina* is regaining her health. Our little chick Antoninus* is coughing somewhat less. Everyone in our little nest offers prayers for you, as far as they know how to do so. May you have good health this year, and next, and far into your old age, my most delightful teacher. I ask you that you do not trouble yourself by coming to Lorium for Cornificia's birthday,* and I hope you obey this. If the gods are in favour of it, you will see us at Rome in a few days' time. But after your birthday is over, if you love me, make sure that you rest peacefully when night comes, without worrying about pressing work. Grant this favour to your Antoninus, who anxiously and genuinely makes this request.

Commentary

I ask the gods: It was traditional to make vows to the gods on the birthdays of friends and family members; these days also functioned as the birthdays of the individual's 'spirit' (*genius* for men, *iuno* for women). Quite often the day was commemorated in writing, with Ovid and Horace composing special birthday poems for their friends (Argetsinger 1992).

daughter, grandchildren, and son-in-law: Fronto's daughter, Cratia, had given birth to two children by this time (see **Letter 40**). Fronto's wife, Cratia, is a puzzling omission, since she was still alive.

Our Faustina: This is either Marcus' wife, or his daughter Annia Galeria Aurelia Faustina, who would have been around ten.

Our little chick Antoninus: This is T. Aurelius Fulvus Antoninus, the twin of the emperor Commodus. He would die approximately four years later in 165 (*HA Commodus* 1.2–4). 'Chick' (*pullus*) is Marcus' pet name for his son.

Cornificia's birthday: Cornificia was Marcus and Faustina's ninth child, born in 160 (Birley 1993: 114). She would outlive her parents and all her siblings, surviving until 213, when the emperor Caracalla forced her to commit suicide.

Letter 39. Fronto to Marcus (late 162)

Ad Anton. Imp. 1.3, VdH² p. 91 = Haines II, pp. 118–21.

Fronto to my lord Antoninus Augustus,

1. I've seen your little chickadees,* and I can be sure that I've looked on nothing else with greater joy in my life. So similar are they in appearance to you, that nothing else could have a stronger resemblance. There is a short-cut on my journey up to Lorium, a short-cut of the slippery road, a short-cut of the steep slopes. There I saw your face, not only right in front of me, but on all sides, as I turned right and left.

2. With the gods' favour, may the little ones have healthy complexions and strong voices. One was holding on very well to a piece of white bread,* like a boy king, the other was grasping a coarser bread, clearly the son of his philosopher father. I pray to the gods for the safety of the sower,* the seed he has sown, and the field that brings forth crops in such a likeness. For their little voices sounded

so sweet, and so delightful to me, that I recognised – I don't know how – the charming and calm tenor of your voice in the chirping of both boys. So now, if you're not careful, you will find me a little more vain, for I now have those whom I can love in your place, not only with my eyes, but also with my ears.

Commentary

I saw your little chickadees: Fronto uses the diminutive form (*pulluli*) to refer to the twin boys Antoninus and Commodus, who would have been between twelve and eighteen months old at the time this letter was written. The date is provided by Marcus' short reply, not included here, in which he urges Fronto to write to Verus, who departed for the eastern frontier in mid-162 (*Ad. Ant. Imp.* 1.4, VdH^2 p. 92 = Haines II, pp. 120–3; van den Hout 1999: 236). Fronto's attitude to the babies is surprisingly tender, but his remarks are also designed to articulate his fondness for Marcus.

One was holding on very well to a piece of white bread: The two boys reflect different aspects of Marcus' own personality, the emperor and the philosopher (Claassen 2007: 53).

I pray to the gods for the safety of the sower: The mention of bread offers Fronto the opportunity to segue into a prayer for Marcus and his family as if he was pleading for a good harvest.

Letter 40. Fronto to Aufidius Victorinus (*c.* 162)

Ad Amicos 1.12, VdH^2 pp. 178–9 = Haines II, pp. 170–3.

Fronto sends greetings to Aufidius Victorinus,

1. The letter, which . . . *[The next page of the letter is lost.]* . . . that [the gods] will favour my daughter and your wife,* and that she will pull through, and that they will enlarge our household with children and grandchildren, and that

they will ensure that those who have been and will be born to you will be made in your likeness.*

2. To tell the truth, there are daily quarrels and disagreements between me and that child, whom we call either our Victorinus or Fronto.* Although you've never asked anyone for compensation for anything you've done or said, our little Fronto jabbers no word more readily or often than the one we know so well: 'give'. In return, I do what I can, providing him with bits of paper or little tablets, as I hope that he will turn out to be someone who requires such things.* He nevertheless shows some signs of his grandfather's character: he has an insatiable appetite for grapes.* It was actually the first food he wolfed down, and he hardly stopped all day, either teasing it with his tongue or kissing it with his lips and popping it on his gums and playing with it. He's also very interested in small birds: he is delighted by the chicks of our hens, doves, and sparrows, and I've often heard from those who were my paedagogues or teachers that I had the same enthusiasm for such things when I was young. And as for how much I am consumed by my enthusiasm for partridges – well there is no one, even those who barely know me, who doesn't know about that.

3. For there is nothing that I have done or said that I would want to keep a secret, for whatever I myself feel, I want all others to know right along with me . . . *[The letter breaks off here.]*

Commentary

that [the gods] will favour my daughter and your wife: It may be, as van den Hout (1999: 417) suggests, that Cratia was about to give birth to her third child, whose subsequent death Fronto mourns in Chapter 8.

made in your likeness: Fronto's feelings are all too human, as many parents are proud if their children choose to follow their profession, or enjoy the same activities. On another level, there is a sense of a real need to continue the family line: Fronto would have been all too aware of the fact that many aristocratic families had died out (Scheidel 1999).

either our Victorinus or Fronto: It was once thought Fronto was referring to two children, but as van den Hout (1999: 417) shows, the conjunction *sive* ('either') is used to discriminate between the different names of polyonymous Romans. Moreover, Fronto uses a singular pronoun (*isto*) to refer to the child. He should be identified as M. Aufidius (Victorinus) Fronto, who remained behind in Rome while his parents went to Germany (see *Dramatis Personae* on pp. 13–14). Van den Hout thinks he would have been around the age of three when this letter was written, but Fronto's description of him suggests he was younger, probably between twelve and twenty-four months old. Babies usually have a few words by one year of age, and most one- to two-year-olds are able to grasp a writing implement and make scribbling movements. We therefore suggest he was born *c.* 160, and that this letter was written *c.* 162.

I hope that he will turn out to be someone who requires such things: Likewise, the orator Quintilian, who held a paid chair of Latin rhetoric in Rome in the Flavian period, wrote of his pride at his son's accomplishments in Latin and Greek. Quintilian had hoped that his *Principles of Oratory* would form part of his son's inheritance, in the hope that he would follow in his father's footsteps, but he and his brother sadly predeceased the orator (see *Principles of Oratory* 6.pref.1–16, especially 1, 11).

an insatiable appetite for grapes: The medical writer Soranus recommended a small number of different foods for babies who were not yet weaned, with the first food being cereal mixed with a honey solution (*Gynecology* 2.46–7). We do not know whether such advice was actually followed. Even in a letter to his son-in-law, Fronto cannot resist using alliteration to describe the baby's activities: '**t**easing it with his **t**ongue' (*__l__ingua __l__ambere*) and '**p**opping it on his gums and **p**laying with it' (*__l__acessere ac __l__udificari*).

Letter 41. Fronto to Marcus (*c.* 161–166)

De fer. Als. 3, VdH^{2} pp. 227–33 = Haines II, pp. 4–18.

To my lord Antoninus Augustus,

1. Now, don't I know that you went to Alsium* with the intention of carrying on in the fashion of the place with games and jokes and leisurely relaxation for

four whole days? I imagine that you've set yourself up to enjoy the holiday at your secluded coastal spot in this fashion: lying around in the midday sun, submitting to the urge to take a nap, then calling Niger,* and telling him to bring your books. Then, when the desire to read strikes you, you might refine your thoughts with some Plautus, or satisfy your appetite with Accius, or soothe yourself with Lucretius, or set yourself aflame with Ennius,* until the hour special to the Muses, the fifth hour, and then . . . *[A fragmentary line.]* . . . if someone came to you with stories, you would listen to them . . . *[Some missing words.]* . . . you would go as far as you could along the seashore and . . . *[Another fragmentary line.]* . . . or, if it seemed a good idea, you might climb aboard some boat, so that in gentle weather you could delight in the sight and sound of the rowers and the time-keeping hammer. From there you could head straightaway to the baths, invigorating your body with plentiful sweat, and then you might launch into a dinner party fit for a king with all kinds of shellfish, the 'hooked and rocky catch' as Plautus says,* birds fattened for a good while,* dainty dishes, fruit, dessert mix, pastries, fortunate wines, and transparent cups without a treacherous mark.

2. You might ask what that actually means. Take note, then: as an eloquent man and emulator of Annaeus Seneca,* I call Faustian wines 'fortunate' after the cognomen of Faustus Sulla; and indeed, when I speak of a cup 'without a treacherous mark', I mean without a blemish. For it does not befit me, a man so learned, to speak, as the common people do, of 'Falernian wine' or a 'flawless' cup. For what reason should I say that you selected Alsium, a seaside pleasure resort and, as Plautus says, 'a lugubrious location',* unless you were enjoying yourself, and, as our forefathers used to say, to take your 'plea'?* How wicked it is to say 'plea'! No, if words cut in half were to be used to speak the truth, you might take it upon yourself to say 'wat' (I say 'watch'), or 'lab' or 'bur' ('labours' or 'burdens', I say). Do you ever use 'plea'? It would be easier to reconcile you with a fox than with pleasure.*

3. Tell me, I beg you, Marcus, did you make for Alsium so that you could be hungry within sight of the sea? Why? Couldn't you wear yourself out with hunger and thirst and tiresome business at Lorium? *[The next six lines are barely legible.]* The sea herself, they say, in halcyon days, takes a holiday: is a kingfisher with her chicks worthier of peaceful leisure than you with your children?

4. *[The next two lines are fragmentary]* 'But,' you say, 'the circumstances surely require . . .' What? Surely not study? Surely not hard work? Surely not continuous, unremitting, daily, and eternal sweat? What bow is continually drawn? What strings are continually tightened? Our eyes actually last longer because we blink, and they would be ruined if they held only one fixed gaze. A garden repeatedly tended will bring forth no herbs and vegetables, if it lacks the help of manure. But we choose land that has lain fallow for grain and staple crops, for its fertility is restored only by rest.

5. What about your forefathers, who strengthened the commonwealth and empire of Rome in great strides? Your great-grandfather, a supreme warrior,* nevertheless occasionally took delight in pantomimes and was also a committed drinker; yet on account of his efforts the Roman people often drank honeyed wine during his triumphs. Likewise, we know that your grandfather – a learned and diligent emperor, who not only ruled the world but actually visited it all faithfully – was fond of music and flute-players, in addition to being a first-class gourmand at extravagant banquets. It is also correct that your father, a truly god-like man, surpassed the virtues of all other emperors in his foresight, self-control, frugality, integrity, sense of duty, and sanctity, but nevertheless still visited the gymnasium, baited a hook, and laughed at clowns.

6. I will say nothing about Gaius Caesar, the bitterest enemy of Cleopatra, and nothing about Augustus, the husband of Livia. Do you think that Romulus, the very founder of our city, really had only a meagre dinner after he cut down the leader of the enemy in hand-to-hand combat and dedicated the *spolia opima** to Jupiter Feretrius? Surely no hungry or abstemious man would have come up with the idea of dragging off ripe young women* from the games? Didn't the old and venerable Numa* spend his time between offering cakes and tithes and the slaughtering of sacrificial animals as the presider of banquets, the offerer of dinners, and the initiator of holidays? I call him a glutton and leisure-seeker. Surely you don't spend your holidays in hunger? Nor will I neglect to mention your Chrysippus,* who apparently spends his days soused, and tends to get his wine directly from the press, filling his cup to the brim. But Socrates,* as you'd know from the Socratic *symposia*, dialogues, and letters, was famous as a man of great knowledge and humour, and this Socrates, you realise, was the student of Aspasia, and the teacher of Alcibiades.

7. Now if you've declared war on play, leisure, abundant food, and on pleasure, at least sleep as much as a free man requires. [You should?] rest [after] having worked to the utmost ... *[The rest of the line is very uncertain.]* ... If no one had snatched fire from heaven,* would the sun not be enough for you to hold court? Don't you think you are caught in a lie on a daily basis, since you say you've set aside the day for judicial investigations, and yet you're still hearing cases at night,* so regardless of whether you condemn the parties or set them free, you yourself are guilty? If you condemn anyone, you say: 'He appears to have provided insufficient guarantees'. But he can hardly 'appear' at all, if the light has vanished.

8. But I implore you, either as a joke or in all seriousness: allow yourself to be persuaded by my words not to cheat yourself of sleep and actually keep to the limits of the day and night. Imagine that the renowned and noble gods, Evening and Morning, are involved in a heated and serious dispute about their boundaries. Each of the two makes a clear case for the limits of his own territory. Sleep demands to step in during the hearing, for he is also involved in this affair and says that he is affected by the injustice. If only I had as much vigour or enthusiasm as when I wrote those trifles in praise of Smoke and Dust.* You can be sure that I would have written in praise of Sleep at the height of my powers! Now then, if you would like to hear a short story on sleep, pay attention.

9. The story goes that father Jove, when he founded the human race at the dawn of time, took one stroke to divide the life of man right down the middle into two equal parts. One he enveloped in light, the other in darkness, naming one 'day' and one 'night', giving over the night for rest, the day for work. At that time Sleep had not yet been born, and all men passed their lives constantly awake, with night spent by watchful men in nocturnal rest, rather than in sleep, as was the law. Then little by little, as it is the nature of men to be restless and eager for action and disruption, they began to use up both night and day with work, saving no hour for rest. Then it is said that Jove, when he saw that disputes and bail suits were taking place at night, and that even the nights were adjourned, gave special attention to the selection of one of his own brothers to take care of night and the repose of men. Neptune objected that he had many and burdensome cares for the sea, taking care that waves did not overwhelm whole lands and their mountains, and that winds did not arise, uproot

everything from their foundations, swallow up the forests and the crops from their roots. Father Dis also objected that the depths of Hades were barely kept in check with his stringent efforts and concern, and that Acheron* was barely fortified by the streams and swamps and Stygian pools. He said that he had appointed a watch dog* to look over the shades in order to intimidate them, since they wanted to escape to the upper air. He had given that dog three throats for barking, and a three-fold jaw and a triple set of terrifying teeth.

10. Then Jove, having asked the other gods, noticed that they were rather more pleased with wakefulness: Juno set most births in motion at night, Minerva (the teacher of arts and crafts) much preferred alertness, Mars swiftly arranged nocturnal sorties and ambushes, and Venus and Liber* were by far the most in favour of night-owls. Then Jupiter conceived of a plan to create Sleep and admit him to the council of the gods, to place him in command of night and rest and deliver to him the keys to men's eyes. Jupiter then used his own hands to blend the sap of herbs with which Sleep could soothe the hearts of men. The herbs of safety and pleasure were brought from the forests of heaven, but the herb of death he took from the plains of Acheron. He sprinkled a single drop of that death, a drop so tiny that it amounted to the tear of a man who usually suppressed his emotions. 'With this sap,' he said, 'wash sleep over men through the doors of their eyes: all of those whom you bathe thus will lie down on the spot, and will lie motionless as if they are dead. But have no fear, for they will soon revive and a little later, when they have woken up, they will arise.'

11. After that, Jupiter tied wings to Sleep, not like those of Mercury attached to his ankles, but like those of Love, attached to the shoulders: 'For you must not attack the pupils and eyelids of men with soles and winged sandals, with the din of chariots and the roar of horses, but fly quietly and softly on delicate wings in the manner of a swallow, not with the clapping wings of the pigeon.'

12. In order that Sleep might be more pleasant for men, he bestowed on him many pleasing dreams, designed to suit each man's individual passions. In this way, a sleeping man might be a spectator watching an actor, or listening to a flute-player, or barracking for a charioteer driving round the track. Soldiers might conquer in their dreams, generals might triumph, and wanderers might return home. These dreams usually turn out to be true.

13. And so Marcus, if you need to sleep after this, I recommend that you sleep for as long as you wish, until your heart's desire – whatever that might be – comes to you when you wake.

Commentary

Alsium: Alsium was a seaside town and famous pleasure resort to the north west of Rome. Archaeological evidence of aristocratic villas has been found in the vicinity of the modern towns of Ladispoli, Palo, and Marina di S. Nicoli (Marzano 2007: 389, 399, 419–21).

Niger: Otherwise unknown, probably an imperial slave or freedman.

Plautus . . . Accius . . . Lucretius . . . Ennius: These writers all figure in Fronto's list of authors in **Letter 1**.

the 'hooked and rocky catch' as Plautus says: This is a reference to a line in Plautus' play *The Rope* (*Rudens*, line 299), which focuses on a group of fishermen.

birds fattened for a good while: Varro (*On Agriculture* 3.3) considers the farming of pigeons and domestic chickens to be a long-standing Italian tradition, and also lists other animals that were farmed at the typical Roman villa, including thrushes, peacocks, geese, ducks, rabbits, and dormice.

Annaeus Seneca: Fronto is lampooning L. Annaeus Seneca the Younger, the philosopher and tutor of the emperor Nero, by adopting his pretentious affectations, which were well known (see Quintillian, *Principles of Oratory* 10.1.125–131). Fronto's dislike for the philosopher's style is well known: it also appears in the letter to Marcus *On Speeches* (*De Orationibus*, VdH[2] pp. 153–60 = Haines II, pp. 100–15; Champlin 1980: 123–4). Thus, instead of referring to the type of wine known as 'Falernian' or 'Faustian' by one of those names, Fronto calls them 'fortunate' (*felicibus*), as if the term 'Faustian' actually derived from Faustus Sulla, son of the dictator L. Cornelius Sulla *Felix*. Then, rather than simply saying that the cups were unblemished, Fronto says they lacked 'a treacherous mark' (*sine delatoria nota*), as if the cups had been betrayed by their maker. The jokes are rather feeble.

as Plautus says, 'a lugubrious location': Plautus uses this term in his play *The Boastful Soldier* (*Miles Gloriosus*, line 853): it refers to the place for the storage of wine (van den Hout 1999: 514).

to take your 'plea'? The archaic form of *voluptas*, the Latin word for 'pleasure', was the shorter *volup*, hence it is translated here as 'plea'. The other abbreviated forms that follow are Fronto's own invention (van den Hout 1999: 515).

It would be easier to reconcile you with a fox than with pleasure: The Latin word for 'fox' was *vulpis* or *volpis*, hence Fronto is making a pun with the word for 'pleasure' (*voluptas*).

Your great-grandfather, a supreme warrior: Fronto goes through Marcus' family tree, praising the qualities of Trajan (his great-grandfather), Hadrian (his grandfather), and Antoninus Pius (his father), and outlining their various pastimes. Most of these are known from other sources: (i) Trajan's fondness for drinking and pantomimes (Dio 68.7.4, 68.10.2; **Letter 49**); (ii) Hadrian's love of music (*HA Hadrian* 14.9; *Epitome concerning the Caesars* 14.2); (iii) Pius' enthusiasm for fishing and the theatre (*HA Pius* 11.2). His love of the gymnasium is not specifically attested elsewhere, though Marcus (*Meditations* 1.16.5–9) wrote that Pius took good care of his body.

dedicated the *spolia opima*: Romulus, the first king of Rome, killed Acro, king of a neighbouring Latin town, in single combat. He then dedicated the deceased ruler's armour to the god Jupiter Feretrius, whose temple he built on the Capitoline Hill (Livy 1.10). Henceforth, booty captured by a Roman general after killing an enemy commander in single combat was known as the *spolia opima* ('rich spoils'). Only two other Romans were officially awarded this honour: A. Cornelius Cossus in 437 BC and M. Claudius Marcellus in 222 BC. The exact etymology of 'Feretrius' was uncertain even to the Romans, but this incarnation of Jupiter was the god of treaties and oaths.

dragging off ripe young women: This is a reference to the so-called 'Rape of the Sabine Women', in which Romulus and his cohorts abducted the women from the nearby Sabine tribe during games in honour of Neptune. This was prompted by the Sabines' refusal to allow inter-marriage with other tribes, including the Romans (Livy 1.9).

Numa: Numa Pompilius was the second king of Rome (traditional dates *c.* 715–673 BC). He reputedly established many of Rome's religious institutions and was know for his peaceful nature. For comparisons between Numa and Antoninus Pius, see **Letter 49**.

Chrysippus: Chrysippus was a Stoic philosopher of the third century BC. Fronto's point is that if a man such as Chrysippus can enjoy himself (perhaps a little too much), then so should Marcus.

Socrates: Socrates was an Athenian philosopher of the fifth century BC. A controversial and provocative figure, he was famously condemned to death for corrupting the youth of Athens and disrespecting the gods. Aspasia was a Milesian woman and companion of the Athenian statesman Pericles, whom Socrates allegedly visited with his pupils (Plutarch, *Pericles* 24.3). Alcibiades was an Athenian politician and general, who was notorious for switching sides several times during the Peloponnesian War.

snatched fire from heaven: This is a reference to the myth of Prometheus, who stole fire from the gods and gave it to men after Zeus had revoked its use by mankind (Hesiod, *Works and Days* 50–1).

you are still hearing cases at night: Marcus' tendency to hold court into the night appears in Dio (72.6.1), while the *Historia Augusta (Marcus* 10.8) says he stayed in the senate at night until elections were complete. Fronto himself had been forced to appear in a case before Hadrian's prefect Marcius Turbo at night (Dio 69.18.3).

those trifles in praise of Smoke and Dust: The *Praise of Smoke and Dust* is a letter written by Fronto to Marcus in the early 140s (*Laudes fumi et pulveris*, VdH^2 pp. 215–7 = Haines I, pp. 38–45). It was a 'paradoxical eulogy', the term given to a serious rhetorical treatise on a decidedly trivial subject (Clarke 1996: 132; van den Hout 1999: 487–8).

Acheron: In Latin texts, Acheron is used as an alternative name for Hades or the Underworld. In Greek myth, Acheron was one of the rivers that flowed through the Underworld.

a watch dog: Fronto is describing Cerberus, the three-headed dog that stood guard over the entrance to Hades.

Venus and Liber: Venus, the Roman goddess of love, was associated with wine, hence her appearance here alongside Liber, the Roman god of wine and, unsurprisingly, fertility.

Letter 42. Fronto to Marcus (*c.* 162/3)

Ad Ant. Imp. 2.1, VdH[2] p. 95 = *Ad M. Caes.* 2.16, Haines II, pp. 94–7.

Fronto to my lord, Antoninus Augustus,

1. *[The beginning of the letter is lost, and we open mid-sentence.]* . . . that 'children of the earth',* as the saying goes – though they're really more like the children of the outhouse in this case – that they should carry off [the inheritance]; that such a great amount from the treasury of Antoninus should be wasted, so that some fattened foster-child, a complete nobody,* will receive it, and Egatheus* will get nothing. But how many hostile rumours and how many complaints will spring up after the estate has been divided up in accordance with the Falcidian law?* Who will buy that renowned – nay, infamous – necklace,* and the other baubles that are worth so much? If your wife were to buy them, it will be claimed that she assaulted and carried off the spoils for virtually nothing, with the result that little would be left for those who were entitled to a legacy. And if Faustina doesn't buy these jewels? Then who will buy the pearls that were bequeathed to your daughters?* Will you deprive your daughters' necks of these pearls so that they might instead adorn the trunk of that bloated glutton?

2. Won't you take up Matidia's estate instead? Shall it be the case that this very noble woman, of exalted status* and with a significant fortune, a woman who deserves the very best from you, will have died intestate? If that happens, you will have deprived of a will the same woman to whom you granted a public funeral.* Up till now you have shown yourself to be a fair, conscientious, and unimpeachable judge: will you now begin to make improper rulings with your wife's case? Then you'll be like a fire, burning those closest to you, but shining bright for those far removed.

Commentary

'children of the earth': This was a common expression describing people of undistinguished origins, which Fronto uses to refer to undesirables who may inherit part of Faustina's fortune. However, he says they should really be 'children of the *cella*', with *cella* meaning basement, servant's quarters, huts, or other confined spaces, hence the translation here as 'outhouse'.

some fattened foster-child, a complete nobody: The Latin word *alumnus* (masc.) or *alumna* (fem.) generally refers to a foster-child, namely one who has been raised by someone other than their natural parents. Many of these were slaves or from otherwise humble birth, but they could also be orphans or children of poor relatives (Rawson 1986; 2003: 251–5). *Alumnus* (and its feminine form, *alumna*) has been defined as a term of 'quasi-adoption', since it indicates a 'warm relationship' between a young person and a parental figure, but not formal adoption into the family (Nielsen 1987). Matidia evidently had a sizeable number of foster children, provisions for some of whom (the 'Varian foster children' in **Letter 44**) were included in her final will, while others, including the 'fattened foster-child', were disinherited when Matidia unsealed the codicils containing their bequests.

Egatheus: T. Aurelius Egatheus was an imperial freedman who held the post of *a codicillis* (*CIL* VI 8840 = *ILS* 1529). The office probably involved oversight of different aspects of imperial correspondence, since the term 'codicil' also referred to letters of appointment or benefactions, as well as appendices to wills (van den

Hout 1999: 247). For other inscriptions attesting the *a codicillis* and his assistants, see *CIL* VI 6190, 8441, 8442, *CIL* XIV 4011 = *ILS* 1530, and *AE* 1975, 55.

the Falcidian law: The Falcidian law, passed in 40 BC, specified that no more than three-quarters of an estate could be distributed through legacies to ensure that the heir (in this case Marcus' wife Faustina) received a share of at least one quarter (*Digest* 35.2.1.pr). The problem stems from the fact that if Marcus allowed the codicils to remain valid, then the amount of the legacies would exceed three-quarters of the estate, and the emperor would have to apply the Falcidian law to ensure his wife received her valid share (Champlin 1980: 71; van den Hout 1999: 245).

necklace: In her will, Matidia had left valuable jewellery to Faustina and her daughters, including a pearl necklace. However, these precious jewels would have to be sold to pay the foster-children's legacies if the codicils were deemed valid. Fronto imagines a situation in which Faustina buys back the necklace at a discount rate in order to cheat the foster-children out of the full amount of their inheritance (Champlin 1980: 71). He was right to call the necklace 'infamous', since the jurist Q. Cervidius Scaevola was called in to give an opinion on the case (*Digest* 35.2.26). Although Scaevola does not mention Matidia, he discusses whether a necklace made of thirty-five pearls should be restored to the heir under the Falcidian law.

bequeathed to your daughters: Matidia appears to have had a close relationship with Marcus' daughters, who were her great-grand nieces (Boatwright 1992: 29). Although they are not named, the daughters in question would be Annia Aurelia Galeria Lucilla and Annia Galeria Aurelia Faustina, in their early teens at the time. In another letter Marcus reports that his daughters stayed with Matidia at one of her residences (*Ad Ant. Imp.* 4.1, VdH[2] p. 105 = *Ad Ant. Imp.* 2.1, Haines I, pp. 300–3).

exalted status: Matidia was honoured with statues in Italy, North Africa, Greece, and Asia Minor, some of which were integrated into larger imperial family groups (Boatwright 1992: 21–3). She was styled the 'maternal aunt' (*matertera*) of Antoninus Pius, as on an inscription from Ephesus (*CIL* III 6070a = *ILS* 327).

a public funeral: Such a funeral would require official authorisation from the senate, and would have involved a procession through the streets of Rome, including the wax images (*imagines*) of Matidia's ancestors, and a public oration by Marcus, probably in the *forum Romanum*. Hadrian's funeral oration for her mother, Matidia the Elder, paid tribute to her chastity after her husband's death, and her dutifulness to her relatives (Jones 2004). Other female members of the imperial family who received such an honour were Augustus' wife Livia, and Poppaea, wife of Nero (Toynbee 1971: 55–61). When Junia Tertia, half-sister of Caesar's assassin, M. Junius Brutus, died in 22, she was honoured with a funeral oration in front of the *rostra* (Tacitus, *Annals* 3.76).

Letter 43. Marcus to Fronto (*c.* 162/3)

Ad Ant. Imp. 2.2, VdH[2] pp. 95–6 = *Ad M. Caes.* 2.17, Haines II, pp. 96–9.

A reply to my teacher,

1. So my teacher will now also be my advocate then!* For my part I can feel secure, since I've always followed the two things that are closest to my heart: good reason and your advice. May the gods see to it that, whatever I do, I'll do it with your seal of approval, my teacher.

2. You'll note the late hour* at which I am replying to you. For after consulting with my advisers,* I carefully marshalled those points that concern us at this moment, in order to write to my brother* so that he could contribute to the discussion as if he were actually present. Then, finally, I will be confident in our decisions once he has approved them. I'll show Faustina the speech in which you came to our defence* at once, and I'll convey her thanks to you. It's been one good outcome of this sordid affair that I've been able to read such a letter from you. Farewell, my good and best teacher.

Commentary

So my teacher will now also be my advocate then! Fronto was not a member of the council assembled by Marcus to discuss the issue of Matidia's will. He may not have expected Fronto to offer such a forthright assessment of the case in **Letter 42**, with its vituperative rhetoric reminiscent of the speech of a prosecuting lawyer.

the late hour: The letter was probably delivered directly to Fronto by a messenger at night. If both men were in Rome, it would have been possible for an envoy to carry the letter from the Palatine to Fronto's house on the Esquiline.

For after consulting with my advisers: Marcus uses the word *amici*, which literally means 'friends', but also functions as a technical term to refer to the emperor's advisers. The *amici* formed part of the imperial council (*consilium*) which, despite its name, had no fixed membership, but was composed of senators and equestrians whom the emperor summoned to provide advice on each occasion (Millar 1977: 110–12; Eck 2000: 195–213).

in order to write to my brother: Lucius Verus was stationed at Antioch, his base for the Parthian War. It is interesting that Marcus postponed his verdict until he received Verus' advice: it would probably have taken about forty days for the letter to reach Syria, and the same amount of time for the reply to return to Rome (Casson 1994: 188). One wonders how many other imperial decisions were made on this basis during their joint rule.

the speech in which you came to our defence: Marcus is not referring to an actual speech, but the impassioned **Letter 42**.

Letter 44. Fronto to Aufidius Victorinus (*c*. 162/3)

Ad Amicos 1.14, VdH^2 pp. 179–80 = Haines II, pp. 98–101.

Fronto sends greetings to Aufidius Victorinus,

1. At the time of reckoning (?) ... *[Over twenty lines are lost.]* ... and to the Varian foster-children,* both male and female, she left one million sesterces, to be held as a collective long-term deposit rather than their own property. For

from this bequest she instructed that they each be given an annual sum of 50,000 sesterces* by the empress. Nearly all those who had attended to her had done so in vain,* since they weren't thought worth even a penny each. But some of them, obviously cunning and quick-thinking men, dared to seal the codicils, which Matidia had voided long ago, while she was lying there unconscious. Then they were so bold as to vouch for and defend those codicils before our emperor, as if they had been executed honestly in the proper fashion.* And I was a little afraid that his devotion to philosophy would persuade him to make the wrong decision. So that you'll know what I wrote, I've attached a copy of the letter I sent to him.

2. I've added many new points to my Bithynian speech,* part of which you say you've read. The additions are not without eloquence, and I think you'll like the passage at the beginning concerning my actions, if you've read the outstanding speech on a similar topic that Marcus Tullius wrote in defence of Publius Sulla,* which still survives today. This isn't so you can judge us to be equals, but so you so can observe how far removed my mediocre talent is from the remarkable eloquence of that man.

Commentary

Varian foster-children: The precise origin and status of the Varian foster-children is unknown. Duncan-Jones (1984: 228) suggests that the original foundation could have been set up by the senator L. Varius Ambibulus, and subsequently augmented by Matidia. Van den Hout (1999: 421) proposes a male relative of Matidia's family, T. Vibius Varus, as a possibility. Matidia was not the first member of the Antonine family to contribute to such an initiative: Nerva and Trajan had established alimentary foundations, and Antoninus Pius created a fund for orphaned girls in honour of his wife Faustina (Duncan-Jones 1964).

an annual sum of 50,000 sesterces: In this translation, we follow the suggested interpretation of Duncan Jones (1984: 379). When Pliny the Younger (*Letters* 7.18) established an alimentary foundation in his hometown of Comum, he promised to donate 500,000 sesterces to establish the fund, but then decided to provide some of his estates instead, the income from which would be worth more than the original sum.

those who had attended to her had done so in vain: These are the hated and vilified 'legacy-hunters' (*captatores*) who are depicted preying upon the elderly and childless of the wealthy classes in many literary sources (Seneca, *On Benefits* 4.20.3; Pliny, *Letters* 8.18).

in the proper fashion: Matidia had cut the thread which tied up the tablets, an accepted practice for voiding a legal document. But the legacy-hunters had retied it to make the codicils valid again (van den Hout 1999: 423).

my Bithynian speech: Fronto's speech *For the Bithynians* was probably delivered while he was prosecuting a proconsul of Bithynia and Pontus on the charge of 'murder by mandate' (that is, the governor did not murder anyone personally, but his actions caused a death or deaths) (Champlin 1980: 67–8). Fronto began to revise the speech for publication, and circulated copies to Victorinus and to his friend Praecilius Pompeianus, though the process took well over a year (*Ad Amicos* 1.15, VdH^2 pp. 180–1 = Haines II, pp. 88–91).

defence of Publius Sulla: In 62 BC, Cicero defended P. Cornelius Sulla, nephew of the dictator Sulla, on the charge of having been involved in the conspiracy of Catiline.

Letter 45. Fronto to Verus (*c.* 164)

Ad Verum Imp. 1.6, VdH^2 pp. 110–11 = Haines II, pp. 150–7.

To my lord Verus Augustus,

1. I am sure that you remember well, my lord, what a significant and long-standing friendship I have with Gavius Clarus.* It is for this reason that I have so frequently spoken about him to you from the very bottom of my heart. And

I do not think it a reason for reproach to remind you of this, as I am sure you remember it anyway.

2. From a very early age, Gavius Clarus cared for me on friendly terms,* and this was not restricted to the terms of his duties, by which a senator lesser in age and position reveres and honours a senator more senior in age and rank.* But gradually our friendship grew to such a point that it neither pained him, nor embarrassed me, for him to show deference to me in the manner that clients and loyal and hard-working freedmen do.* This was not the result of any arrogance of mine, nor any desire on his part to flatter me, but because our mutual esteem and genuine affection removed from both of us any desire to evade our obligations.

3. Why should I recall his dedication in attending to my affairs in the forum, whether large or small? At home, when I wanted anything taken care of correctly, put away, signed off, or completed, I entrusted and committed the task to him alone.

4. Clarus was always so eager to take care of my health, even though a foster-child would find the task difficult. He paid such constant attention to me that he even kept watch over me when I was sick,* and when I was not able to use my hands because of my illness, he brought the food to my mouth with his own hand. Finally, if anything might happen to me when Victorinus and my dear brother are absent – for every man's time must come eventually* – I have entrusted the proper care for my body to him. Even if these men should be present, I want my body to be handled by Clarus first and foremost, so that my brother and son-in-law would escape the distress of having to come in contact with my corpse.

5. These are the bonds that exist* between Gavius Clarus and me. And so, if I had greater financial resources,* I would not be remiss in helping him as much as I could to carry out the duties of a senator without difficulty, nor would I ever force him to cross the sea on business such as this. But now dire straits and strict poverty have compelled me to send him away unwillingly to Syria to pursue his claims to the legacies that have come to him in the will of a close friend.*

6. This poverty has fallen on my friend Clarus through no fault of his own. He received no inheritance either from his father's or mother's estates: the result of being his father's heir was having to pay off his father's creditors.* Still,

he carried out his duties as quaestor, aedile, and praetor with frugality, hard work, and honesty. When Clarus was away from the city, your deified father paid out the expenses of his praetorship from the treasury, but as soon as Clarus returned to health and came back to Rome, he paid back the whole amount* to the imperial coffers.

7. There is no one who is more dutiful than this man I am writing about, no one who is more disciplined, or more modest. There is no one more honourable either, if you place any faith in my judgement, nor as generous as he can be, given his poor financial situation. His candour, integrity, honesty, and loyalty are clearly Roman. But I do not think his humanitarian nature is Roman,* for there is nothing I have seen less often in my life at Rome than a man who is truly humanitarian. This is why, I think, there is no word at Rome for 'humanitarian',* as no Roman really has any of this virtue.

8. This is the one man, my lord, whom I commend to you with every prayer. If you ever loved me, or ever will love me in the future, I ask that you watch over this man whom I have introduced to you. But perhaps you may ask, what for him . . . *[The rest of the letter is lost.]*

Commentary

Gavius Clarus: L. Gavius Clarus was a senator, who was probably in his mid-thirties when this letter was written, since he had been praetor. His father, L. Gavius Aelianus, was the first member of the family to enter the senate, though he is not known to have risen far. Clarus himself resided with Fronto at his house on the Esquiline hill (Champlin 1980: 46).

From a very early age, Gavius Clarus cared for me on friendly terms: For this stylistic convention in a letter of recommendation, see **Letter 28**.

a senator more senior in age and rank: Fronto's words make it clear that he is acting as Clarus' patron (*patronus*), but he never refers to the younger senator as his client (*cliens*). Roman aristocrats were reluctant to use the technical terms *patronus* and *cliens* because they were seen as degrading. Instead they preferred to talk about relationships in terms of 'friendship' (*amicitia*), even if such friendships were unequal because of differences in status (Saller 1982: 8–10; Konstan 1997: 135–7; Garnsey 2010: 46).

in the manner that clients and loyal and hard-working freedmen do: Fronto explicitly compares his relationship with Gavius Clarus with that between patrons and their clients (*clientes*) and freedmen (*liberti*). Such men owed their patrons official duties (*officia*), in return for which they received legal and financial protection. Fronto, in writing that Clarus behaved 'in the manner' of clients, implies that the young man was not actually his client, but that he was nevertheless prepared to act as if he were (Saller 1989: 59). This passage demonstrates how Fronto manipulated the terminology of Roman social relations to make a point about Clarus' dutifulness.

he even kept watch over me when I was sick: The care Clarus gave to Fronto in his poor health is presented as the highest level of service that the young senator has rendered to his master. It was considered especially dutiful to render assistance in times of ill-health, regardless of whether the sick party was socially superior or inferior. Cicero's correspondence is full of paternalistic concern for the health of his freedman Tiro (see especially the sequence of letters in *Ad Fam.* 16.1–18), and Pliny the Younger makes much of his anxiety for his sick freedman Zosimus, as a way of demonstrating to his correspondents that he was a conscientious patron (Joshel 2011: 235–8). At the other end of the social scale, it was the mark of a 'good emperor' (the so-called *civilis princeps*) to visit senators at home when they were ill (Wallace-Hadrill 1982: 40).

for every man's time must come eventually: The Latin adverb *humanitus* 'in the manner of men' is translated here as 'for every man's time must come eventually' to show that Fronto is referring to his own death; a near-identical phrase is used by Cicero (*Philippics* 1.10). Van den Hout (1999: 272) argues that Fronto is referring to his body functions ('the motions'), but the context shows this is not the case.

the bonds that exist: Fronto's point is reinforced by the use of the vocabulary of patronage and kinship (Bernstein 2008: 225). Clarus is not a client or freedman, but is so dutiful that he behaves as if he were; he is not a relative, but he steps in to render assistance when Fronto's son-in-law and brother are away, as if he was actually related to the senator. Fronto is building up to requesting a favour from the emperor on his protégé's behalf in the second half of the letter.

if I had greater financial resources: The 'duties of a senator' included numerous financial obligations, such as maintaining property in Italy and a house in Rome, and paying for games as quaestor, aedile, praetor, and consul (Talbert 1984: 54–66).

the legacies that have come to him in the will of a close friend: Although Fronto states that the deceased was a 'close friend', one did not have to be on intimate terms to receive a legacy (Pliny, *Letters* 7.20.6). Instead, legacies often functioned as displays of *amicitia* to peers and associates (Saller 1982: 124–5). Sometimes they could be quite small gestures, particularly if one was not a family member (Champlin 1989).

to pay off his father's creditors: In Roman legal terminology, Clarus was presumably a *heres suus et necessarius*, which meant that he inherited all his father's property, including his debts. This law was not modified until the sixth century, during the reign of Justinian (Saller 1994: 155–80).

he paid back the whole amount: Antoninus Pius had evidently given Clarus a loan of money so that he could pay for the games he was supposed to sponsor as praetor. Emperors often subsidised senators who had fallen on hard times (Millar 1977: 297–9). Praetors were responsible for six festivals held throughout the year that involved various combinations of chariot racing, plays, and public feasts (Talbert 1984: 59–66).

I do not think his humanitarian nature is Roman: In this passage, Fronto praises Clarus for possessing a number of 'Roman' virtues: *simplicitas* ('candour'), *castitas* ('integrity'), *veritas* ('truth') and *fides* ('loyalty'). But what makes Clarus unique is that he possesses φιλοστοργία (*philostorgia*), a Greek word that means 'warm-heartedness', or as translated here, 'humanitarian nature'. By drawing attention to this quality, Fronto aims to demonstrate that his protégé is more than just an ordinary Roman, and thus worthy of Lucius Verus' patronage and protection. Marcus Aurelius (*Meditations* 1.9) himself credits one of his tutors, the philosopher Sextus of Chaeronea, for teaching him how to be 'the most humanitarian man' (φιλοστοργότατος).

there is really no word at Rome for 'humanitarian': The Greek word φιλόστοργος, here translated as 'humanitarian', has no true equivalent in Latin, as Fronto himself had to transliterate it as *philostorgus* in another letter (*Ad Amicos* 1.3, VdH[2] pp. 172–3 = Haines I, pp. 278–83).

7

Fronto and the Parthian War

Introduction

The reign of Antoninus Pius was a relatively peaceful age compared with the long years of warfare that the empire endured under Marcus and Verus. In 161, the Parthian king Vologaesus III placed his relative Pacorus on the throne of Armenia, deposing its previous ruler. Since Armenia was a Roman client kingdom immediately adjacent to the province of Cappadocia, the move represented a major challenge to Roman power in the region (Birley 1993: 121–2). The governor of Cappadocia, M. Sedatius Severianus, launched an ill-fated invasion of Armenia, having been convinced by the false prophet Alexander that he would win a great victory if he launched such an attack (Lucian, *Alexander* 27; Xiphilinus = Dio 71.2.1). The venture ended in disaster and Severianus committed suicide. Later the same year, the Parthian invasion of the province of Syria resulted in the death of the consular governor, L. Attidius Cornelianus (*HA Marcus* 8.6). Fronto wrote a letter to Marcus to console him on these setbacks, reminding the emperor of all the tragedies that had befallen Rome in the past (*De Bello Parthico*, VdH^2 pp. 220–6 = Haines II, pp. 20–31).

Lucius Verus was chosen to take command of the Roman forces in the east on the grounds of his youth, though he had never before seen active combat. He departed Rome in the summer of 162 and arrived in Syria later in that year or early 163 (Champlin 1974: 147; Birley 1993: 122–6). Verus took a circuitous route through Greece and Asia Minor, visiting numerous pleasure resorts along the way, and marrying Marcus' daughter Lucilla in Ephesus (*HA Verus* 6.9; Barnes 1967: 70–1). Upon reaching Antioch in Syria, he chose to remain in the city rather than leading the armies personally, relying upon his senatorial generals to win battles for him. Verus is said to have enjoyed the pleasures of pantomimes, actors, and musicians during his sojourn (*HA Verus* 7.1–5, 8.10–11; *Marcus* 8.12; Xiphilinus = Dio 71.2.2). Fronto initially kept in touch with Verus while he was travelling, writing to his former pupil when he fell ill at Canusium in Italy (*Ad Verum Imp.* 1.5, VdH[2] pp. 109–10 = *Ad Verum Imp.* 2.6, Haines II, pp. 84–7). However, after this, their correspondence lapsed, as Verus confessed in an apologetic letter dated to 163 or 164 (*Ad Verum Imp.* 1.1, VdH[2] pp. 107–8 = *Ad Verum Imp.* 2.2, Haines II, pp. 116–19).

After the Roman forces had recaptured Armenia, Fronto sent the very long, but unfortunately now very fragmentary, **Letter 46** to Verus. Fronto argues that Verus' accomplishments in warfare pale in comparison with his rhetorical achievements, claiming that eloquence is the true mark of a king. This encapsulates Fronto's attitude towards the Parthian War, revealed throughout this correspondence: it is the perspective of a man who has little or no acquaintance with warfare, or any sympathy with its practitioners. Fronto's understanding of such conflicts was largely shaped by what he had read, and the same can probably be said of Verus, given his pupillage under the orator (see Kemezis 2010: 293–5). Fronto consistently compares Verus to the great generals of the Republican past, such as Cato, but there was a significant difference in that Cato had a long military career, whereas Verus had been brought up at the court of Antoninus Pius, and spent his youth in Italy.

Still, Verus was concerned that his accomplishments should be remembered by posterity. He wrote to Fronto in late 165, after the capture of the Parthian cities of Ctesiphon and Seleucia, providing Fronto with instructions as to how he should write a history of the war (**Letter 47**). Fronto's lack of military experience did not disqualify him for such a task. The most important criteria were his rhetorical prowess and his relationship with the imperial house, which would enable him to produce a worthy account of Verus' exploits and achievements (Kemezis 2010: 305–7). In writing the history, Fronto was instructed to use the official reports of Verus' generals, including the legionary commander Avidius Cassius. In 166, Fronto wrote to Cassius himself to praise his friend Iunius Maximus, who had been a junior officer in the campaign and whom he hoped would benefit from the general's patronage (**Letter 48**).

Letter 49, from Fronto to Marcus, is particularly famous. In the original manuscript, it bears the title of *Principia Historiae* ('The beginnings of a history'). This was not Fronto's title, and should not lead us to assume that the letter was ever published in his lifetime as a historical work. It was surely only intended for Marcus, as a way of showing how he would commemorate Verus' achievements in prose (van den Hout 1999: 462–3; Kemezis 2010: 290–1). Fronto himself calls it a 'treatment' (*thema*) that is a 'sample' (*gustus*) of the larger history he intends to write. When he penned the letter, he had not yet received Verus' accounts of the campaign promised in **Letter 46**, and this may explain the lack of concrete historical detail in the letter. Indeed, Fronto focuses on comparing Verus' character and achievements with his predecessors (particularly his great-grandfather Trajan). Fronto would not have been the first man to embark on a history of the Parthian War. In 162, the orator Polyaenus had dedicated his *Stratagems* to Marcus and Verus, and even offered to compose an account of Verus' campaigns (*Stratagems* 6 pref.; Wheeler 2010: 16). More famously, the satirist Lucian recalled the cottage industry of flattering histories that sprang up in response to the war (*How to Write History* 13–14). Although Fronto's 'sample' certainly bears some of the same traits as the works cited by Lucian, it is hardly likely that the satirist knew of this letter.

Letter 46. Fronto to Verus (164)

Ad Verum Imp 2.1, VdH[2] pp. 118–32 = Haines II, pp. 128–50.

Greetings to my lord Verus Augustus,

1. Now, emperor, behave however you want towards me, and act in whatever way you think is best. Either neglect me, shun me, or show me no respect at all*; treat me as the lowest of the low, if you want to. There is nothing so harsh or unjust that you can do to me, even if you really want to, that will prevent me from deriving enduring happiness from my relationship with you.

2. You may think that I am praising your military abilities and your decisions and accomplishments in war. These deeds are certainly very fine, as they are outstanding and glorious achievements for the state and the empire of the Roman people. I have derived my own share of pleasure from these accomplishments, along with your other subjects. But now it is my moment to triumph,* thanks to your eloquence, which you have made clear in your letters

to the senate. I have received – yes, I have received – and I retain and hold fast to this suitable remuneration that you have repaid me with interest. Now I can depart my life with a happy heart, since I have received an appropriate reward for my efforts, and I leave behind a magnificent monument to my eternal glory. After they hear you or your brother, everyone knows, suspects, or believes that I was your teacher. You can be sure that I myself would only invite this recognition reluctantly, if you both did not make it publicly known. But since you make no secret of it, I cannot deny it.

3. You have many assistants in your pursuit of glory and distinction in warfare, many thousands of armed men, who have been summoned from every nation to assist you and strive for victory on your behalf, but your excellence in eloquence was acquired under my generalship and auspices,* Caesar, if I might be so bold to say so . . .

[The text breaks off here and two pages are entirely missing in the manuscript. When it resumes, sections 4 and 5 are still very fragmentary, so we re-join the letter in section 6.]

6. The imperial rule has been passed down, from hand to hand, to a number of undeserving individuals, simply because their father was king.* This is no different from the case of chickens, since the distinguishing features of their species are implanted in them from conception: their comb and feathers, their crow, and their watchfulness. Supreme power is assigned to the children of kings in their mother's womb: they gain their empire through the hand of the midwife. There are different traditions regarding this: in the presence of the people . . . *[The next lines are very fragmentary, but refer to the acclamation of Darius as the Persian king because his horse neighed first, and Romulus and Remus taking the auspices from different hills of Rome.]* . . . we know that imperial rule is often snatched away, sometimes by treachery and sometimes by conspiracies, and then bestowed on others, but eloquence cannot be stolen from the living, nor can it be transferred to another when we are carried off by death.

7. You and your brother are right to approve of those deeds of Romulus . . . *[The text breaks off here, with over seventy fragmentary or entirely unreadable lines. We resume in section 8.]*

8. Nor would lightning cause as much terror as it does if it did not strike together with thunder. And the ability to make thunder is not bestowed on

Father Dis, or Neptune, or the other gods, but only on the supreme emperor Jupiter himself, so that through the crashing of the clouds and the clamour of tempests, which resound like voices from heaven on high, he protects his lofty realm from disrespect.

9. Therefore, if you seek out a veritable ruler* of the human race, it is the eloquence of your majesties that rules, your eloquence that governs the minds of the people. It is eloquence that excites fear, produces love, represses insolence, encourages excellence, checks vices, and soothes, teaches, and consoles. I issue a bold challenge to you, in accordance with our ancestral procedure: disregard eloquence and then govern, cease giving speeches in the senate and then subjugate Armenia. Other generals have conquered Armenia* before you, but – by Hercules! – your one letter, and that single speech given by your brother* about you and your virtues will add greater nobility to your glory and be celebrated more in times to come than plenty of princes' triumphs. The infamous Ventidius,* after he had ruined and routed the Parthians, obtained a speech from Sallust in order to announce his victory, and Nerva expounded his accomplishments in the senate with borrowed words. Likewise, most of the emperors before your own fathers* were like babies and mutes, who could say nothing more about their accomplishments in warfare than their own helmets could.

10. In the period after the Roman commonwealth had been transferred from annually elected magistrates to Julius Caesar,* and then to Augustus, I observe that Caesar possessed a facility in speaking that was worthy of a general. I think that Augustus was endowed with the eloquence that remained in his time and the charm of the Latin language that was still intact, rather than any richness of speech. After Augustus, there were only some dwindling and decaying remains left over for the infamous Tiberius. As for all the emperors who succeeded him up until Vespasian, they were of such a breed that their words were more shameful than their behaviour was disgusting and their actions disappointing.

11. Now, someone might object: 'It was because they had not been taught.' Why, then, did they exercise imperial power? I imagine they ruled through their gestures, much like pantomimes, perhaps by nodding in the manner of mutes, or maybe through an interpreter, like the barbarians. Which of these emperors could address the senate with a speech they had written, which of

them could compose an edict or a letter in their own words?* It was as if they had been afflicted by a state of delirium, and their eloquence derived from others, like pipes that are silent without another's lips to blow on them.

12. For 'imperial rule' is a term not only of relevance to power, but also to oratory. Indeed, imperial authority is exercised by giving orders and issuing prohibitions. If an emperor did not praise good deeds, if he did not find fault with wrongs, if he did not encourage virtuous behaviour, if he did not deter men from vices, he would forsake his own title, and would be called 'emperor' in vain . . .

[The next two sections of the text are very fragmentary, and are omitted here. A note in the margin of the manuscript indicates that Fronto discussed a speech of Hadrian that showed 'a semblance of the quality of our former eloquence'.]

15. There are letters written in both Latin and Greek, some composed by the generals themselves, others by historians or annalists,* like that celebrated letter which the general Nicias sent from Sicily. In the work of Sallust, we find the accusatory letter of Mithridates to king Arsaces requesting his help, the serious missive of Cn. Pompeius to the senate concerning the army pay, and the hostile letter of Adherbal, sent when besieged on all sides at Cirta. In truth, all these letters were short and did not contain any detailed account of events, as the circumstances demanded. But as regards that style in which you wrote, there survives the letter of Catulus,* in which [he detailed] his defeats and disasters in a sober manner, to prove he deserved a laurel wreath. It is certainly inflated language, written in a proud style with words that are almost sensitive. History, however, must be set forth in a more illustrious vein, and even cautiously, if it is written to the senate. If Cicero, our role model, had recast the delights of his pamphlet, *On his Policies*,* in the form of a letter (by necessity shorter, more lucid and concise, and if the matter calls for it, somewhat plainer), he would have written it better.

16. Your letter is eloquent, just as we would expect from an orator; vigorous, as befitting a general; serious, as appropriate for the senate, but not overflowing with detailed military matters. For the subject does not call for serious accounts or epitomes in Livy's style, nor like those short, but still suitable, *Annotations* of Titius Aristo,* treatments made point-by-point, in which the requirements of brevity almost result in obscurity because the parts have been compressed together . . . *[The next five lines are fragmentary.]* . . . I am unwilling to expose

and exacerbate those infamous happenings again.* He was accused of making merry when our sluggish and defenceless army had been defeated, and questions were raised as to why he himself had not supported the province with part of the army ... *[Two illegible words.]* ... [it is said] that this was the situation when the truce with the enemy had been broken, and when he had given the kingdom of Armenia to Sohaemus* rather than to Vologaesus, because he had removed Pacorus from his throne.

17. Surely you do not want to detail such matters in a speech,* as Nepos wrote in a letter concerning the Numantine affair* (for it was not quite a war) which he inserted into his work: 'Men drawn from all sides and from the nations of Spain were there to assist: the infantry were distinguished by golden helmets on their heads which made their cloaks look faded.' *[The remainder of section 17 of the letter is fragmentary, and we return with section 18.]*

18. Certainly, emperor, it was not your shield or breastplate that inspired you with this advice in your childhood, but books and literary studies. Since you often read many helpful examples of this kind* in histories and speeches, you employed eloquence as your teacher in military affairs.

19. The army that was handed over to you was corrupted by luxury, lasciviousness, and a long-standing laziness. The soldiers stationed at Antioch had grown accustomed to applauding pantomimes continually, and were more frequently found in the garden of a neighbourhood eatery than under our standards. The horses were shaggy from neglect, while their riders were shaved smooth; hairy arms or legs were rare on these soldiers. These men were dressed up in all their finery rather than in armour, with the result that Pontius Laelianus,* a serious man who believed in old-fashioned discipline, could tear apart their cuirasses with his fingertips, then turn his attention to the horses bedecked with little cushions. At his command, the corners were cut open, and the stuffing plucked out from the pillows on the horses like feathers from geese. Few of the soldiers were able to leap high onto their horses, while the rest crawled up using their withered feet, knees, and calves. Only a few could throw spears swiftly, with most of them hurling them without any strength or stamina as if they were actually using lightweight javelins. Dice games were common in camp, and they slept all night, or kept watch with the company of wine.

20. As regards the orders necessary for restraining these types of soldiers, and for turning them to honest work and diligence – did not the severity of

Hannibal,* the discipline of Africanus, and the examples of Metellus which appear in the histories prove instructive to you? That decision you made in accordance with your established prudence, that you would not join battle with the enemy under our standards before you had broken in your forces with light skirmishes and minor victories – did not Cato,* unsurpassed in oratory and generalship, teach you that? I add now Cato's own words, in which you can see the roots of your decision clearly: 'Meanwhile I made a trial of each and every squadron, maniple, and cohort, to determine its capabilities. I ascertained each man's qualities through light skirmishes. If any one man had excelled, I bestowed suitable honours on him, so that his comrades would want to emulate him, and I praised him at great length in my official address. During this time, I established a few camps, and winter quarters when the season came upon us.'

[There is another whole page missing here, and section 21 is very fragmentary. We return with section 22.]

22. But training in eloquence is the very source and foundation of liberal arts and literary studies, and neither military affairs nor attention to duty, which is called 'philosophy', can be perfectly formed unless it is created in company with eloquence. If one of these arts lacks eloquence . . . *[Seven lines of fragmentary text omitted.]* . . . providing that it can add colour to events, which are more or less embellished at any rate: first, how to march forward; how to draw up the battle line behind the first ranks; when to bear down using heavy ballistas; when the troops should regroup if good reasons present themselves; when, if circumstances are pressing, they must join the fight; when the matter must be discussed in eloquent fashion and with free rein; and when the speech comes to an end and the retreat is sounded.

23. Even Viriathus, even Spartacus* possessed knowledge of warfare and were proficient in combat. But if one was to count all those orators who have ever lived, going right back to the foundation of Rome – and even include those whom Cicero endowed wholesale with membership of the republic of eloquence in his *Orator* – you could barely manage three hundred, when three hundred of the bravest soldiers from one clan of the Fabii* died fighting for the fatherland on one single day. For I am not a lenient assessor ... *[The text becomes fragmentary again, and more than two pages are lost, before we resume in section 24.]*

24. . . . and you replied to the [king of the] Parthians* promptly and severely. Evidently, you learned this from those most graceful of public speakers – your centurions and chief centurions! Dausara, Nicephorium, and Artaxata* were captured by our armies under your leadership and auspices. But as for that well-defended fortress which lies in your brother's chest, unconquered and unassailable against the assumption of the title of 'Conqueror of the Armenians',* which he refused – who else was it but you who made the assault, and with what weapon other than eloquence? You adopted an army as your comrade in making this offensive, but it was an army of words that fought with rhetoric. In that section of your letter, as befitted a devoted brother, you employed rich and rather delightful sentiments and composed your words very melodiously. When I read the letter (for I could not be there in the senate on account of sickness), I imagined your brother backed into a corner by your eloquence. Thus, I began to address him in my mind with these words: 'How do you respond to this, Antoninus? For I think you must accept the title which you declined, and recant your previous position. Well now, what's the point of my letters, or those of the philosophers? We have been defeated by the letter of a soldier. Come, hasn't he written in a fine fashion? Did he use unsuitable or unusual language? Or do you think I have mentored a boastful soldier?* On the contrary, you have that which you sought with all your prayers: a bold brother, a good man accomplished in the arts of rhetoric. For he says the same things that you do, but does so more concisely.'

25. At the moment when I was thinking these things to myself, the speech of Antoninus followed yours, and good gods, how beautiful, true, and extensive it was! All his sentiments and words were truly captivating, imbued with fraternal affection, loyalty, love, and longing. How shall I decide between both of my protégés? Should I praise the petitioner or the petitioned more? Antoninus was compliant while holding the imperial power, but because of your love, it was you, Lucius, who acted like an emperor in your compliance. As I carried both these speeches, one in my right hand, the other in my left, I thought I was even more noble and dignified than the Eleusinian torchbearers* as they carry their brands, than kings wielding sceptres, and the members of the board of fifteen priests* unrolling their books. Thus I prayed to the gods of my homeland, 'Jupiter Ammon, from Libya (?) . . .'* *[The rest of the letter is lost.]*

Commentary

either neglect me, shun me, or show me no respect at all: Verus had recently apologised for his lack of correspondence with Fronto in the early years of the war (*Ad Verum Imp.* 1.1, VdH[2] pp. 107–8 = *Ad Verum Imp.* 2.2, Haines II, pp. 116–19).

But now it is my moment to triumph: This is the first of several military metaphors which Fronto employs throughout the letter.

under my generalship and auspices: Traditionally, Roman magistrates who possessed *imperium* (the power of command, especially in wartime) had their position confirmed by taking the auspices, which involved the interpretation of portents as a sign of divine validation.

their father was king: The passage has been seen as an attempt on Fronto's part to validate the Antonine practice of adopting successors (Fleury and Demougin 2003: 203). However, there was no real practice of choosing the best man for the throne, since both Hadrian and Antoninus Pius promoted men from within a close family group (Hekster 2002: 15–30). Instead, the remark reveals Fronto's true argument, that eloquence is innate and cannot be transferred. This sentiment is very similar to that expressed by Iulius Pollux in a letter he sent to Marcus' son, Commodus, when he dedicated his *Onomasticon* to the young prince *c.* 175. Pollux wrote that Commodus would inherit kingship and wisdom from his father, but that the *Onomasticon* would assist in endowing the prince with eloquence (1.1 = Trapp 2003: no. 59).

a veritable ruler: The Latin is *verus imperator*, clearly a pun on Verus' own name.

Armenia: Armenia was a kingdom in the Caucasus to the east of Cappadocia, forming a buffer between the Roman and Parthian empires. The Romans preferred to install a loyal client king on the Armenian throne rather than convert it into a province. Although Armenia did briefly become a province in the reign of Trajan, Hadrian rescinded this decision (Birley 1997a: 78–9).

that single speech given by your brother: The fact that Verus' letter was not only read to the senate, but also received with a speech given by Marcus, emphasises the collegiality of the imperial office.

Ventidius: In 39 BC, P. Ventidius Bassus was given a command against the Parthians, and won a series of victories that culminated in the defeat and death of Pacorus, the Parthian king. Ventidius had started his career procuring supplies for Julius Caesar's Gallic campaigns, which might explain the story that he could not write his own speeches.

before your own fathers: Pius wrote his own speeches, according to the *Historia Augusta* (*Pius* 11.3). It is somewhat surprising that Nerva is criticised in this same section, since Marcus Aurelius and Lucius Verus were described as his 'great-great-grandsons' (*abnepotes*) (*CIL* III 10632; *CIL* VIII 2348). But it does accord with Fronto's argument that eloquence cannot be inherited.

Julius Caesar: Caesar and Augustus fared rather well in the assessment of Suetonius (*Julius* 55.1; *Augustus* 86.1), who also reported that Tiberius spoke better when not giving a prepared speech (*Tiberius* 70.1).

compose an edict or a letter in their own words? The most famous example of an emperor relying on a speechwriter is Nero, whose speeches are said to have been written by Seneca (Dio 61.3.1; Tacitus, *Annals* 13.3, 14.11). Scholarly studies of the authorship and style of imperial constitutions have established that each emperor did have their own distinct style, at least in the second century (Williams 1976, 1979).

some composed by the generals themselves, others by historians or annalists: Fronto acknowledges that the letters which appear in historical works were not genuine historical documents. They served a similar function to speeches, which were designed to contribute to the characterisation of the speaker, develop a moral or didactic theme, or to demonstrate the rhetorical talents of the historian (Pelling 2000: 112–22; Trapp 2003: 1–4; Marincola 2007). Fronto cites four such letters composed by historians. The first is the letter of Nicias in Thucydides' *History of the Peloponnesian War* (7.11–15), in which he informs the Athenian people of the desperation of the situation in Sicily. The remaining three come from the works of Sallust, with the letters of Mithridates and Pompey appearing in the *Histories* (IV.67 and II.82, respectively), and that of Adherbal in the *Jugurthine War* (24).

Catulus: Q. Lutatius Catulus was victorious at the Battle of Vercellae in 101 BC, a success which he shared with Gaius Marius. Catulus tried to claim equal credit with Marius, and the two men shared a triumph (Plutarch, *Marius* 27).

***On his Policies*:** Cicero wrote the work *On his Policies* as a defence of his own career, especially the execution of the Catilinarian conspirators in 63 BC. He is said to have attacked both Crassus and Caesar in the work (Dio 39.10.2).

Titius Aristo: Aristo was a Roman jurist and contemporary of Pliny the Younger. His writings included the *Annotations.*

to expose and exacerbate those infamous happenings again: This passage seems to refer to criticisms levelled against Verus' conduct of the campaigns in the east (see the Introduction to this chapter).

given the kingdom of Armenia to Sohaemus: After the recapture of Armenia in 163, Verus successfully installed his own appointee, Sohaemus, on the throne (Birley 1993: 121–31). The achievement was commemorated on coins struck with the legend 'The king bestowed on the Armenians' (*REX ARMEN(IIS) DAT(US): BMCRE* IV 300–302).

Surely you do not want to detail such matters in a speech: Fronto makes the point that Verus does not need to defend himself against the accusations of 'making merry' in an official speech to the senate. Given Verus' reputation, they were probably at least partially true.

Numantine affair: Numantia was a settlement in northern Spain which resisted a series of sieges by the Romans, before it was finally captured by P. Cornelius Scipio Aemilianus in 133 BC. Scipio, like Verus, was forced to take over the command after the defeats of two previous commanders. The topic was covered in a biography of Scipio written by Cornelius Nepos.

many helpful examples of this kind: There was a whole range of manuals written for the edification of prospective generals. These handbooks featured *exempla* drawn from the lives and careers of great generals of the past, covering topics such as battlefield tactics, siege warfare, and military discipline (Campbell 1987). They did not, however, always offer good advice (Sallust, *Jugurthine War* 85.14).

Pontius Laelianus: The senator M. Pontius Laelianus Larcius Sabinus (*PIR*^{2} P 806) was an 'official companion' (*comes*) of Verus during the Parthian War, and earned several military decorations for his service. He would later accompany Marcus against the Marcomanni, and was honoured with a statue in the forum of Trajan in Rome for his long years of service (*CIL* VI 41146).

the severity of Hannibal: Fronto describes the depths to which the Roman army in Syria had sunk prior to the emperor's intervention, a standard *topos* that he also uses to praise the general Avidius Cassius in a later **Letter 48**.

Cato: M. Porcius Cato, first mentioned in **Letter 1**, was sent to Spain after his consulship in 195 BC to take command of the armies, winning a reputation for his strict discipline (Livy 34.8–18).

Even Viriathus, even Spartacus: Viriathus (sometimes called Viriatus) was a Lusitanian chieftain who held the Romans at bay in Spain between 147–139 BC, when he was murdered on the orders of the Roman general Q. Servilius Caepio. Spartacus was a Thracian gladiator who led a successful revolt against Rome in Italy in 73–71 BC. He was eventually defeated by M. Licinius Crassus. The pairing of these two characters recurs in **Letter 49**.

three hundred of the bravest soldiers from one clan of the Fabii: This is a reference to the Battle of the Cremera fought between Rome and Veii in 477 BC in which 306 members of the Fabii were allegedly killed. According to Livy (2.50), only one boy survived to carry on the family name.

you replied to the [king of the] Parthians: Verus had tried to conclude a peace with the Parthian monarch Vologaesus after his forces had captured Armenia, but he was rebuffed (**Letter 49**; *Pan. Lat.* IV(X).24.6–7).

Dausara, Nicephorium, and Artaxata: Artaxata was the capital of Armenia, captured in 163, while Dausara and Nicephorium were Parthian settlements on the Euphrates, which were seized in early 164 (Birley 1993: 130).

'Conqueror of the Armenians': After the conquest of Armenia, Verus received the triumphal *cognomen*, or surname, *Armeniacus* ('Conqueror of the Armenians'). This continued a Republican practice of bestowing the name of defeated peoples on victorious Roman generals. The last private citizen who received this honour was Lentulus Gaetulicus in 6 BC, after which such names were restricted to the emperors themselves (Campbell 1984: 122–33). Marcus initially refused the title of *Armeniacus*, but accepted it in a speech to the senate in 164 after receiving the letter from Verus (*HA Marcus* 9.1). After Verus' death in 169, he gave up this name, as well as the two other titles later gained by Verus: 'Conqueror of the Medes' (*Medicus*) and 'Conqueror of the Parthians' (*Parthicus*) (*HA Marcus* 12.9).

a boastful soldier? This is a clear reference to Plautus' play *The Boastful Soldier* (*Miles Gloriosus*). Fronto alludes to the play again in **Letter 48**.

Eleusinian torchbearers: The sanctuary at Eleusis, close to Athens, was sacred to the goddess Demeter. It was the home of the Eleusinian Mysteries, whose mysterious rites were revealed only to the initiates. The torchbearer (*dadouchos*) ranked second in the Eleusinian hierarchy, as he had the important task of leading the ceremonial procession.

members of the board of fifteen priests: The 'board of fifteen priests for conducting sacred rites' (*quindecimviri sacris faciundis*) were charged with oversight of the Sibylline Books. These books, written in Greek, allowed the priests to interpret signs and portents. All members were senators, and the board always included the reigning emperor.

'Jupiter Ammon, from Libya (?) . . .': Ammon, king of the Egyptian pantheon, was associated with Zeus (in Greece) and Jupiter (in Rome). It is one of several references in his letters to Fronto's African origin, but this does not speak to any particular 'African' identity: he regarded himself as Roman (Claassen 2009: 64–7).

Letter 47. Verus to Fronto (*c.* 165)

Ad Verum Imp. 1.2, VdH² pp. 108–9 = *Ad Verum Imp.* 2.3, Haines II, pp. 194–7.

[To my teacher]

1. *[The opening of the letter is lost.]* . . . they attached to their letters. You will learn about the events that occurred after I set out from the letters that were written to me by the generals* placed in charge of those affairs. Fulvianus – my very own Sallust* – will give you copies of these. And so you can discuss the reasons for my decisions, I'll send you my own letters, which explain why things were done in certain ways. If you want some paintings* as well, you can get these from Fulvianus. Moreover, so that you can understand events as if you were really there, I've instructed Avidius Cassius* and Martius Verus* to put together some memoranda, which I'll send to you. From these you'll be able to ascertain the character and thought processes of these men. But if you want me to compose such memoranda too, tell me what you want me to do, and I'll do what you wish. I'm prepared to go along with whatever you want, provided that my accomplishments are highlighted. Naturally, you will not overlook my reports sent to the senate and addresses to the army.* I'll send you transcripts of my negotiations with the Persians, as these will be of great benefit to you.

2. There is one thing that I, a mere student writing to his teacher, do not wish to mandate, but to offer for consideration:* you should spend quite a bit of time on the causes and opening stages of the war, and especially on the things that went badly before I arrived.* There's no need to rush to the part where I come in. Besides, I think that it is necessary to shed light on the fact that the Parthians were getting the better of us before my arrival, so that it becomes

clear how much I've accomplished. As to whether you ought to explain this by abridging everything in the manner of Thucydides' *Pentekontaetia*,* or whether you should spend a little more discussing things (though without going completely overboard), I'll leave it up to you to consider.

3. In short, my achievements, of whatever kind, are only as great as they actually are, but they can seem as great as you want them to seem.*

Commentary

the generals: M. Statius Priscus (*PIR*[2] S 880) was sent from his post as governor of Britain take control in the east (Birley 1997a: 126). His deputies included M. Claudius Fronto (*PIR*[2] C 874), legate of the Legion I Minervia, C. Avidius Cassius (*PIR*[2] A 1402), legate of the Legion III Gallica, and P. Martius Verus (*PIR*[2] M 348), legate of the Legion V Macedonica.

Fulvianus – my very own Sallust: Fulvianus, about whom nothing is else is known, must have accompanied Verus on his campaign with the intention of writing an account of the Parthian War in the manner of Sallust. He was hardly the first such 'court historian' of a military campaign, the most famous example being Callisthenes, who accompanied Alexander the Great. In the Roman world, Aulus Licinius Archias composed poems about Gaius Marius' wars against the Cimbri and Lucius Lucullus' campaign against Mithridates, and Pompey honoured Theophanes of Mytilene with Roman citizenship for writing histories chronicling his achievements (Cicero, *Pro Archia* 19, 21, 24).

paintings: Van den Hout (1999: 266) suggests that the Latin *picturas* should be translated as 'topographical maps'. Although the Roman army used and compiled itineraries, some of which had images, these were not maps in the modern sense (Mattern 1999b: 26–9, 41–4). It is more likely that Verus is referring to actual paintings, as there is rich evidence for a tradition of representing battles and conflicts in the Hellenistic and Roman world (Hölscher 2004: 23–46). For example, L. Hostilius Mancinus commissioned paintings of the capture of Carthage to help his consular bid (Pliny, *Natural*

History 35.23), while the emperor Maximinus ordered paintings of his battle against the Germans be erected in front of the senate house (Herodian 7.2.8).

Avidius Cassius: See *Dramatis Personae* at p. 16 and **Letter 48**.

Martius Verus: P. Martius Verus was legate of the Legion V Macedonica. He was praised in the Suda (= Dio 71.3.1[1]) for his strategic and diplomatic talents. After the war, he became suffect consul in 166 and governor of Cappadocia, *c.* 172–175. Martius Verus remained loyal to the emperor during the rebellion of Avidius Cassius and replaced Cassius in Syria after his defeat.

my reports sent to the senate and addresses to the army: Speeches were an integral part of any ancient historical work, as they added drama and a sense of immediacy to the narrative (Marincola 2007). Perhaps even more importantly, they allowed the historian to display their own rhetorical talents, a task to which Fronto would have been well suited. Presumably, Verus intended to provide Fronto with copies or summaries of his formal addresses to the army (*adlocutiones*). Battle speeches were also common in war histories, although their historicity is debatable (Hansen 1993; Zoido 2007).

but to offer for consideration: Cicero (*Ad Fam.* 5.12) wrote to the historian Lucius Lucceius to offer advice about the part he should play in his account of the Italian and Civil Wars. Cicero even suggested to Lucceius that he might compose a monograph on his own life from the conspiracy of Catiline in 63 BC to his return from exile in 57 BC. Likewise, Pliny the Younger (*Letters* 7.33) confessed to Tacitus that he was anxious to appear in his *Histories*, and wrote a description of a minor incident in the senate in which he was involved so that it could be included. He also famously sent Tacitus an account of the eruption of Vesuvius (*Letters* 6.16). Verus' remarks here are therefore not without parallel, though they have added force coming from an emperor.

the things that went badly before I arrived: This is a clear reference to the deaths of Severianus and Cornelianus (see the Introduction to this chapter).

Thucydides' *Pentekontaetia*: Book One of Thucydides' *History* of the Peloponnesian War features an account of the 'Fifty-Year Period' (*pentekontaetia*) between the end of the Persian War in 479 BC and the outbreak of hostilities between Athens and Sparta in 431 BC (1.89–118).

as great as you want them to seem: The satirical writer Lucian penned a work called *How to Write History* in reaction to the vast number of substandard histories of the Parthian War. He claimed that he heard these histories being recited during his visits to Asia Minor and Greece. Since *How to Write History* was written in the middle of 166, before Lucius Verus' triumph in Rome, there must have been a significant outpouring of literary effort devoted to the war, even allowing for some satirical exaggeration on Lucian's part (Jones 1986: 59–60; Kemezis 2010: 288–90). One of Lucian's particular complaints was that many of the histories sounded more like panegyrics (*How to Write History* 7).

Letter 48. Fronto to Avidius Cassius (166)

Ad Amicos 1.6, VdH[2] pp. 175–6 = Haines II, pp. 190–3.

Fronto sends greetings to Avidius Cassius,

The tribune Iunius Maximus,* who carried the letters decorated with laurel* to Rome, not only attentively performed his public duty, but also his private obligation towards you, as a friend should. He could always be found in the busiest public places crowing about your exertions, strategies, enthusiasm, and vigilance. He came to see me in my villa on the outskirts of the city when I was not in the best of health, and did not stop telling tales until the evening about your expeditions and the discipline that you established* and restored to the standards of old. Then he spoke about your tireless vigour while leading the army, and your ability to seize the moment when engaged in close combat.* Certainly, no Plautine soldier* declaimed as boastfully about his own talents as Maximus spoke about yours. But while Plautus wrote about his soldier in a satirical fashion, Maximus spoke of you with love and true loyalty. He is worthy of your esteem, and you should distinguish him with your support.* Your efforts to increase his public standing will only serve to enhance your own glory.

Commentary

Iunius Maximus: Iunius Maximus served as *tribunus* (junior officer) of the Legion III Gallica under Avidius Cassius, and received military decorations (*AE* 1979: 601; Alföldy and Halfmann 1979). Maximus is known to have received two letters from Fronto (*Ad Amicos* 1.23, VdH[2] p. 185, no longer extant; *Ad Amicos* 1.26, VdH[2] p. 185 = Haines II, p. 245, of which only a few lines remain).

letters decorated with laurel: Laurel leaves were regarded as a symbol of triumph, according to Pliny the Elder (*Natural History* 15.133), and were used to decorate dispatches sent to Rome announcing a victory. When Maximus brought the letters to the senate, he was promoted to the post of quaestor to read them out (*AE* 1979: 601).

the discipline that you established: It was customary to praise Roman generals for restoring discipline to lax units. The Syrian legions were often criticised as they allegedly preferred luxury and decadence to the rigours of military life. This *topos* can be found in authors such as Livy, Sallust, and Tacitus (Wheeler 1996). The author of the *Historia Augusta* seized upon the notion of Cassius as a stern disciplinarian in his largely fictional biography of the general.

your ability to seize the moment when engaged in close combat: The portrait of Avidius Cassius as a successful general is supported by the account of the Byzantine writer Xiphilinus (= Dio 71.2.1–4). Little is known of his exploits in battle, however, apart from a brief mention in the Suda (= Dio 71.3.1) of him directing missiles against the enemy.

Plautine soldier: Fronto compares Maximus with Pyrgopolynices, the title character in Plautus' *The Boastful Soldier*, as a way of demonstrating the extent of the young man's enthusiasm for Cassius (van den Hout 1999: 409–10, cf. Whitehorne 1977a).

distinguish him with your support: The Latin word *suffragium*, translated here as 'support', originally meant 'vote' or 'voting', but came to refer to the type of support provided by patrons for their clients (Ste Croix 1954). Like Fronto, Pliny the Younger (*Letters* 2.1.8) used the verb *ornare*, which means 'to distinguish' or 'to embellish', to refer to the bestowal of such support. As the governor of Syria, Cassius was one of the most prominent senators in the empire, and in a prime position to assist Maximus.

Letter 49. Fronto to Marcus (166)

Principia Historiae, VdH² pp. 202–14 = Haines II, pp. 198–219.

[Fronto to my lord Antoninus Augustus]

[Over fifty lines at the beginning of the letter are unreadable.]

1. . . . a history written responsibly and with forethought would bring a certain level of attention and fame to the great accomplishments of your brother, just as a light gust of air still helps to fan a fire, regardless of how large it already is.

2. As soon as your brother sends me his memoranda of his achievements, we will start to write, so long as this treatment, sent as a sample, does not displease you . . . *[Some thirty illegible lines.]* . . . we approach these deeds, which Achilles wishes he could have accomplished, and Homer* wishes he had written . . . *[Over ten unreadable lines.]*

3. What should I add? [*The first half of the chapter is fragmentary, though there is a reference to 'the unbridled morals of Antioch'.*] . . . the series of defeats before the Taurus mountains* [were retold] after the disasters through alluring tales. Indeed the abundant talents of these men would have been exercised in vain, if they had not occupied themselves with writing of great deeds. The same would also be true if the talents of the writers did not match – or at least adapt themselves to – the greatness of the accomplishments. And the poems of

Homer would be ruined if they lacked battles, which is apparent in the second book, but which he made known even in the very first lines of book one. Certainly Xenophon the Athenian,* a worthy guardian of Greek knowledge, voluntarily served under Cyrus ... *[Two lines missing.]* ... and the labours of Hercules were famous, if not for the facts themselves, then for their lessons.

4. *[This section is lacunose, so we include only a few lines.]* ... for indeed, Porcius Cato the censor, praised by far the most among all men for his oratorical ability and leadership ...

5. *[The fragmentary section 5 includes brief references to the defeat of Crassus at Carrhae and Alexander the Great.]*

A note in the margin of the manuscript: ... the empire of the Roman people was extended by the emperor Trajan across hostile rivers.*

6. *[Over fifty lines at the beginning of this section are lost.]* ... those nations, which caused defeats by their acts of plundering and pillaging, I regard as brigands, rather than enemies. It is the Parthians, unique among the races of men, who bear the title of the enemy who must never be underestimated. That is sufficiently demonstrated, not only by the defeat of Crassus and the reprehensible retreat of Antonius,* but even by the massacre of a legionary commander* with his army, under the overall command of Trajan, the mightiest emperor, and the retreat – hardly easy or free from bloodshed – of that prince as he was departing for his triumph.

7. Therefore, I will proceed to make a comparison between the two greatest wars* that were waged against the Parthians within living memory, wars conducted with equal success by the two greatest emperors. I will do this by focusing on the circumstances of each emperor and his situation. This will be done in full knowledge of the fact that the fearsome feats of living men are treated quite critically, while those of the dead are treated more generously; past events are looked on with favour, those of the present with hostility. For jealousy always ... *[The second half of this section is illegible.]*

8. As soon as the Roman state called for a great general, who would be worthy of the weighty responsibilities, one man stood out who was more suited for war than all those who came from poverty in Arpinum or the harsh environment of Nursia ...* *[The rest of this chapter is illegible, and then there are sixteen lost pages.]*

10. *[Section 9 and the beginning of 10 are very fragmentary.]* ... he embarked on the war with veteran soldiers who despised the Parthian enemy.* They

regarded the sting of their arrows with contempt, compared with the sizeable wounds inflicted by the curved swords of the Dacians.* The emperor used to call many of his soldiers by their own name* and the humorous nicknames given by their camp-mates. He promoted a great number* to the rank of centurion or *cornicularius* or gave them double pay, while others received positions as centurion *pilus, princeps*, or *hastatus* ... *[The next five lines are missing or fragmentary.]*

11. For the Parthian War, Lucius had either new recruits* chosen by a levy or those men who had been broken in by harsh years of required enlistment, since the general soldiery had been corrupted by their sorrowful and lax service conditions.* For after the reign of Trajan, the soldiers were almost entirely lacking in discipline, and when Hadrian was emperor, he travelled around and spoke eloquently to the armies* in an active enough fashion, but avoided wars as much as possible. Indeed, he preferred to relinquish, rather than hold with a garrison, the provinces which Trajan had seized with his own hand,* of which the Dacian (?) regions were not yet pacified.* One can see the monuments of his journeys located in a large number of cities in both Asia and Europe, and his tombs that were constructed from stone,* along with many others. He journeyed not only into frosty lands, but also into other lands in southern locations, in order to safeguard the provinces which, lying across the rivers of the Euphrates and the Danube, Trajan had annexed to the Roman empire ... *[A word is missing.]* ... with the hope of adding them to the provinces of Moesia and Asia. He [Hadrian], in contrast, gave back these provinces (Dacia, and the regions lost by the Parthians) in their entirety.* The army in Asia used to entertain itself by engaging in banter in their tents rather than with shields and swords:* the army never saw another general of this ilk.

12. Aurelius Antoninus,* the sacred emperor, is said to have restrained himself by shunning the need for bloodshed, and he alone of all Roman emperors was the equal of king Numa ... *[A word or two missing.]* ... for after Hadrian similar tasks and the state were to be administered by him ... *[The end of this line and the beginning of the next are indecipherable.]* ... nor was there anyone in favour of renewing war against the Parthians,* and thus the Roman soldiery was reduced to idleness from a long period without experience of warfare. For sloth is damaging to all of life's practical skills, and to military

training above all. It is of the utmost importance for soldiers to endure the vagaries of fortune and to train vigorously in camp.

13. The soldiers stationed in Syria were truly the most corrupted of all, being prone to mutiny, obstinate, rarely reporting for duty, wandering in front of their camp stations, roaming about like scouts, intoxicated from noon until the next day. They were not even used to putting on their armour, but since they could not invest the necessary effort, they laid down their arms one after another so that they were half-naked just like light-armed soldiers and slingers. In addition to this sort of disgrace, they were so disheartened by poorly-fought battles that they turned their backs as soon as they caught sight of the Parthians, and interpreted the sounds of trumpets as if they were giving the signal for retreat.

14. Lucius checked this great decline in military discipline as the circumstances demanded, and he served as an example of how to act like a soldier* through his own zeal. Positioning himself at the head of the column, he usually exercised himself by walking on foot rather than being carried on horseback. He endured the blazing sun just as easily as a clear sky, and he suffered a thick dust cloud as if it was merely fog. He did not worry about sweating in his armour, acting like he was just engaging in sport. He kept his head uncovered in the sun, pouring rain, hail, and snow, or in the face of weapons. He devoted himself to examining the soldiers in camp and doing the rounds of the sick. He paid close attention when he visited the soldiers' quarters, but casually observed the effeminate behaviour of the Syrians and the doltishness of the Pannonians, working out the natural character of each of the men from their habits.

After his daily duties were completed, he took a bath in the evening, and then, at a modest table, he enjoyed the common soldiers' fare in the camp, drinking the local wine and the water that was to hand. He took the first watch without complaint, and was already up and at the ready for a long time before the last one came about. He enjoyed working more than his leisure time, and spent his leisure time engaged in work. When he had time free from military duties, he devoted it to administrative tasks. When there was a period of rationing, he sometimes simply used twigs and leaves as his bedding, occasionally lying down on the ground as if it were a bed. He took his rest when he had earned it through hard work, rather than seeking a time for rest.

He enforced severe punishments only for truly serious wrongdoings, and pretended not to know about the more trivial ones, giving the men an opportunity to show contrition. For many men correct their own transgressions when they think no one knows about them, but when they realise they have become public knowledge, they are only confirmed in their shamelessness.

15. *[This section is almost non-existent, with over thirty unreadable lines. Only part of one sentence in the middle can be translated.]* ... through countless provinces, the manifest dangers of innumerable sieges, battles, and destruction of citadels, armed posts, and strongholds, he offered them his concern and his counsel,* not luxuries ...

16. *[The first two lines are missing.]* ... Lucius, in the ingenuity of his plans, was far the superior of Trajan ... *Most of the rest of the section is illegible, though there are two interesting notes in the margin of the manuscript:* (i) he knew that the mailed cavalry were just like beasts of the sea,* somersaulting as they leap from the high sea, as they prance along the great open plains; (ii) horses are unstable on the slippery ground, their hands are useless due to the cold, their bows weakened by the rain. *[After twenty missing lines, we return to the end of the section.]* ... a few days beforehand [Lucius] had sent a letter to Vologaesus* of his own initiative, stating that he could settle the war by a treaty, if he wished. Since the barbarian spurned the peace that had been offered, he suffered a serious injury.

17. This action clearly shows how much deep-seated concern Lucius had for the safety of his soldiers,* since he was a man who preferred to obtain a bloodless peace at the cost of his own glory. Many people have surmised that Trajan would have rated his own glory more highly than the blood of his soldiers based on his other actions, for it is said that he often dismissed the ambassadors of the Parthians who had pleaded in vain for peace.

18. Lucius had an unblemished reputation for justice and clemency* among the barbarians; Trajan was not as blameless in everyone's eyes. No one regretted entrusting his kingdom or fortunes to Lucius' trust, but one cannot excuse Trajan in the same way for his slaughter of king Parthamasirus* when he offered himself as a suppliant. Although the king himself was responsible for initiating the violence, when the struggle began, he was justly killed. However, it would have been better for Rome's reputation if a suppliant had departed unharmed, rather than suffer such a punishment. For, as happens in matters

such as these, the reason for the act lies hidden, while the act itself is seen by all. Therefore, it is much better to disregard the affront and have people speak of you favourably, than to seek vengeance and suffer negative reports.

19. In each of the Parthian wars a man of consular rank was cut down while in command of armies. Severianus* was killed when Lucius had not yet even made his departure from Rome. But Appius Santra* was killed by Arbaces* while returning to Balcia in the Taurus mountains, and when Trajan himself was present, revising the toll charges for horses and camels* on the Euphrates and Tigris rivers.

20. *[The first two lines of this section are fragmentary.]* . . . a pantomime came from Rome to Syria.* But indeed, just as the very highest trees are shaken rather violently by squalls, spite attacks the greatest virtues in a very accusatory manner. I think it is uncertain whether the emperor Trajan should be regarded more brilliant in military affairs or peacetime government, except that even Spartacus and Viriathus* had considerable skill in warfare, but as far as the arts of peace are concerned, there is scarcely anyone more acceptable to the people than Trajan,* and there is perhaps no one to equal him in this regard. It was these topics, along with some aspects of his life as a private citizen, which were stirred up by his critics.* These charges seem to have emerged from the chief principle of political philosophy: the emperor did not neglect pantomimes and other shows on the stage, circus, or amphitheatre,* as he knew that the Roman people were principally controlled by two things – grain hand-outs and spectacles.*

The people's acceptance of imperial rule thus depended on these frivolities just as much as on serious matters of state: although disregard for important matters could result in great harm, overlooking the people's pleasures would result in rather serious discontent. Cash hand-outs are less effective incentives than public shows, for they only expressly placate individual plebeians eligible for the grain dole,* whereas shows are enjoyed by everyone at once . . .* *[The next four lines are fragmentary and difficult to read.]* . . . or are placated [less] by purifying sacrifices than by games and the rites of public shows. In this matter, the processions, ornamental carriages, the chariots of the gods* with their trappings dedicated by our ancestors, and even elephants (who appeared in peacetime even though the Roman people never used them during their battles) were employed in night-time spectacles . . .* *[The next line is* *fragmentary.]* ... these things are recorded by me for the purpose of rebutting slander.

21. *[The opening line is fragmentary.]* ... but Lucius himself, wherever he had accomplished something, wrote letters to senators,* which were composed in an elegant fashion to shed light on the state of affairs, as he was the sort of man who possessed a great enthusiasm for restoring eloquence.... *[Some fifty lines are lost here.]* ... as for the question of whether the great-grandfather or the great-grandson should be regarded as the more outstanding in virtue,* the outcome is only really of concern to the imperial house.

Commentary

Outline

This is a long letter, so for ease of reference we provide the following outline of the parts translated here:

1–2	Fronto outlines his reasons for writing
3–4	Warfare and history
5–6	Rome's relationship with the Parthian empire
7	Fronto outlines his intention to compare the Parthian wars of Trajan and Verus
8–10	Trajan and his well-disciplined soldiers
11	The decline of the army under Hadrian
12	Hiatus in warfare under Antoninus Pius
13	Corruption and laxity of the Syrian legions
14	Verus' efforts to restore discipline to the Syrian legions
15	Fragments about warfare
16–17	Verus' superiority to Trajan; his attempts to make peace with Parthia
18	Verus' clemency compared with Trajan
19	The death of a leading senator in each war
20	Trajan and public entertainment: pantomimes, bread, and circuses
21	Verus' eloquence; conclusion

Homer: Fronto writes of the epic qualities of Verus' achievements, and then in a statement of false modesty, wonders whether he is equal to the task of committing them to paper. Fronto's remark shows the debt owed by ancient historiography to epic poetry (on which see Funke 2011; Rutherford 2012). The sentiment was a commonplace one: Alexander the Great is said to have exclaimed at Achilles' tomb how fortunate the young warrior had been to have Homer as the herald of his glory (Cicero, *Pro Archia* 24). The historian Arrian would later lament at the beginning of his *Anabasis* (1.12) that Alexander himself had no 'Homer' to record his exploits.

Taurus mountains: The Taurus mountains lie in southern Turkey. The reference is to a number of calamities which befell Roman troops in Syria, discussed in more detail in section 6.

Xenophon the Athenian: Xenophon was one of the most significant Greek historians and philosophers of the Hellenistic period. In 401 BC, he served as a mercenary in the army of Cyrus the Younger, pretender to the Persian throne, until Cyrus' death at the Battle of Cunaxa. He subsequently led the remaining Greek mercenaries out of Persia, a journey recorded in his *Anabasis.*

extended by the emperor Trajan across hostile rivers: This is a marginal note, added by a second hand in the manuscript. It refers to Trajan's short-lived annexation of Parthian territory across the Tigris and the Euphrates, which was subsequently relinquished by Hadrian.

the defeat of Crassus and the reprehensible retreat of Antonius: M. Licinius Crassus, a member of the so-called 'first triumvirate' along with Pompey and Caesar, was killed after being defeated by the Parthians near Carrhae in 53 BC (Plutarch, *Crassus* 31). Less than twenty years later, M. Antonius renewed war against the Parthians in 36 BC, but was defeated and had to retreat in disgrace through Armenia (Plutarch, *Antony* 37–50).

a legionary commander: This is Maximus, who was killed while trying to restore order in the provinces conquered by Trajan (Dio 68.30.1–2). He may be identical with Appius Santra, a former consul whom Fronto mentions in section 19 as being killed during Trajan's reign.

a comparison between the two greatest wars: Trajan's successes in wars in Dacia and Parthia, not to mention his public image as a benefactor of the people, meant that he had quickly become the standard by which other emperors would be judged (Bennett 1997: 205–13). The historian Arrian wrote a *Parthica* in seventeen books, ten of which focused on Trajan's war (Stadter 1980: 135–44). In the fourth century, it would be Trajan's war that was remembered as a success worthy of Alexander the Great, despite the fact that the campaign was costly and only achieved short-term success (Lightfoot 1990).

poverty in Arpinum or the harsh environment of Nursia: The Republican general C. Marius, victor against the Germans and famously seven times consul, was born near Arpinum (Plutarch, *Marius* 3). Nursia was the birthplace of Q. Sertorius (Plutarch, *Sertorius* 2), another excellent military leader, who held the Spanish provinces against Sulla's supporters in the 70s BC. Despite Fronto's implications about humble and rustic origins, both men came from families of equestrian status.

veteran soldiers who despised the Parthian enemy: Fronto outlines the superior capabilities of Trajan's soldiers, owing to their experience in the emperor's Dacian wars.

the curved swords of the Dacians: These swords (the Latin word is *falx* sing., *falces* pl.) are clearly shown on Trajan's Column in Rome and the *Tropaeum Trajani* in Adamklissi. They have a wooden handle, with a long blade curved at the top, and need to be held in two hands (Sim 2000).

their own name: This is a common *topos* of a good commander in historical works (e.g. Sallust, *War of Catiline* 59), and was specifically attributed to Trajan by Pliny in his *Panegyricus* (15.5).

He promoted a great number: Fronto lists various ranks in the Roman army. The centurion commanded eighty men: there were six such centuries in the cohort of the imperial army (apart from the first, which had five). The senior centurion in each cohort was the *pilus prior*, and beneath him came the *princeps prior, hastatus prior, pilus posterior, princeps posterior, hastatus posterior.* The titles are based on the old Republican divisions of the cohort (Southern 2006: 332–3). The post of *cornicularius* ranked below that of centurion, and was primarily an administrative position, which came with double pay (Breeze 1974).

new recruits: No new legions were actually raised for this war; instead, reinforcements were sent from the Rhine and Danube frontiers (Birley 1993: 123).

general soldiery had been corrupted by their sorrowful and lax service conditions: It is ironic that Fronto goes on to lament the decline in the Roman army under Hadrian in particular: the author of the *Historia Augusta (Hadrian* 10.3) praises Hadrian for his efforts in restoring army discipline for the first time since Augustus. This only goes to show the extent to which this was a *topos*, and provides little historical insight into the reign of either Verus or Hadrian.

spoke eloquently to the armies: Cassius Dio (69.9.1–6) records, in a much more complimentary fashion, Hadrian's inspections of the garrisons of the empire, his addresses to the troops, and his training of the men, as does the *Historia Augusta (Hadrian* 10.1–11.2). Records survive of Hadrian's addresses to the Legion III Augusta and several auxiliary units in Numidia, which were inscribed on the base of a column at the legionary headquarters at Lambaesis (Birley 1997a: 210–13).

the provinces which Trajan had seized with his own hand: This criticism of Hadrian is hardly fair, since he had but little choice to withdraw from the provinces across the Euphrates, which had been consumed by revolts even while Trajan was still alive (Dio 68.29.3–30.2; Birley 1997a: 78).

the Dacian (?) regions were not yet pacified: The manuscript is very corrupt at this point, leading van den Hout to conjecture that the uncertain word should be 'Dacian'. This is plausible: although the province of Dacia itself continued to exist, some of the new territory added to Moesia Inferior by Trajan after the first Dacian War was given back to the Sarmatians (Birley 1997a: 84–5).

his tombs which were constructed from stone: This is a reference, first and foremost, to the magnificent mausoleum which Hadrian began for himself on the left bank of the Tiber in Rome, and which was completed by Antoninus Pius (Davies 2004: 34–40). His favourite Antinoüs was probably buried at Hadrian's villa at Tivoli (Opper 2008: 181). Hadrian erected a tomb for his horse Borysthenes at Apte in Gallia Narbonensis (Dio 69.10.2; *HA Hadrian* 20.12; *CIL* XII 1122), and rebuilt the tomb of Pompey the Great at Pelusium in Egypt (Dio 69.11.1; *HA Hadrian* 14.4).

He [Hadrian], in contrast, gave back these provinces (Dacia, and the regions lost by the Parthians) in their entirety: The subject of the sentence has been the focus of scholarly debate. Although van den Hout (1999: 474) argues that 'he' refers to Trajan, we think that Fronto is actually talking about Hadrian. In order to support this interpretation, we need to engage in a more technical discussion of the Latin than usual (this is indebted to comments provided by an anonymous referee for the press).

If we look at section 11 as a whole, Fronto begins by referring to the sad state in which Lucius Verus found the soldiery, which he attributes to the period after Trajan (*post imperatorem Traianum*), i.e., the reign of his successor, Hadrian. Fronto proceeds to discuss Hadrian's travels around the empire, and describes his actions in the perfect tense (e.g. *omittere maluit*, 'he preferred to relinquish'). We then reach the difficult passage at the end of this section, which we give in Latin and in English translation:

> *non solum in gelosas, sed etiam bis in meridionalis sedis terras* ***profectus est*** *saluti his provinciis, quas trans Euphratis et Danuvii ripas sitas Traianus spe Moesiae et Asiae provincias addere ... e.. imperio Romano* ***adnexuerat****. has omnino provincias, Daciam et Parthis omissas partes, ultro* ***restituit****. exercitus in Asia se pro scutis atque gladiis salibus sub pellibus* ***delectare****: neminem umquam ducem post eiusmodi vidit.*

> He [Hadrian] **journeyed** not only into frosty lands, but also into other lands in southern locations, in order to safeguard the provinces which, lying across the rivers of the Euphrates and the Danube, Trajan **had annexed** to the Roman empire . . . *[A word is missing.]* . . . with the hope of adding them to the provinces of Moesia and Asia. He [Hadrian], in contrast, **gave back** these provinces (Dacia, and the regions lost by the Parthians) in their entirety. The army in Asia **used to entertain** itself by engaging in banter in their tents rather than with shields and swords: the army never saw another general of this ilk.

The subject of the perfect tense verb *profectus est* ('he journeyed') is Hadrian, as Fronto is still describing his travels. When Fronto refers to the regions that Trajan 'had annexed' to the empire, he uses the pluperfect tense of the verb *adnexuerat*, which places Trajan's actions further back in time than those of Hadrian. We then reach the crucial sentence in which the subject is left unstated, but the perfect tense of the verb *restituit* ('he gave back') indicates that Fronto is referring to Hadrian again, rather than Trajan. The verb *restituo, restituere* can be used, as here, in the sense 'to give back' something that has been lost or captured (*OLD* s.v. *restituo* 8). Fronto uses the adverb *ultro*, which means 'at the opposite end of the scale, conversely' (*OLD* s.v. *ultro* 4), to contrast Hadrian's actions with those of his predecessor. In the next line, Fronto changes the subject to *exercitus* ('the army'), and employs the historic present infinitive *delectare*. The historic present is best interpreted as an imperfect, hence our translation, 'the army . . . used to entertain itself'. This implies Fronto is once again discussing events under Hadrian, rather than the more distant reign of Trajan. It is clear that Fronto is moving through history chronologically, covering the army under Trajan in sections 8–10 and Hadrian in section 11, before moving to Antoninus Pius in section 12.

The army in Asia used to entertain itself by engaging in banter in their tents rather than with shields and swords: The manuscript reads *salibus*, 'with jokes, witticisms' (*OLD* s.v. *sal* 6b), which we have translated more colloquially as 'engaging in banter'. Davies (1968) proposed that the text should be amended to read *salicibus* ('willows'), which would refer to the wooden practice swords used by the Roman army. He translated the line as follows: 'The army in the East amused itself under canvas with practice weapons instead of real swords and shields.' The emendation is enticing, but unnecessary; either way, the reference is clearly to the decline in conditions in the reign of Hadrian (Holford-Strevens 2000: 462). Van den Hout (1999: 474–5) interprets the line as a reference to Trajan, whose troops 'cracked jokes instead of loitering about and drinking like Verus' soldiers'. He also believes that the final remark, 'the army never saw another general of this ilk', is a positive assessment of Trajan's military prowess. However, as we argued above, the final lines of section 11 still refer to Hadrian, rather than Trajan, so Fronto's tone is obviously sarcastic. This accords well with his remarks about Hadrian elsewhere in the correspondence (**Letter 12**).

Antoninus: Although Fronto had no hesitation in criticising Hadrian, Antoninus Pius is a different matter. He therefore praises Pius for not shedding blood by engaging warfare, much like Numa. It is striking that the *Historia Augusta (Pius* 13.4) makes a very similar statement at the end of its biography of Pius, and comparisons to Numa can be found in Eutropius (8.8) and the *Epitome concerning the Caesars* (15.2–3). These could derive from Fronto's speeches in honour of Pius (Champlin 1980: 84–6; **Letter 14**).

anyone in favour of the renewal of war against the Parthians: The text of the preceding section is very corrupt, and thus the interpretation of this sentence is uncertain. But Fronto appears to be absolving Antoninus Pius of personal responsibility for the declining standards of the army by stating that public opinion was not in favour of war.

how to act like a soldier: This passage is full of historical commonplaces, found in authors such as Livy and Tacitus (van den Hout 1999: 477). For example, Tacitus (*Histories* 2.5) praises Vespasian for marching at the head of his forces, eating whatever was at hand, and acting like a common soldier. It is particularly ironic that Hadrian – whom Fronto contrasts unfavourably with Verus – is also praised by other authors for similar actions, such as enduring climatic changes with a bare head and for visiting sick soldiers in camp (Dio 69.9.2, 4; *HA Hadrian* 10.6, 23.1).

he offered them his concern and his counsel: Van den Hout (1999: 479) thinks this refers to Trajan, rather than Verus, but this is uncertain, given how fragmentary the text is.

the mailed cavalry were just like beasts of the sea: The Latin term used by Fronto for 'mailed cavalry', *catafracti*, is a transliteration of the Greek word κατάφρακτοι, from the verb καταφράσσω, 'to protect'. The first clear evidence for the use of *catafracti* in the Roman empire comes from an *ala catafractata* ('mailed cavalry unit') in the reign of Hadrian (*CIL* XI 5632 = ILS 2735), but the horses themselves do not seem to have been coated in armour. The *catafractarii clibanarii* – mailed cavalry with armoured horses – were not introduced into the Roman army until the third century (Eadie 1967; Speidel 1984). Here, Fronto is referring to the mailed cavalry belonging to the Parthian forces, and Verus' knowledge of them (see below).

. . . a few days beforehand Lucius had sent a letter to Vologaesus: The panegyric of Constantine delivered by the orator Nazarius in 321 sheds some light on this fragmentary section. The relevant passage is as follows:

> When Antoninus, an outstanding emperor in peacetime and not without energy and capacity in war, made trial of the Parthians in combat, after he had seen their men clad in mail he lapsed so completely into fear that on his own he sent the King a letter promoting peace. And when the overly proud king had spurned it, the barbarian's insolence was vanquished indeed, but it was made clear that there was so much potential power in that type of armour that he who was to be overcome felt confident and he who was to conquer was afraid. (*Pan. Lat.* IV (X).24.6–7, trans. Nixon and Rodgers 1994: 369).

Putting the mistaken reference to 'Antoninus' (meaning Marcus Aurelius) to one side, Nazarius is clearly referring to this very passage (van den Hout 1999: 608). The detail that Vologaesus rejected the peace offering, but then paid the price, is identical in both authors. Nazarius would have been able to read Fronto's letter in full, and his discussion shows that the strength of the Parthian forces, particularly their mailed cavalry, was connected to Verus' decision to sue for peace. This probably occurred in 163 after the capture of Armenia (Birley 1993: 130).

the safety of his soldiers: Many a Roman general had made the claim that the safety of their soldiers was their primary concern (e.g. Caesar, *Civil Wars* 3.90).

Fronto explains Verus' attempt to make peace not as a sign of weakness, but as a desire to protect his soldiers from being slaughtered by the mailed cavalry, whose armour was superior to that of the Roman forces (Bivar 1972: 277–8). Although this statement is designed to introduce another point of comparison with Trajan, Fronto was not alone in thinking that Trajan's Parthian War was motivated by a desire for glory (Dio 68.17.1; *Epitome concerning the Caesars* 48.10; cf. Eutropius 8.2–5; Victor, *On the Caesars* 13, who are more flattering). Dio, in particular, supports Fronto's claim that Trajan dismissed the Parthian ambassadors (68.17–18).

justice and clemency: Justice (*iustitia*) and clemency (*clementia*) were two virtues which formed part of the ethical profile of a good Roman emperor. The expression of these virtues towards barbarians can be found in monumental form on the so-called 'Panel Reliefs of Marcus Aurelius', which originally formed part of an arch (or arches) erected in honour of the emperor (Kleiner 1992: 288–95).

Parthamasirus: The Parthian king Osroes installed Parthamasirus on the Armenian throne in 113. The following year, Trajan agreed to receive Parthamasirus in person, and the Armenian king removed his diadem before the emperor, expecting to receive it back and have his throne officially confirmed. Trajan would not agree to this, stating that Armenia would henceforth be a Roman province. He ordered a unit of cavalry to escort the king away (Dio 68.17.1–20.4). Other sources confirm Fronto's statement that Parthamasirus was killed on Trajan's orders (Arrian, *Parthica* fr. 40; Eutropius 8.3).

Severianus: Fronto attempts to draw a parallel between the death of Sedatius Severianus and that of Trajan's legate, by stating that he was slain by the Parthians (see also *HA Verus* 6.9; Xiphilinus = Dio 71.2.1). However, Lucian (*How to Write History* 21) records that Severianus committed suicide after a three-day siege, censuring those historians who claimed that he starved himself to death.

Appius Santra: Dio (68.30.1) refers to a Maximus who was killed in battle when he was sent by Trajan to quell revolts in the Parthian regions. Maximus is usually identified with this Appius Santra (*PIR*[2] A 950), although the reading of Santra in the manuscript is uncertain. On the other hand, it has been been suggested that Dio's Maximus should be identified with T. Iulius Maximus, suffect consul in 112 (*PIR*[2] I 426; Bennett 1997: 200).

Arbaces: The identity of 'Arbaces' is uncertain. Potter (1979) proposed that the text should be read as 'Abgar', king of Edessa in the Trajanic period, though Gerhardt and Hartmann (2000: 135–40) have identified him with the Parthian general Arsaces, who appears in the *Chronicle of Arbela*. The location of Appius' death is also problematic, with the Latin term *ad Balcia Tauri* best interpreted as a place near Armenia (Gerhardt and Hartmann 2000: 131).

toll charges for horses and camels: Tolls (*portoria*) were levied at the border of the Roman empire, and at specific regional boundaries within the empire, such as Gaul, Illyricum, and Asia. Merchants who did not declare the goods they intended to sell in an attempt to evade the penalty risked having them confiscated. Two inscriptions dating to the late second century attest to a particularly high toll of 25 per cent exacted on Rome's eastern border (*AE* 1947: 179–80).

a pantomime came from Rome to Syria: The *Historia Augusta (Verus* 8.7, 10–11) refers to pantomimes which Verus brought from Syria to Rome, rather than vice versa. These included a certain Agrippus, who was called Apolaustus Memphius after gaining his freedom. A fragmentary letter from Verus to Fronto, usually dated prior to the Parthian War, also refers to a pantomime called Apolaustus (*Ad Verum Imp.* 1.10 VdH[2] p.114 = *Ad Verum Imp.* 1.2, Haines I, pp. 304–7). Apolaustus was a stage name borne by several different pantomime artists, and epigraphic evidence shows that these are two different men (Barnes 1967: 72). L. Aelius Aurelius Apolaustus (*CIL* IX 344 = *ILS* 5188; *CIL* X 3716 = *ILS* 5189) is to be identified with the 'first' pantomime mentioned in *Ad Verum Imp.* 1.10, while L. Aurelius Apolaustus Memphius Senior was the dancer brought from Syria (*CIL* VI 10117 = *ILS* 5190; *CIL* X 2619 = *ILS* 5187; *CIL* XIV 4254 = *ILS* 5191).

Van den Hout (1999: 484) supposes this line refers to Verus. It is certainly not implausible that the emperor summoned a favourite pantomime to join him at Antioch. But the context of the passage itself, which deals with Trajan, suggests that the same accusations of cavorting with artists and dancers in the east were levelled against him. Fronto himself states as much in **Letter 41**, in which he says that Trajan enjoyed the company of pantomimes. His point is that both Verus and Trajan endured the same rumours about their conduct.

Spartacus and Viriathus: The same sentiment is found in **Letter 46**.

anyone more acceptable to the people than Trajan: Trajan cultivated a public image which emphasised his benefactions to the people of Rome and Italy, as described in Pliny's *Panegyricus* and monumentalised on the arch at Beneventum (Bennett 1997: 63–73. 205–8; Roche 2006, 2011).

were stirred up by his critics: The reference is also to Trajan rather than Verus. The stock charges against Trajan were his devotion to boys and wine and his desire for glory (Dio 68.7.4; Victor, *On the Caesars* 13.10; *Epitome concerning the Caesars* 13.4; 48.10; **Letter 41**).

the emperor did not neglect pantomimes and other shows on the stage, circus, or amphitheatre: Trajan initially banned pantomime performances, a move which won him considerable praise from Pliny (*Panegyricus* 46.4). In commending Trajan's actions, Pliny was contrasting him with Domitian, but it was actually Trajan's adoptive father Nerva who allowed pantomimes to be performed again (Bennett 1997: 121). As Dio (68.10.2) reveals, Trajan enjoyed pantomimes and authorised their performances again later in his reign (for epigraphic evidence of his pantomimes, see *CIL* V 2185, *CIL* VI 10114). Pliny (*Panegyricus* 54.1–2) had a rather disdainful attitude towards theatrical performances, especially when they were used to curry favour with the mob, whereas Fronto clearly recognised the reality that Roman emperors had to appeal to the populace (Veyne 1990).

grain hand-outs and spectacles: Fronto echoes Juvenal's (*Satires* 10.80–1) famous statement that the Roman people no longer bestowed commands and offices as they had in the days of the Republic, but now only desired 'bread and circuses' (*panem et circenses*). Julius Caesar, Augustus, and successive emperors placed different limits on the number of male citizens eligible for the grain hand-outs, so the precise proportion of the population who received them fluctuated. This was a privilege for a section of the citizen body, and should not be considered a form of welfare (Yavetz 1988: 141–6).

the plebeians eligible for the grain dole: Citizens who were enrolled to receive the grain dole were also entitled to receive 'cash hand-outs' (*congiaria*) from the emperors. The first Roman to promise such a handout was Julius Caesar in 49 BC, and the emperors followed this practice, making distributions on special occasions, such as their accession to the throne, imperial anniversaries, marriages, and promotions of sons to the rank of Caesar or Augustus (Duncan-Jones 1994: 78–84).

shows are enjoyed by everyone at once: Admission to the theatre and amphitheatre was open to all, from the lowliest slaves through freedmen, equestrians, and senators. The emperors still distributed coins and other gifts (known as *missilia*) at these events, but they were scattered randomly (Millar 1977: 137–8).

the processions, ornamental carriages, the chariots of the gods: The Roman circus games (*ludi circenses*) began their lives as religious festivals, and retained a strong religious character throughout the imperial period. The games were inaugurated by a procession from the Capitoline hill to the Circus Maximus, described by Dionysius of Halicarnassus (7.72.1–13). This included images of the gods, which were removed from temples around Rome and placed in ceremonial carriages drawn by horses (Ovid, *Amores* 3.2).

elephants . . . were employed in night-time spectacles: This is a reference to Julius Caesar's triumph for the conquest of Gaul in 46 BC, in which he approached the Capitoline at night accompanied by elephants with torches (Suetonius, *Iulius* 37.2; Cassius Dio 43.22.1).

wrote letters to the senators: Fronto once again returns to the theme of eloquence from **Letter 45**, and presumably he would have continued to develop the idea further in the remainder of the passage, which is now lost.

whether the great-grandfather or the great-grandson is regarded as the more outstanding in virtue: Fronto concludes the comparison between Trajan and Verus which has been a major theme of his 'sample'. The conclusion, that 'the outcome is only really of concern to the imperial house', is a fitting note to end on for what is essentially a private letter sent to Marcus.

8

Fronto's Grief

Introduction

These letters were written following the death of Fronto's wife Cratia and his three-year-old grandson in 165. We know nothing about the circumstances of Cratia's death, except that it took place within a few months of the child's passing (**Letter 50**). The grandson, who seems to have had the nickname Decimanus, died in Germany, where his parents were stationed (**Letter 54**). The original editor of Fronto's correspondence included four letters between Marcus and Fronto under the title 'On the loss of his grandson' (*De nepote amisso*). The surviving portions of three of them are translated in this chapter as **Letters 52–54**; the text of the remaining one is far too uncertain to include here.

The death of a child was a devastating blow for those who loved them, regardless of the high rate of mortality in ancient Rome (Golden 1988: 152–3). There were legal regulations and cultural practices that guided appropriate behaviour, such as fixed mourning periods and burial rituals. Official limits on mourning depended on the age of the deceased and their relationship to the bereaved. A wife was required to mourn her husband for eight months, while children under the age of three were to be mourned for one month for each year of life (Paulus, *Opinions* 1.21.13). However, there were still many differences in the ways in which individuals expressed their grief. Marcus Aurelius, whose attitude was shaped by his Stoic beliefs, wrote of the inevitability of death and the necessity not to become overwhelmed by grief (*Meditations* 4.48, 5.36, 7.43). When his son M. Annius Verus died in 169 aged seven, Marcus was said to have mourned for only five days, and even then, still occupied himself with official business when necessary (*HA Marcus* 21.3–4). Cicero wrote that grief was a self-indulgence and should be laid aside (*Tusculan*

Disputations 3.28; *Ad Fam.* 5.16.2–3), yet his own correspondence shows that he was so crushed by the death of his daughter Tullia that he withdrew from public life, and even from his friends (*Ad Att.* 12.14.3, 12.20.1; *Ad Fam.* 5.14.1–3). The preface to book six of Quintilian's *Principles of Oratory* (6.pref.1–16) is likewise full of raw emotion concerning the death of his wife and both his sons, as the orator describes how he decided to continue with his work, despite the personal tragedy that had befallen him (cf. Leigh (2004), who argues that this expression of grief is itself a form of rhetorical performance).

Consolation was offered to grieving friends and family members through letters, speeches, essays, poetry, and philosophical treatises (Stowers 1986: 142–4). For members of the senatorial and equestrian elite, letters of consolation were an expected part of maintaining relationships with their peers, and were even sent to people who were not intimate friends (Stowers 1986: 144; Wilcox 2005). The most elevated examples of the genre take on a distinct form, with an introduction expressing commiseration, followed by encouragement to behave in a particular manner, and sometimes metaphysical or philosophical musings about life and death. We have already seen some of these elements in Fronto's letter to Herodes Atticus on the death of his son (**Letter 19**), and similar sentiments can be found in other examples of the genre (Cicero, *Ad Fam.* 4.6) Letters of consolation were not restricted to aristocratic elites, as is vividly demonstrated by papyrus letters from Egypt, though these generally tend to be shorter and more to the point (*P. Oxy.* 115 = Trapp 2003: no. 46).

Men often wrote of the deaths of women by focusing on their roles as child-bearers. This is exemplified by Pliny's remarks on the death of the Helvidiae sisters during childbirth (*Letters* 4.1). In contrast, in his eulogy for Gaius Fannius, Pliny praises his pursuits, ambitions, and literary accomplishments, valuing him as a real individual (*Letters* 5.5). Fronto himself expressed pride in one of his grandsons, whom he hoped would grow up to share his interests (**Letter 40**); he never made such remarks about his daughter Cratia. The deaths of children had implications for the continuation of the family name and fortune, and men often wrote of their passing in these terms (Pliny, *Letters* 5.16; Quintilian, *Principles of Oratory* 6.pref.13; **Letter 52**). On sarcophagi and other funerary monuments, children were often represented as miniature adults as a way of recognizing the life they did not have (Dixon 1992: 105; Rawson 2003: 356–63).

The highly rhetorical nature of many of these letters of consolation does not mean that they are not expressions of real emotion; indeed, the expected formulaic phrases and rhetorical maxims may have helped the bereaved to convey their grief. Latin has a particularly rich vocabulary of loss that enabled them to do this. Describing himself as 'weary' (*fatigatus*) with 'prolonged illness' (*diutina valetudo*), Fronto gives the impression of long drawn-out suffering, which is reinforced by alliteration and rhythmic sequences of words. Fronto frequently uses the superlative forms of adjectives, such as 'in just a few months' (*in paucissimis mensibus*); 'most burdensome' (*gravissimus*); 'most wretched' (*miserrimus*). His verbs are also particularly vivid: 'I was tortured' (*cruciabar*), 'I waste away' (*tabesco*), 'I melt away' (*conliquesco*).

We begin this chapter with a letter from Fronto to Verus, in which he reveals his grief to his former pupil (**Letter 50**). Fronto takes solace in the fact that Verus still needs him, even though his formal instruction had long ceased, and writes eagerly of his preparations for the history of the Parthian War. Verus' reply is unfortunately fragmentary, but reveals that he felt himself ill-equipped to console Fronto properly on his loss – a common sentiment in such letters of consolation (**Letter 51**). Fronto did not tell Marcus himself about the death of his grandson, but when the emperor heard through other channels, he wrote to his teacher immediately (**Letter 52**). The letter is much more intimate than the correspondence with Verus, revealing the close relationship between the two men which had lasted for more than twenty-five years.

Fronto responded with what is probably one of his most famous letters, and certainly the most moving (**Letter 53**). Much of the language seems self-centred, focusing on Fronto's own feelings rather than those of his daughter, who has just lost her baby boy (Richlin 2011: 180). Yet one cannot help but be moved by passages such as the one in which Fronto recalls being haunted by the voice and image of his deceased grandson. Our interpretation of this letter is that Fronto does sympathise with his daughter's situation, but cannot properly express his grief at the situation in terms that are anything other than resolutely 'male'. The letter concludes with Fronto acutely conscious of his own mortality, as he reviews his relationships with his brother, the emperors, friends, and associates. Marcus' reply is all but lost, and is not included here. Fronto then sent one more letter on the subject, of which only the last few lines are readable (**Letter 54**). He informs Marcus that he cannot write anymore, and instead sends a book that encapsulates his feelings. The prince and the tutor thus end their epistolary relationship as it had begun, with literature.

Letter 50. Fronto to Verus (165)

Ad Verum Imp. 1.8, VdH[2] p. 113 = *Ad Verum Imp.* 2.9, Haines II, pp. 232–5.

To my lord Aurelius Verus Augustus,

1. I am weary with a prolonged illness that is more serious that usual, and afflicted with sorrows that are not only painful but almost interminable – for in only just a few months I have lost both my most beloved wife and my little three-year-old grandson – and though I have been struck down by these many terrible things, I nevertheless admit that my mood was lifted a little when I heard that you had remembered us and wanted something from me. And so I've sent what my lord, your brother, recommended* that I send to you after he had received your letter. I've also attached the speech for Demostratus.* When I initially offered it to your brother, I learned from him that you do not disapprove of Asclepiodotus, who is rebuked in the speech. When I found this out, I naturally wanted to destroy the speech.* What then – what then, I say – would you recommend? Since Asclepiodotus is regarded favourably by you, he will become my greatest friend too – just as, by Hercules, Herodes is now my firm friend – even though the speech is on record.

2. Moreover, your brother animatedly pressed me regarding that work which I want to embark on with great eagerness. When you send me your memoranda,* I will make a start and put all my efforts into the project. For you, who have deemed me qualified for the task, will see that it is done by providing the appropriate resources.

Commentary

I've sent what my lord, your brother, recommended: Earlier in 165, Marcus had written to Fronto to tell him that Verus wished to read some of

Fronto's speeches (*Ad Ant. Imp.* 3.3, VdH[2] p. 102 = *Ad Ant. Imp.* 2.8, Haines II, pp. 218–19).

speech for Demostratus: Many scholars – listed in full by van den Hout (1999: 278) – have identified Demostratus with the Athenian archon Ti. Claudius Demostratus who played a part in bringing Herodes Atticus to trial before Marcus Aurelius at Sirmium *c.* 174. This very famous case, in which Herodes was accused of tyranny by the people of Athens, is discussed in Philostratus' *Lives of the Sophists* (559). The identification of Demostratus and the archon has been reinforced by Fronto's mention of Herodes in this very letter. Furthermore, Bowersock (1969: 98–9) has argued that Fronto's speech for Demostratus was actually delivered at the trial in which Fronto was required to attack Herodes (Chapter 2). Bowersock regarded Demostratus as the accused, Fronto as the defense counsel, and Herodes as the prosecution. His argument has been followed by a number of scholars (Champlin 1980: 63–4; Birley 1993: 77; Tobin 1997: 30–2).

This does not seem to be convincing. Fronto never mentions Demostratus at all in connection with the events of the 140s, and as we have seen, a close reading of **Letters 7–8** shows that Herodes was the man on trial. If we turn to the evidence from this letter, we find that Fronto had once delivered a speech for a certain Demostratus, which contained criticisms of a man called Asclepiodotus, whose identity remains a mystery. In another letter to Marcus Aurelius concerning this very speech, Fronto appears to give Demostratus a *cognomen* beginning with *P*, but the exact word is illegible (*Ad Ant. Imp.* 3.4, VdH[2] p. 102 = *Ad Ant. Imp.* 2.8, Haines II, pp. 220–1). Demostratus could be identical to the Athenian archon, he could be a relative, or there could be no connection whatsoever: we simply do not know.

The reference to Herodes can be explained in the following manner: since the emperor approves of Asclepiodotus, Fronto will regard him as a friend. This is comparable to the situation in the past, when Fronto, who had been hostile to Herodes Atticus, was reconciled with him through the efforts of the emperor, and now thinks of Herodes as a friend. This is the explanation proposed by van den Hout (1999: 278), and we think it is the most natural interpretation of the text.

When I found this out, I naturally wanted to destroy the speech: Fronto quotes this letter in a separate missive to Marcus Aurelius (*Ad Ant. Imp.* 3.4, VdH^2 p. 102 = *Ad Ant. Imp.* 2.8, Haines II, pp. 220–1). However, the end of the letter reads a little differently:

> As soon as I found this out, I naturally took steps to destroy the speech, but it had already found its way into the hands of too many people to be destroyed. But what is to be done next? What, I say, is to be done, except that Asclepiodotus, since you regard him favourably, should become my greatest friend? Just as, by Hercules, Herodes is now my firm friend, although I have spoken [against him].

The differences are probably to be explained by the fact that Fronto did not write to Marcus with a copy of the letter to Verus directly in front of him, and could not remember exactly what he said. It must be emphasised that the last word or two is unreadable, hence the supplement [against him] (*contra eum*).

when you send me your memoranda: This is a reference to **Letter 47**, in which Verus promised to compile the official records of the Parthian War for Fronto's history.

Letter 51. Verus to Fronto (165)

Ad Verum Imp. 1.9, VdH^2 pp. 113–4 = *Ad Verum Imp* 2.9, Haines II, pp. 234–7.

Lucius Verus to Fronto.

To my teacher,

1. There is no doubt, my dearest teacher, that even if I did not reply I would still feel insurmountable anguish whenever misfortunes befall you, regardless of whether they are trivial or all-consuming. What is more, since you have lost both your wife – dear to you for so many years – and your sweetest grandson, almost at the same time, the greatest compassion . . . *[The next six lines are lost.]* . . . you have experienced misfortunes that are greater than anything for which I could dare to console my teacher in appropriate terms. But it is a father's duty to pour forth his heart full of love and duty . . . *[The rest of the line is fragmentary.]*

2. Now I shall turn to the rest of your letter:* in my delight at your speech, I would wish that you would both aim at peace, and be forgetful of that bitter quarrel of yours. What do you think, my teacher? I will grow angry, unless you . . . *[The rest of the letter is not readily intelligible.]*

Commentary

Now I shall turn to the rest of your letter: It is striking that Lucius Verus and Fronto compartmentalise their thoughts in this way. While Verus writes very sympathetically to Fronto about the loss of Cratia and his grandson, he quickly gets back to business, urging a reconciliation between Fronto and Asclepiodotus.

Letter 52. Marcus to Fronto (165)

De Nepote Amisso 1, VdH[2] p. 235 = Haines II, pp. 220–3.

Greetings my teacher,

1. I've only just heard of your plight.* Since I'm usually tortured when but a single joint of yours gives you pain, my teacher, what do you imagine I suffer when your soul grieves? In my distressed state, I can think of nothing else except to ask you take care of yourself for me, my sweetest teacher. For it's in you that I find more solace in this life than anything that anyone could possibly offer to you as a remedy for your grief.

2. I've not written in my own hand* because it was still shaking after my evening bath. Farewell, my most delightful teacher.

Commentary

I've only just heard of your plight: This shows that the letter was written after word came through a messenger, rather than being in response to correspondence from Fronto.

I've not written in my own hand: Fronto and Marcus usually wrote to each other themselves, rather than dictating their letters to slaves, and usually apologised for not doing so (Freisenbruch 2007: 251–4). Dictation had an air of an 'official' response, as noted by Fronto in **Letter 8**, when he rebukes Marcus for not writing himself. In this case, Marcus is particularly concerned to note his inability to write so that he does not seem unfeeling. The Roman bathing habit involved moving between hot and cold baths quite quickly, which would probably be enough to cause Marcus' hands to shake.

Letter 53. Fronto to Marcus (165)

De Nepote Amisso 2, VdH[2] pp. 235–9 = Haines II, pp. 222–33.

Fronto to Antoninus Augustus,

1. Fortune has tested me throughout my whole life* with many sorrows of this kind. For, although I could pass over my other misfortunes, I have lost five children* in the most wretched circumstances during the course of my life. Yes, I lost all five, and each I lost as an only child, enduring a succession of bereavements in such a way that no child was born to me except when I was already childless. And so I have always lost my children when there were no others left to offer comfort, and I became a father again with grief fresh upon me.

2. However, I steadfastly endured those bereavements that tortured me alone.* My mind made a stand as it struggled resolutely against my own grief, like one man against another in single combat, adversary against adversary. But now, with my grandson lost, my grief is compounded by the anguish of my daughter and by the anguish of my son-in-law. I withstood my own emotions, but I cannot bear the grief of my loved ones: I waste away at the tears of my Victorinus,* I melt away beside him.

3. Sometimes I even complain to the immortal gods and accost them with this kind of abuse: was it in any way fair or just that Victorinus, a man outstanding in his sense of duty, his gentility, honesty, integrity, humanity, and truly preeminent in all the very best qualities of men, be crushed by the

bitterest blow that was the death of his son? If everything is governed by Providence, was this event correctly preordained?* If all human affairs are determined by Fate, did Fate decree that this should happen? Shall there be no discrimination between the fortunes of good men and wicked men? Shall there be no determination by the gods or by the Fates as to what kind of man will have his son snatched away? Some villainous and wicked human being – though the world would be a better place if he had never been born – raises his children unharmed, and at his own death leaves them to survive him. Victorinus, a faultless man – though it would be the best thing for the state if as many as possible were born in his likeness – has been robbed of his son. And this terrible thing, Providence foresaw? It is said that the Fates got their name because they speak fairly.* Is *this* speaking fairly? In addition, the poets assign a distaff and thread to the Fates.* Surely no weaver would be so cruel and ignorant to weave for her master a hard and knotty fabric for a toga, but a fine and delicate fabric for a slave. That good men can be afflicted with grief, while bad men have earned a household that is safe and sound – I regard this cloth woven from the loom of the Fates to be both ill-fitting and of poor value.

4. Unless, perhaps, we are making another error and, in our ignorance, we ardently desire evil things, as if they were actually favourable, and turn ourselves away from good things as if they were bad. If this is the case, death itself, which seems so grievous to us all, in fact brings an end to our labours and worries and troubles, and carries men who have been freed from the bonds of a wretched body to a tranquil and beautiful place replete with everything that is good – that is, the assembling places of our spirits.* And so, I would more easily place faith in this than think that everything is not governed by Providence at all, or by someone that is unjust.

5. But if we are to rejoice at our death rather than lament it,* the younger a man is when he reaches the end, the more fortunate and popular with the gods he must be, since he has been relieved more quickly of his wretched body, more quickly summoned for those honours granted to a free soul. But though this may be true, it matters little to us who pine for those we have lost. The immortality of the soul can offer no comfort for those of us who are still alive, yet have lost those dearest to us. We long for the presence, voice, beauty, and spirit of our children, we grieve over the distressing countenance of the deceased, the closed lips, the eyes rolled back, the colour lost from every

feature. And even if our souls are immortal, it is an argument to be examined by philosophers, not a comfort for parents in mourning.

6. Regardless of how such matters are ordained by the gods, they are not of long-lasting concern to me, since my own death is imminent. As to whether we are dead forever, it has been my desire for a long time ... *[Over twenty fragmentary lines follow here.]* ... I could not because of my weeping and grief. Indeed, it is my most darling grandson, whom I am raising in my own bosom,* who increasingly now tears me to pieces and tortures me. For in his countenance I behold the grandson I have lost, and I fancy that I see an image of his face, and imagine that I hear the actual sound of his voice. This is the vision that my grief creates of its own volition, but since I have never seen the face of my dead grandson, I torture myself by imagining what he looked like.

7. My daughter will be sensible:* she will follow the lead of her husband, who is an excellent man. He will console her by weeping with her, commiserating with her, talking with her, and simply by sitting in silence with her. I, her ageing father, am not a suitable person to offer consolation. For it would have been more appropriate for me to die before the child. Nor would the poets' verses or the sayings of wise men banish the grief and the pain of my daughter so much as the voice of her husband, emerging as it does from lips so dear and a heart so close to her own.

8. As far as I am concerned, my age is a consolation, since it is almost now at a close, and death is very near. When the moment arrives, regardless of whether it happens at night or during the day, I will salute the heavens as I descend, and I will testify as my conscience dictates. In the long span of my life I have done nothing shameful, or disgraceful, or scandalous. In my life I have done nothing out of greed, committed no treacherous crime. On the contrary, I have always done many things graciously, out of friendship, faithfully, and loyally, even when my life was placed in danger.

9. I have lived in complete harmony with an excellent brother,* and I am pleased that he has gained the highest offices* thanks to the benevolence of your father. I now see that he rests safely and securely in your friendship. As for those offices, which I myself obtained, I never desired to acquire them by inappropriate means. I have devoted myself to cultivating my mind rather than my body. I have placed the pursuit of learning above the wealth of my house:* I preferred to be a pauper than be supported by another's wealth, to be left

wanting rather than asking for charity. I have never been lavish in my spending, and any profit I made was only what was necessary. I have spoken the truth carefully, I have listened to it receptively. I have considered it preferable to ignore rather than to engage in sycophancy, to keep quiet rather than make things up, to be an inconstant friend rather than a constant flatterer. I have sought little, I have earned much. I have provided people with what I could, according to my resources. I have rendered assistance readily to the worthy, and courageously to the innocent. If anyone proved too sparing in his gratitude, that did not make me any slower in bestowing a favour to the extent of my abilities, nor did I ever take offence at the ungrateful. *[The final twenty lines of the letter are very fragmentary.]*

Commentary

Fortune has tested me throughout my whole life: Fortuna, the goddess of chance, was responsible for both good and bad luck. We may contrast Fronto's thoughts on Fortune with those of Pliny (*Letters* 1.12) responding to the death of Corellius Rufus: he considered it all the more distressing that the death was not due to fate, but to suicide. Van den Hout (1999: 534) suggests that Fronto modelled this letter on Cicero's *Book of Consolation*, for which see Erskine (1997).

I have lost five children: This is the only place in the extant letter collection in which Fronto reveals this fact, but it is probable that all five babies had been born and died before *c.* 141, when Cratia the Younger was born (Richlin 2011: 196–7).

However, I steadfastly endured those bereavements that tortured me alone: Richlin (2011: 181) suggests that Fronto neglects the grief of his wife Cratia, possibly because she was dead when this letter was written. In his other correspondence, Fronto always refers to the deaths of Cratia and his grandson in that order (**Letters 50** and **54**). The motif of a man struggling against his emotions appears in Seneca (*Moral Letters* 99.16) and Cicero's letters following the death of Tullia (*Ad Att.* 12.14, 12.35–7).

Victorinus: Throughout the letter, Fronto places greater emphasis on the bereavement of Victorinus, rather than his own daughter, Cratia. The language of grief is resolutely male, written in terms that other Roman men (such as Marcus) could understand. Fronto describes Victorinus' virtues that make him the ideal Roman man in order to emphasise the unjustness of the situation. He has lost a son who was born in his likeness, who would go on to serve the Roman empire, language which echoes Fronto's earlier statements concerning his first grandson in **Letter 40**. Roman men could hope for nothing more than sons who would follow in their footsteps: the orator Quintilian (*Principles of Oratory* 6.pref.1, 13) had looked forward to his son emulating his achievements in rhetoric and rising high in the senatorial order before the boy's untimely death. Roman men expected their daughters to provide them with grandchildren to safeguard the family inheritance (see most recently Späth (2010) on Cicero's attitudes in this regard). The feelings of Cratia, the baby's mother, do not figure prominently in the letter, as Richlin (2011: 182) has noted. But this can be attributed to the fact that Fronto does not speak the language of a Roman woman: he cannot articulate the loss of a son in terms other than those familiar to a man.

If everything is governed by Providence, was this event correctly preordained? Fronto questions the tenets of Stoic philosophy to which Marcus subscribed. The Stoics believed that man must live in harmony with nature and that the world was fundamentally rational. In his *Meditations* (1.8), Marcus writes how the philosopher Apollonius taught him to be always guided by reason (λόγος in Greek, *ratio* in Latin), even when in pain or faced with the loss of a child. In Stoic thinking, Providence represented the will of the gods, and they always worked for the common good, as Marcus himself believed (*Meditations* 6.44). Since Fate had already predestined the course of events, Stoic philosophers believed that Providence and Fate were essentially the same thing (Sellars 2006: 99–106).

It is said that the Fates got their name because they speak fairly: It was commonly thought that *fatum*, the Latin word for fate, was related to the verb *fari*, which means 'to speak' and 'to predict'.

the poets assign a distaff and thread to the Fates: The Fates were three goddesses who spun out the thread of a man's life, measured its length, and then severed it at the end.

the assembling places of our spirits: There were diverse views in the Roman world on the nature of life after death. The concept of the migration of the souls was espoused by Protagoras and Plato, and in this they were followed by the Stoics. In his *Meditations* (4.21, 12.24), Marcus writes of the transference of souls into the air and the spirits that populated the heavens. This was in contrast to Epicurean philosophy, which taught that the body and soul perished simultaneously, for one could not live without the other (Lucretius, *On the Nature of Things* 3.323–49).

But if we are to rejoice at our death rather than lament it: This topic was explored by a number of authors in their philosophical writings. For example Cicero, in his *Tusculan Disputations* (1.11.25) wondered whether the dead went to a happy place, or ceased to be conscious. The fortunate, those who had lived good lives, could go to the Elysian Fields, so beautifully described by Vergil in the *Aeneid* (6.638–92).

it is my most darling grandson, whom I am raising in my own bosom: This is M. Aufidius (Victorinus) Fronto, who had been left in Fronto's care when his parents went to Germany (**Letter 40**). The boy must have lived with Fronto in Rome for about three to four years.

My daughter will be sensible: Fronto's attitude to Cratia and her reliance on Victorinus is remarkably similar to that of Marcus, who praised his wife Faustina for being so obedient to him in times of illness (**Letter 27**). Yet we should not believe Fronto is unfeeling: it is apparent, as we read on, that he does not know how he can offer her consolation. He is wracked by guilt that he, an old man, survives, while a child does not. He could turn to literature and rhetoric, as he had so often in the past, but they would not be sufficient. In response to his inability to communicate properly with his daughter, in the remainder of the letter Fronto turns back to what he knows: the virtues and qualities of a good Roman man.

I have lived in complete harmony with an excellent brother: Quadratus lived with Fronto in his house on the Esquiline. Van den Hout (1999: 541) argues that Quadratus also died in 165, based on a very fragmentary line in **Letter 54:** 'since I have lost him, [I hate] the size of my [ho]use' (*illo amisso vastitatem <do>mus meae <odi>*). Elsewhere, van den Hout (1999: 418) says this line refers to the putative 'fourth' grandson. We regard the Latin as too uncertain to draw any firm conclusions, and in the present letter, Fronto certainly speaks of Quadratus as if he is still living.

the highest offices: Quadratus was suffect consul in 147, and obviously continued to enjoy imperial favour.

the wealth of my house: Fronto was of course very wealthy compared to the majority of Romans, but does not seem to have flaunted it. As Champlin (1980: 25) observes, 'as a topic of correspondence it holds no interest for him'.

Letter 54. Fronto to Marcus (165)

De Nepote Amisso 4, VdH^2 p. 240 = *De Nepote Amisso* 2, chapter 10, Haines II, pp. 232–3.

. . . I've endured many serious bouts of poor health, my dearest Marcus. Then I've been struck down by these truly awful events: I've lost my wife, I've lost my grandson in Germany* – yes, I am truly miserable, because I've lost my Decimanus (?).* Even if I were made of iron, I wouldn't be able to write any more at the moment. I've sent you a book* which you can take as representative of my feelings.

Commentary

I've lost my grandson in Germany: For reasons that are inexplicable to us, van den Hout (1999: 533) argues that this letter deals with a different grandson from that mentioned in **Letter 53**. We can find no evidence to support this conclusion.

I've lost my Decimanus (?): The manuscript is very uncertain at this point. If Decimanus ('tenth') is the correct reading, it could be a nickname derived from an aspect of the military camp or legion under the command of his father Victorinus, as suggested by van den Hout (1999: 543).

I've sent you a book: It was a commonplace sentiment that reading and literary pursuits brought solace to the grieving (Cicero, *Ad Att.* 12.14–15; Quintilian, *Principles of Oratory* 6.pref.14; Erskine 1997: 38), and it is likely that Fronto had adopted this as a coping strategy.

Epilogue

Fronto, now about seventy years old, probably died shortly after these letters were written (Champlin 1980: 139–41). Marcus Aurelius asked the senate to dedicate a public statue of his former teacher in Rome (*HA Marcus* 2.5). We can only speculate as to what the honorific inscription inscribed on the base of the statue said, but it probably would have made reference to Fronto's tutorship of the emperors. This was certainly the case with the sarcophagus of his great-grandson, M. Aufidius Fronto, who died as a child sometime in the early third century:

> To Marcus Aufidius Fronto, great-grandson of Marcus Cornelius Fronto, orator, consul, and teacher of the emperors Lucius and Antoninus, grandson of Aufidius Victorinus, urban prefect and twice consul, Fronto the consul (dedicated this) to his sweetest son. (*CIL* XI 6334 = *ILS* 1129)

Bibliography

Aberth, J., 2011, *Plagues in World History*, London.

Adams, J. N., 2007, *The Regional Diversification of Latin, 200 BC–AD 600*, Cambridge.

Alföldy, G., 1977, *Konsulat und Senatorenstand unter den Antoninen: prosopographische Untersuchungen zur senatorischen Führungsschicht*, Bonn.

Alföldy, G. and Halfmann, H., 1979, 'Iunius Maximus und die victoria Parthica', *Zeitschrift für Papyrologie und Epigraphik* 35, 195–212.

Anderson, R. D., 2000, *Glossary of Greek Rhetorical Terms*, Leuven.

Andreau, J., 1999, *Banking and Business in the Roman World*, Cambridge.

Argetsinger, K., 1992, 'Birthday rituals: friends and patrons in Roman poetry and cult', *Classical Antiquity* 11, 175–93.

Arnaud, P., 1994, '*Transmarinae provinciae*: réflexions sur les limites géographiques et sur la nature des pouvoirs en Orient des 'corégents' sous les règnes d'Auguste et de Tibère', *Cahiers du Centre Gustav Glotz* 5, 221–53.

Bablitz, L., 2007, *Actors and Audience in the Roman Courtroom*, London.

Barden Dowling, M., 2006, *Clemency and Cruelty in the Roman World*, Ann Arbor.

Barnes, T. D., 1967, 'Hadrian and Lucius Verus', *Journal of Roman Studies* 57, 65–79.

Barnes, T. D., 1986, 'Proconsuls of Asia under Caracalla', *Phoenix* 40, 202–5.

Beard, M., 2002, 'Ciceronian correspondence: making a book out of letters', in Wiseman, T. P. (ed.), *Classics in Progress: Essays on Ancient Greece and Rome*, Oxford, 103–144.

Bennett, J., 1997, *Trajan: Optimus Princeps*, London.

Bernstein, N. W., 2008, 'Each man's father served as his teacher: constructing relatedness in Pliny's *Letters*', *Classical Antiquity* 27, 203–30.

Birley, A. R., 1993, *Marcus Aurelius: A Biography*, London.

Birley, A. R., 1997a, *Hadrian: The Restless Emperor*, London.

Birley, A. R., 1997b, 'Hadrian and Greek senators', *Zeitschrift für Papyrologie und Epigraphik* 116, 209–45.

Birley, A. R., 2003, 'The commissioning of equestrian officers', in Wilkes, J. J. (ed.), *Documenting the Roman Army: Essays in Honour of Margaret Roxan*, London, 1–18.

Birley, A. R., 2005, *The Roman Government of Britain*, Oxford.

Bivar, A. D. H., 1972, 'Cavalry equipment and tactics on the Euphrates frontier', *Dumbarton Oaks Papers* 26, 271–91.

Boatwright, M. T., 1992, 'Matidia the Younger', *Echos du Monde Classique/Classical Views* 36, 19–32.

Bonner, S. F., 1977, *Education in Ancient Rome*, London.

Börner, S., 2012, 'Coins', in Van Ackeren, M. (ed.), *A Companion to Marcus Aurelius*, Oxford and Malden, MA, 278–93.

Bowersock, G., 1969, *Greek Sophists in the Roman Empire*, Oxford.

Bowman, A. K., 1994a, *Life and Letters on the Roman Frontier: Vindolanda and its People*, London.

Bowman, A. K., 1994b, 'The Roman imperial army: letters and literacy on the northern frontier', in Bowman, A. K. and Woolf, G. (eds), *Literacy and Power in the Ancient World*, Cambridge, 109–25.

Breeze, D. J., 1974, 'The career structure below the centurionate during the principate', *ANRW* II.1, 435–51.

Brunt, P. A., 1961, 'Charges of provincial maladministration under the early principate', *Historia* 10, 189–227.

Burns, J., 2007, *Great Women of Imperial Rome: Mothers and Wives of the Caesars*, London and New York.

Burton, G. P., 1975, 'Proconsuls, assizes and the administration of justice under the empire', *Journal of Roman Studies* 65, 92–106.

Burton, G. P., 2004, 'The Roman imperial state, provincial governors and the public finances of provincial cities, 27 BC–AD 235', *Historia* 53, 311–42.

Campbell, B., 1984, *The Emperor and the Roman Army*, Oxford.

Campbell, B., 1987, 'Teach yourself how to be a general', *Journal of Roman Studies* 77, 13–29.

Carey, C., 2010, 'Epideictic oratory', in Worthington, I. (ed.), *A Companion to Greek Rhetoric*, Oxford and Malden, MA, 236–52.

Carlon, J. M., 2009, *Pliny's Women: Constructing Virtue and Creating Identity in the Roman World*, Cambridge.

Casson, L., 1994, *Travel in the Ancient World*, Baltimore.

Champlin, E., 1974, 'The chronology of Fronto', *Journal of Roman Studies* 64, 136–59.

Champlin, E., 1980, *Fronto and Antonine Rome*, Cambridge, MA.

Champlin, E., 1989, '*Creditur vulgo testamenta hominum speculum esse morum:* why the Romans made wills', *Classical Philology* 84, 198–215.

Champlin, E., 1991, *Final Judgments: Duty and Emotion in Roman Wills*, Berkeley.

Church, A. J., 1884, *Roman Life in the Days of Cicero: Sketches Drawn from His Letters and Speeches*, London.

Claassen, J.-M., 2007, '*Fronto avus*: the tale of a grandfather', *Akroterion* 52, 49–59.

Claassen, J.-M., 2009, 'Cornelius Fronto: a "Libyan nomad" at Rome', *Acta Classica* 52, 47–71.

Clarke, M. L., 1996, *Rhetoric at Rome: An Historical Survey*, London.

Coarelli, F., 2007, *Rome and Environs: An Archaeological Guide*, trans. Clauss, J. J. and Harmon, D. P., Berkeley.

Connolly, J., 2011, 'Rhetorical education', in Peachin, M. (ed.), *The Oxford Handbook of Social Relations in the Roman World*, Oxford, 101–118.

Cooper, C., 2010, 'Forensic oratory', in Worthington, I. (ed.), *A Companion to Greek Rhetoric*, Oxford and Malden, MA, 203–19.

Corbeill, A., 2010, 'Rhetorical education and social reproduction in the Republic and early empire', in Dominik, W. and Hall, J. (eds), *A Companion to Roman Rhetoric*, Oxford and Malden, MA, 69–82.

Cotton, H. M., 1985, '*Mirificum Genus Commendationis*: Cicero and the Latin letter of recommendation', *American Journal of Philology* 106, 328–34.

Crawford, M. H., 1996, *Roman Statutes*, London.

Crook, J. A., 1967, *Law and Life of Rome*, Ithaca.

D'Arms, J. H., 1970, *Romans on the Bay of Naples: A Social and Cultural Study of the Villas and their Owners from 150 BC to AD 400*, Cambridge, MA.

Davies, P. J. E., 2004, *Death and the Emperor: Roman Imperial Funerary Monuments from Augustus to Marcus Aurelius*, Austin.

Davies, R. W., 1968, 'Fronto, Hadrian and the Roman army', *Latomus* 27, 75–95.
Dench, E., 1995, *From Barbarians to New Men: Greek, Roman, and Modern Perceptions of Peoples from the Central Apennines*, Oxford.
Dickey, E., 2002, *Latin Forms of Address: From Plautus to Apuleius*, Oxford.
Dillery, J., 1995, *Xenophon and the History of his Times*, London.
Dixon, S., 1992, *The Roman Family*, Baltimore.
Donahue, J. F., 2004, *The Roman Community at Table during the Principate*, Ann Arbor.
Dover, K. J., 1989, *Greek Homosexuality*, updated edition, Cambridge, MA.
Duncan-Jones, R. P., 1964, 'The purpose and organization of the *alimenta*', *Papers of the British School at Rome* 32, 123–46.
Duncan-Jones, R. P. 1984, *The Economy of the Roman Empire: Quantitative Studies*, 2nd edition, Cambridge.
Duncan-Jones, R. P., 1994, *Money and Government in the Roman Empire*, Cambridge.
Duncan-Jones, R. P., 2006, 'Who were the *equites*?', in Deroux, C. (ed.), *Studies in Latin Literature and Roman History* XIII, Brussels, 183–223.
Eadie, J. W., 1967, 'The development of Roman mailed cavalry', *Journal of Roman Studies* 57, 161–73.
Eck, W., 1998, 'M. Cornelius Fronto, Lehrer Marc Aurels, *consul suffectus* im J. 142', *Rheinisches Museum* 141, 193–96.
Eck, W., 2000, 'Government and civil administration' in Bowman, A. K., Garnsey, P., and Rathbone, D. (eds), *The Cambridge Ancient History, Second Edition, Volume XI: The High Empire, AD 70–192*, Cambridge, 195–292.
Eck, W., 2002, 'Imperial administration and epigraphy: in defence of prosopography', in Bowman, A. K., Cotton, H. M., Goodman, M., and Price, S. (eds), *Representations of Empire: Rome and the Mediterranean World. Proceedings of the British Academy* 114, Oxford, 131–52.
Eck, W. and Roxan, M., 1995, 'Two new military diplomas', in Frei-Stolba, R. and Speidel, M. A. (eds), *Römische Inschriften: Neufunde, Neulesungen und Neuintepretationen. Festschrift für Hans Lieb*, Basel, 77–99.
Edwards, R., 2008, 'Hunting for boars with Pliny and Tacitus', *Classical Antiquity* 27, 35–58.
Erskine, A., 1997, 'Cicero and the expression of grief', in Braund, S. and Gill, C. (eds), *The Passions in Roman Thought and Literature*, Cambridge, 36–47.
Fagan, G. G., 2006, 'Bathing for health with Celsus and Pliny the Elder', *Classical Quarterly* 56, 190–207.
Fantham, E., 1996, *Roman Literary Culture from Cicero to Apuleius*, Baltimore.
Fentress, E., Goodman, C. and Mauiro, M., 2007, 'Excavations at Villa Magna (Anagni-FR) 2007', *Fasti Online*: http://www.fastionline.org/docs/FOLDER-it-2007-96.pdf (last accessed 17 June 2013).
Fentress, E. and Maiuro, M., 2011, 'Villa Magna near Anagni: the emperor, his winery and the wine of Signia', *Journal of Roman Archaeology* 24, 333–69.
Fishwick, D., 1990, *The Imperial Cult in the Latin West: Studies in the Ruler Cult of the Western Provinces of the Roman Empire: Volume II.1*, Leiden.
Flemming, R., 2000, *Medicine and the Making of Roman Women: Gender and Authority from Celsus to Galen*, Oxford.
Fleury, P., 2001, 'La flûte, le général et l'esclave: analyse de certaines métaphores rhétoriques chez Fronton', *Phoenix* 55, 108–23.
Fleury, P., 2012 'Marcus Aurelius' Letters', in Van Ackeren, M. (ed.), *A Companion to Marcus Aurelius*, Oxford and Malden, MA, 62–76.

Fleury, P. and Demougin, S., 2003, *Fronton: Correspondance*, Paris.

Freisenbruch, A., 2007, 'Back to Fronto: doctor and patient in his correspondence with an emperor', in Morello, R. and Morrison, A. D. (eds), *Ancient Letters: Classical and Late Antique Epistolography*, Oxford, 235–56.

Funke, H., 2011, 'Poetry and historiography: a study in the uses of sources', in Marincola, J. (ed.), *Greek and Roman Historiography*, Oxford, 413–32.

Gatti, S., 1996, 'Anagni (Frosinone): Localita S. Cecilia – Indagini nel santuario ernico: il deposito votivo arcaico', *Notizie degli scavi di antichità* 1994/5, 5–153.

Garnsey, P., 2010, 'Roman patronage', in McGill, S., Sogno, C., and Watts, E. J. (eds), *From the Tetrarchs to the Theodosians: Later Roman History and Culture, 284–450 C.E.*, Yale Classical Studies 34, Cambridge, 33–54.

Geer, R. M., 1935, 'The Greek games at Naples', *Transactions and Proceedings of the American Philological Association* 66, 208–21.

Gerhardt, T. and Hartmann, U., 2000, '*Ab Arsace caesus est*: Ein parthischer Feldherr aus der Zeit Trajans und Hadrians', *Göttinger Forum für Altertumswissenschaft* 3, 125–42.

Gibson, R., 2012, 'On the nature of ancient letter collections', *Journal of Roman Studies* 102, 56–78.

Gibson, R. and Morello, R., 2012, *Reading the Letters of Pliny the Younger: An Introduction*, Cambridge.

Golden, M., 1988, 'Did the ancients care when their children died?', *Greece & Rome* 35, 152–63.

Gourevitch, D., 2010, 'The sick child in his family: a risk for the family tradition', in Dasen, V. and Späth, T. (eds), *Children, Memory and Family Identity in Roman Culture*, Oxford, 273–92.

Gowing, A. M., 1992, *The Triumviral Narratives of Appian and Cassius Dio*, Ann Arbor.

Gunderson, E., 2009, *Nox Philologiae: Aulus Gellius and the Fantasy of the Roman Library*, Madison.

Haines, C. R., 1919–20, *Fronto: Correspondence*, 2 vols., London and Cambridge, MA.

Hansen, M. H., 1993, 'The battle exhortation in ancient historiography: fact or fiction?', *Historia* 42, 161–80.

Harris, W. V., 1992, 'An inscription recording a proconsul's visit to Samothrace in 165 AD', *American Journal of Philology* 113, 71–7.

Harrison, S. J., 1998, 'The Milesian Tales and the Roman novel', in Hofmann, H. and Zimmerman, M. (eds), *Groningen Colloquia on the Novel IX*, Groningen, 61–73.

Hekster, O., 2002, *Commodus: An Emperor at the Crossroads*, Amsterdam.

Hoffer, S., 1999, *The Anxieties of Pliny the Younger*, Atlanta.

Holford-Strevens, L., 1991, 'The new Fronto', *Classical Review* 41, 76–80.

Holford-Strevens, L., 2000, 'Fronto', *Classical Review* 50, 460–62.

Holford-Strevens, L., 2005, *Aulus Gellius: an Antonine Scholar and his Achievement*, revised edition, Oxford.

Holford-Strevens, L., 2010, 'Current and ancient colloquial in Gellius', in Dickey, E. and Chahoud, A. (eds), *Colloquial and Literary Latin*, Cambridge, 331–38.

Hölscher, T., 2004, *The Language of Images in Roman Art*, trans. A. Snodgrass and A. Künzel-Snodgrass, Cambridge.

Hope, V. M., 2007, *Death in Ancient Rome: A Sourcebook*, London.

Horster, M., 2011, '*Princeps iuventutis*: concept, realization, representation', in Benoist, S., Daguet-Gagey, A., and Hoët-van Cauwenberghe, C. (eds), *Figures d'empire, fragments de mémoire: pouvoirs et identitiés dans le monde romain impérial (IIe s. av. n. è – VIe. s. de n. è)*, Villeneuve d'Ascq, 73–103.

Jones, C. P., 1986, *Culture and Society in Lucian*, Cambridge, MA.

Jones, C. P., 2004, 'A speech of the emperor Hadrian', *Classical Quarterly* 54, 266–73.

Jones, C. P., 2007, 'Three new letters of the emperor Hadrian', *Zeitschrift für Papyrologie und Epigraphik* 161, 145–56.

Joshel, S. R., 2011, 'Slavery and Roman literary culture', in Bradley, K. and Cartledge, P. (eds), *The Cambridge World History of Slavery: Volume 1: The Ancient Mediterranean World*, Cambridge, 214–40.

Kemezis, A. M., 2010, 'Lucian, Fronto, and the absence of contemporary historiography under the Antonines', *American Journal of Philology* 131, 285–325.

Kennedy, G., 1972, *The Art of Rhetoric in the Roman World, 300 BC–AD 300*, Princeton, NJ.

Kleiner, D. E. E., 1992, *Roman Sculpture*, New Haven.

König, J., 2005, *Athletics and Literature in the Roman Empire*, Cambridge.

Konstan, D., 1997, *Friendship in the Classical World*, Cambridge.

Laes, C., 2009, 'What could Marcus Aurelius feel for Fronto?', *Studia Humaniora Tartuensia* 10.A.3, 1–7: http://www.ut.ee/klassik/sht/2009/index.html (last accessed 17 June 2013).

Leigh, M., 2004, 'Quintilian on the emotions (*Institutio Oratoria* 6 Preface and 1–2)', *Journal of Roman Studies* 94, 122–40.

Levick, B., 2000, *The Government of the Roman Empire: A Sourcebook*, 2nd edition, London.

Lightfoot, C. S., 1990, 'Trajan's Parthian war and the fourth-century perspective', *Journal of Roman Studies* 80, 115–26.

Liukkonen-Anttila, T., Uimaniemi, L., Orell, M., and Lumme, J., 2002, 'Mitochondrial DNA variation and the phylogeography of the grey partidge (Perdix perdix) in Europe: from Pleistocene history to present day populations', *Journal of Evolutionary Biology* 15, 971–82.

McDonnell, M., 1996, 'Writing, copying and autograph manuscripts in ancient Rome', *Classical Quarterly* 46, 469–91.

McLynn, F., 2009, *Marcus Aurelius: A Life*, Cambridge, MA.

Manuwald, G., 2011, *Roman Republican Theatre*, Cambridge.

Marchesi, I., 2008, *The Art of Pliny's Letters: A Poetics of Allusion in the Private Correspondence*, Cambridge.

Marincola, J., 2007, 'Speeches in classical historiography', in idem (ed.), *A Companion to Greek and Roman Historiography*, Malden, MA, 118–32.

Marzano, A. 2007. *Roman Villas in Central Italy: A Social and Economic Study*, Leiden.

Mattern, S. P., 1999a, 'Physicians and the Roman imperial aristocracy: the patronage of therapeutics', *Bulletin of the History of Medicine* 73, 1–18.

Mattern, S. P., 1999b, *Rome and the Enemy: Imperial Strategy in the Principate*, Berkeley.

Mattern, S. P., 2008, *Galen and the Rhetoric of Healing*, Baltimore.

Matthews, J. F., 1975, *Western Aristocracies and Imperial Court*, Oxford.

Mayer, R., 2003, 'Pliny and *Gloria Dicendi*', *Arethusa* 36.2, 227–34.

Mellor, R., 1999, *The Roman Historians*, London.

Millar, F. G. B., 1977, *The Emperor in the Roman World*, London.

Morgan, T., 1998, *Literate Education in the Hellenistic and Roman Worlds*, Cambridge.

Mountford, J., 1938, *'Bradley's Arnold' Latin Prose Composition*, London.

Mouritsen, H., 2011, *The Freedman in the Roman World*, Cambridge.

Mousourakis, G., 2003, *The Historical and Institutional Context of Roman Law*, Aldershot.

Nicols, J., 1980, '*Tabulae patronatus*: a study of the agreement between patron and client-community', *ANRW* II.13, 535–61.

Nicols, J., 1988, 'Prefects, patronage and the administration of justice', *Zeitschrift für Papyrologie und Epigraphik* 72, 201–17.

Nielsen, H. S., 1987, '*Alumnus*: a term of relation denoting quasi-adoption', *Classica et Mediaevalia* 38, 141–88.

Nixon, C. E. V. and Rodgers, B. S., 1994, *In Praise of Later Roman Emperors: The Panegyrici Latini*, Berkeley.

North, H., 1966, *Sophrosyne: Self-Knowledge and Self-Restraint in Greek Literature*, Ithaca.

Nutton, V., 1971, 'Lucius Gellius Maximus: physician and procurator', *Classical Quarterly* 21, 262–72.

O'Gorman, E., 2007, 'The politics of Sallustian style', in Marincola, J. (ed.), *A Companion to Greek and Roman Historiography*, Oxford and Malden, MA, 379–84.

Opper, T., 2008, *Hadrian: Empire and Conflict*, London.

Panayotakis, C., 2010, *Decimus Laberius: The Fragments*, Cambridge.

Parkin, T. G., 1992, *Demography and Roman Society*, Baltimore.

Parkin, T. G., 2003, *Old Age in the Roman World*, Baltimore.

Parsons, P. J., 1980, 'Background: the papyrus letter', in Veremans, J. and Decreus, F. (eds), *Acta colloqui didacti classici,* Didactia Classica Gandensia 20, Ghent, 3–19.

Paterson, J., 2007, 'Friends in high places: the creation of the court in the Roman empire', in Spawforth, A. (ed.), *The Court and Court Society in Ancient Monarchies*, Cambridge, 121–56.

Pelletier, D. L., Frongillo, E. A. Jr, Schroder, D. G., Habicht, J. P., 1995, 'The effects of malnutrition on child mortality in developing countries', *Bulletin of the World Health Organization* 73, 443–8.

Pelling, C., 2000, *Literary Texts and the Greek Historian*, London.

Plant, I. M., 2004, *Women Writers of Ancient Greece and Rome: An Anthology*, London.

Pomeroy, S. B., 2007, *The Murder of Regilla: A Case of Domestic Violence in Antiquity*, Cambridge, MA.

Potter, D. S., 1979, 'The mysterious Arbaces', *American Journal of Philology* 100, 541–2.

Purcell, N., 1985, 'Wine and wealth in ancient Italy', *Journal of Roman Studies* 75, 1–19.

Rawson, B., 1986, 'Children in the Roman *familia*', in idem (ed.), *The Family in Ancient Rome: New Perspectives*, London and Sydney, 170–200.

Rawson, B., 2003, *Children and Childhood in Roman Italy*, Oxford.

Reay, B., 2005, 'Agriculture, writing, and Cato's aristocratic self-fashioning', *Classical Antiquity* 24, 331–61.

Rees, R., 2007, 'Letters of commendation and the rhetoric of praise', in Morello, R. and Morrison, A. D. (eds), *Ancient Letters: Classical and Late Antique Epistolography*, Oxford, 149–68.

Rees, R., 2011, 'Afterwords of praise', in Roche, P. (ed.), *Pliny's Praise: The Panegyricus in the Roman World*, Cambridge, 175–88.

Reynolds, L. D., 1983, *Texts and Transmission: A Survey of the Latin Classics*, Oxford.

Richlin, A., 2006a, *Marcus Aurelius in Love*, Chicago.

Richlin, A., 2006b, 'Fronto + Marcus: love, friendship, letters', in Kuefler, M. (ed.), *The Boswell Thesis: Essays on Christianity, Social Tolerance, and Homosexuality*, Chicago, 111–29.

Richlin, A., 2011, 'Parallel lives: Domitia Lucilla and Cratia, Fronto and Marcus', *Eugesta* 1, 163–203.

Richlin, A., 2012, 'The sanctification of Marcus Aurelius', in Van Ackeren, M. (ed.), *A Companion to Marcus Aurelius*, Oxford and Malden, MA, 497–514.

Riggsby, A. M., 2010, *Roman Law and the Legal World of the Romans*, Cambridge.

Roche, P. A., 2006, 'Selling Trajan's *Saeculum*: destiny, abundance, assurance', *Athenaeum* 94, 199–229.

Roche, P., 2011, 'Pliny's thanksgiving: an introduction to the *Panegyricus*', in idem (ed.), *Pliny's Praise: The Panegyricus in the Roman World*, Cambridge, 1–28.

Rogers, R. S., 1959, 'The emperor's displeasure: *amicitiam renuntiare*', *Transactions of the American Philological Association* 90, 224–37.

Russell, D. A., 1983, *Greek Declamation*, Cambridge.

Rutherford, R. B., 2012, 'Structure and meaning in epic and historiography', in Foster, E. and Lateiner, D. (eds), *Thucydides and Herodotus*, Oxford, 13–38.

Saller, R. P., 1982, *Personal Patronage under the Early Empire*, Cambridge.

Saller, R. P., 1989, 'Patronage and friendship in early imperial Rome: drawing the distinction', in Wallace-Hadrill, A. (ed.), *Patronage in Ancient Society*, London, 49–62.

Saller, R. P., 1994, *Patriarchy, Property and Death in the Roman Family*, Cambridge.

Scheidel, W., 1999, 'Emperors, aristocrats, and the grim reaper', *Classical Quarterly* 49, 254–81.

Sciarrino, E., 2007, 'Roman oratory before Cicero: the Elder Cato and Gaius Gracchus', in Dominik, W. and Hall, J. (eds), *A Companion to Roman Rhetoric*, Oxford and Malden, MA, 54–67.

Sear, F., 2006, *Roman Theatres: An Architectural Study*, Oxford.

Sellars, J., 2006, *Stoicism*, Berkeley.

Shaw, B., 1984, 'Bandits in the Roman empire', *Past and Present* 105, 3–52.

Sim, D., 2000, 'The making and testing of a *falx*, also known as the Dacian battle scythe', *Journal of Roman Military Equipment Studies* 11, 37–42.

Southern, P., 2006, *The Roman Army: A Social and Institutional History*, Oxford.

Späth, T., 2010, 'Cicero, Tullia, and Marcus: gender-specific concerns for family tradition', in Dasen, V. and Späth, T. (eds), *Children, Memory and Family Identity in Roman Culture*, Oxford, 147–72.

Speidel, M. P., 1984, '*Catafractarii clibanarii* and the rise of the later Roman mailed cavalry', *Epigraphica Anatolica* 4, 151–6.

Stadter, P. A., 1980, *Arrian of Nicomedia*, Chapel Hill.

Ste Croix, G. E. M. de, 1954, '*Suffragium*: from vote to patronage', *The British Journal of Sociology* 5, 33–48.

Stewart, P., 2003, *Statues in Roman Society: Representation and Response*, Oxford.

Stowers, S. K., 1986, *Letter Writing in Greco-Roman Antiquity*, Philadelphia.

Swain, S., 1996, *Hellenism and Empire: Language, Classicism, and Power in the Greek World, AD 50–250*, Oxford.

Swain, S., 2004, 'Bilingualism and biculturalism in Antonine Rome: Apuleius, Fronto and Gellius', in Holford-Strevens, L. and Vardi, A. (eds), *The Worlds of Aulus Gellius*, Oxford, 3–40.

Syme, R., 1980, 'Guard prefects of Trajan and Hadrian', *Journal of Roman Studies* 70, 64–80. Reprinted in Birley, A. R. (ed.), 1984, *Roman Papers III*, Oxford, 1276–302.

Syme, R., 1987, 'Avidius Cassius: his rank, age, and quality', in Straub, J. (ed.), *Bonner Historia-Augusta-Colloquium 1984/1985*, Bonn, 207–22. Reprinted in Birley, A. R. (ed.), 1988, *Roman Papers V*, Oxford, 789–801.

Talbert, R. J. A., 1984, *The Senate of Imperial Rome*, Princeton, NJ.
Tobin, J., 1997, *Herodes Attikos and the City of Athens: Patronage and Conflict under the Antonines*, Amsterdam.
Toynbee, J. M. C., 1971, *Death and Burial in the Roman World*, Baltimore.
Trapp, M., 1990, 'Plato's *Phaedrus* in second-century Greek literature', in Russell, D. A. (ed.), *Antonine Literature*, Oxford, 141–73.
Trapp, M., 2003, *Greek and Latin Letters: An Anthology with Translation*, Cambridge.
Treggiari, S., 1991, *Roman Marriage: Iusti Coniuges from the time of Cicero to the time of Ulpian*, Oxford.
Usher, S., 2010, 'Symbouleutic oratory', in Worthington, I. (ed.), *A Companion to Greek Rhetoric*, Oxford and Malden, MA, 220–35.
Van Ackeren, M. (ed.), 2012, *A Companion to Marcus Aurelius*, Oxford and Malden, MA.
van den Hout, M. P. J., 1988, *M. Cornelius Fronto: Epistulae*, Leipzig.
van den Hout, M. P. J., 1999, *A Commentary on the Letters of M. Cornelius Fronto*, Leiden.
Veyne, P., 1990, *Bread and Circuses: Historical Sociology and Political Pluralism*, trans. B. Pearce, London.
Von Albrecht, M., 1997, *A History of Roman Literature: From Livius Andronicus to Boethius*, 2 vols, Leiden.
Wallace-Hadrill, A., 1981, 'The emperor and his virtues', *Historia* 30, 293–323.
Wallace-Hadrill, A., 1982, '*Civilis princeps*: between citizen and king', *Journal of Roman Studies* 72, 32–48.
Warmington, B., 1954, 'The municipal patrons of Roman North Africa', *Papers of the British School at Rome* 22, 39–55.
Weaver, P. R. C., 1965, 'Freedmen procurators in the imperial administration', *Historia* 14, 460–9.
Weaver, P. R. C., 1972, *Familia Caesaris: A Social Study of the Emperor's Freedmen and Slaves*, Cambridge.
Weaver P. R. C., 2002, '*Consilium praesidis*: advising governors', in McKechnie, P. (ed.), *Thinking Like a Lawyer: Essays on Legal History and General History for John Crook on his Eightieth Birthday*, Brill, 43–62.
Wheeler, E. L., 1996, 'The laxity of Syrian legions', in Kennedy, D. L. (ed.), *The Roman Army in the East, Journal of Roman Archaeology*, supplementary series no. 18, Ann Arbor, 229–76.
Wheeler, E. L., 2010, 'Polyaenus, *Scriptor Militaris*', in Brodersen, K. (ed.), *Polyainos. Neue Studien / Polyaenus. New Studies*, Berlin, 7–54.
White, P., 2010, *Cicero in Letters: Epistolary Relations of the Late Republic*, Oxford.
Whitehorne, J., 1977a, 'Fronto's letter to Avidius Cassius', *Prudentia* 7, 41–5.
Whitehorne, J., 1977b, 'Was Marcus Aurelius a hypochondriac?', *Latomus* 36, 413–21.
Wiedemann, T., 1989, *Adults and Children in the Roman Empire*, London.
Wilcox, A., 2005, 'Sympathetic rivals: consolation in Cicero's Letters', *American Jounral of Philology* 126, 237–55.
Wilcox, A., 2012, *The Gift of Correspondence in Classical Rome: Friendship in Cicero's Ad familiares and Seneca's Moral Epistles*, Madison.
Williams, C., 2012, *Reading Roman Friendship*, Cambridge.
Williams, W., 1976, 'Individuality in the imperial constitutions. Hadrian and the Antonines', *Journal of Roman Studies* 66, 67–83.
Williams, W., 1979, 'Caracalla and the authorship of imperial edicts and epistles', *Latomus* 38, 67–89.

Williams, S. C., 2009, 'Scorpions', in Resh, V. H. and Cardé, R. T. (eds), *Encyclopedia of Insects*, second edition, New York.

Whitmarsh, T., 2005, *The Second Sophistic*, Greek & Rome New Surveys in the Classics 35, Cambridge.

Woodman, A. J., 1988, *Rhetoric in Classical Historiography*, London.

World Health Organisation, n.d., http://www.who.int/inf-new/child.htm (last accessed 19 June 2013).

Yavetz, Z., 1988, *Plebs and Princeps*, revised edition, Oxford.

Yunis, H., 2011, *Plato: Phaedrus*, Cambridge.

Zanker, P., 2002, 'Domitian's palace on the Palatine and the imperial image', in Bowman, A. K., Cotton, H. M., Goodman, M. and Price, S. (eds), *Representations of Empire: Rome and the Mediterranean World*, Proceedings of the British Academy 114, Oxford, 105–30.

Zoido, J. C. I., 2007, 'The battle exhortation in ancient rhetoric', *Rhetorica* 25, 141–58.

General Index

Roman individuals are usually listed by their *gentilicium*, e.g. C. Censorius Niger appears under C, M. Gavius Maximus under G. The exceptions are those Romans who are best known by other names, such as Augustus, Cicero and Pliny the Younger, who are listed under the name most familiar to modern-day audiences.

Index of Letters in this Edition

The index of letters gives the full reference to van den Hout and Haines (as indicated on p. xii), followed by the letter number of this edition in bold, followed by the page numbers in this edition.

www.ingramcontent.com/pod-product-compliance
Lightning Source LLC
Chambersburg PA
CBHW070527100726
47907CB00004B/1009